D0264597

THE SHOPPING EXPERIENCE

edited by
Pasi Falk and Colin Campbell

SAGE Publications
London • Thousand Oaks • New Delhi

First published 1997

 SAGE Publications Ltd
6 Bonhill Street
London EC2A 4PU

SAGE Publications Inc
2455 Teller Road
Thousand Oaks, California 91320

SAGE Publications India Pvt Ltd
32, M-Block Market
Greater Kailash - I
New Delhi 110 048

British Library Cataloguing in Publication data
A catalogue record for this book is
available from the British Library

ISBN 0 7619 5066 4
ISBN 0 7619 5067 2 (pbk)

Library of Congress catalog card number 97-068532

Typeset by Photoprint, Torquay, Devon
Printed in Great Britain by The Cromwell Press Ltd,
Broughton Gifford, Melksham, Wiltshire

CONTENTS

LIST OF FIGURES

NOTES ON CONTRIBUTORS

Rachel Bowlby is Fellow of St Hilda's College, Oxford University. Her books include *Just Looking* (1985), *Still Crazy After All These Years: Women, Writing and Psychoanalysis* (1992), *Shopping with Freud* (1993) and *Feminist Destinations and Further Essays on Virginia Woolf* (1997). She is currently completing a book on supermarkets.

Colin Campbell is Reader in Sociology and Head of Department at the University of York. He has written widely on sociological theory, culture and cultural change, religion, and the sociology of consumption. He is editor of *Studies in Consumption* (Harwood Academic Press), and European Editor of *Consumption, Culture, Markets*. He is also author of *The Romantic Ethic and the Spirit of Modern Consumerism* (1987) and *The Myth of Social Action* (1996).

Mary Douglas is a distinguished anthropologist who has held positions in both the UK (University College, London) and the USA (Princeton University and Northwestern University, Illinois). Since her book *Purity and Danger* (1966), now a classic, she has published numerous articles, edited books and monographs. Her recent books include *How Institutions Think* (1986), *How Classification Works* (1992) and *Risk and Blame* (1992). Her latest book, *Thought Styles*, was published by Sage in 1996.

Pasi Falk is Senior Research Fellow and Docent of the Department of Sociology at the University of Helsinki. He has published extensively on social theory, sociosemiotics and historical anthropology. From the early 1980s onwards his research has been focused on the cultural dynamics of modern society, with a specific emphasis on human embodiment and modern consumption. He is the author of *The Consuming Body* (1994). He is currently completing a book on Finnish lottery winners (with Pasi Mäenpää) and preparing a book on the history of civilization illnesses (*Modernity Syndrome*).

Cecilia Fredriksson is a PhD candidate in the Department of Ethnology at the University of Lund. She is writing her thesis on the modernization of Sweden as this is reflected in everyday consumption. In addition to her research on the department store, she has also conducted fieldwork on fleamarkets (1991, 1996) and consumption of the outdoor life (1997).

Paul Hewer graduated from the University of Leeds in 1989 before taking an MA at the University of York. He then embarked on a PhD programme on the sociology of consumer behaviour and men. He completed his thesis in 1995, and has since worked as a research assistant and as an undergraduate and post-graduate tutor.

Turo-Kimmo Lehtonen is a PhD candidate in the Department of Sociology at the University of Helsinki. He is currently completing his PhD thesis on the everyday practices of consumption and shopping. He has also recently published a study (in Finnish) on the changing history of hygienic habits in Finland.

Pasi Mäenpää is a PhD candidate in the Department of Sociology at the University of Helsinki. He is currently preparing his PhD thesis, in which the sites and practices of shopping are contextualized in the broader perspective of urban culture. He has also worked as a researcher on Pasi Falk's project on Finnish lottery winners and is the co-author of a forth-coming book on the topic.

Daniel Miller is Professor of Anthropology at University College, London. He has recently completed a year's ethnography of shopping in a north London street. Prior to that he undertook an ethnography of commerce and consumption in Trinidad. His recent monographs include *Modernity – An Ethnographic Approach* (1994) and *Capitalism – An Ethnographic Approach* (1997). He has also recently edited the following books: *Unwrapping Christmas* (1993), *Acknowledging Consumption* (1995), *Worlds Apart* (1995) and *Material Cultures* (1997). He is a founding editor of the *Journal of Material Culture*.

Mica Nava is a Reader in the Department of Cultural Studies and co-director of the Centre for Consumer and Advertising Studies at the University of East London. She is author of *Changing Cultures: Feminism, Youth and Consumerism* (1992) and co-editor of *Modern Times: Reflections on a Century of English Modernity* (1996) and *Buy This Book: Studies in Advertising and Consumption* (1997). Her current research is on cosmo-politanism and consumption.

ACKNOWLEDGEMENTS

Two chapters in this book – Mary Douglas's 'In Defence of Shopping' (Chapter 1) and Mica Nava's 'Women, the City and the Department Store' (Chapter 3) – have been published previously. The former was originally published in Mary Douglas's collection of essays titled *Objects and Objections* published by the Toronto Semiotic Circle (Monograph Series of the TSC, no. 9, 1992, pp. 66–87) and the latter, with the title 'Modernity's Disavowal: Women, the City and the Department Store' in the book *Modern Times: Reflections on a Century of English Modernity*, edited by Mica Nava and Alan O'Shea and published by Routledge (1996). We would like to thank the publishers for their permission to reprint these texts.

INTRODUCTION

Pasi Falk and Colin Campbell

Why should anyone not directly involved in marketing or retailing choose to do research on shopping? This is a natural enough question given that at first sight shopping does not appear to be a phenomenon of any particular societal significance, especially when compared with the long list of serious social, political, economic and environmental issues that face modern Western societies at the end of the second millennium. When set against such widely debated issues as globalization versus localization, communal integration versus disintegration, and individualization versus tribalization, not to mention the growing anxiety over the threat to the planet itself (environmental pollution and so on), shopping appears to be a topic of very marginal significance.

However, the last decade has witnessed a considerable growth of interest in shopping as a research topic, not only within sociology but also in other disciplines. This has been the case in anthropology (Appadurai, 1986) – especially in the context of material culture studies (Miller, 1995) – in certain branches of psychology (Csikszentmihályi and Rochberg-Halton, 1987; Dittmar, 1992), and in human geography (Goss, 1993; Jackson and Thrift, 1995; Sack, 1992; Zukin, 1991); an upsurge of interest that can be set against the background of a small but significant literature on the history of shopping in general (Adburgham, 1964), which, in the 1980s, was given a fresh impetus through the publication of a number of studies on the department store (Benson, 1986; Leach, 1993; Miller, 1981; Williams, 1982).[1]

How, then, are we to explain this recent trend? In fact there are many reasons why shopping might be considered an important and relevant topic of research other than the traditional concern with 'selling goods' that has characterized marketing and consumer research for many decades. Actually contemporary research on shopping tends to be characterized by a lack of interest in – if not a rejection of – this narrow economic concern; a feature that links what otherwise constitutes a various and far from homogeneous field of research.

The new significance accorded to shopping as a research topic may, in part, be explained by reference to the central role this phenomenon is accorded as a cultural phenomenon in contemporary 'postmodern' society, where it is identified as a realm of social action, interaction and experience which increasingly structures the everyday practices of urban people. This thesis does not necessarily lead directly into speculative theorizing about 'postmodernity', even though there is an obvious trend towards this kind of symptomatic reading of cultural phenomena. At a more concrete and empirical level such a thesis implies a research interest in many aspects of the lives of contemporary people, especially the growing number who live in urban surroundings. How, for example, do such people structure their lives? What is the actual nature of their daily routines and what kind of meaning do they give to them? These general questions are then concretized into more specific queries concerning what people are actually doing, thinking and experiencing when spending time moving around in urban, public spaces; ones which, although structured in a variety of ways, are commonly dominated by shopping sites. Consequently, the next step in specifying the research topic is to pose these questions in the context of shopping: what is it that people actually do when they shop – whether this is understood as *shopping for* and/or just *shopping around*?

When formulated in such simple terms, this question would also be of interest to those engaged in the traditional forms of consumer research. However, the new approach rejects this perspective because – in addition to viewing shopping as a significant realm of 'public behaviour' and a predominant aspect of people's lives in general – it also regards shopping as a paradigmatic case illustrating the fundamental *shift in the structuring principle of society from production to consumption*. Consequently, there is a complete rejection of any framework of analysis that simply treats people as economic agents and prioritizes production.

The shift from production to consumption is not the only way of envisaging the 'great transformation' but it is obviously the most relevant in the present context; one that involves understanding change in the well-established tradition of contrasts: in effect as a move from traditional or pre-modern to modern society. In this respect it echoes many of the contrasts on which sociology as a distinct theoretical discipline was itself constituted, such as Tönnies's *Gemeinschaft versus Gesellschaft* and Durkheim's *mechanical versus organic solidarity*. However, this schema is taken one stage further, postulating continuing changes of and within modern society itself, such as that from industrial to post-industrial, or from early modern to 'late modern', 'consumer', 'affluent', 'information', 'post-materialistic', 'high modern', 'hyper-real' or, perhaps finally(?), 'postmodern'.

These contrasting distinctions and synthetizing characterizations of 'our' world, culture and society are important instruments for the intellectual reflection and diagnosis of the age (Ger. *Zeitdiagnose*). However, although many of these labels and their associated discussions have certainly produced valuable and insightful conceptualizations, interpretations and synthetizing visions of 'our age', all too often there has been a tendency to treat these concepts and distinctions as unquestioned postulates; ones which are then in their turn used as taken-for-granted conceptual filters through which to 'read' the signs and symptoms of the contemporary 'postmodern' world and its various realms, including, in particular, the sites and practices of shopping.

The problem with such a symptomatic reading is that it builds on a kind of inverted perspective. First, the starting point lies in an abstract theoretical outline of 'the state of the world', a vision assembled by extrapolating all those presumed emergent characteristics of 'our society or age' into a full-blown social and cultural condition. Then, second, comes the actual inversion in which this completed model – which, as an extrapolation, is actually a vision of tomorrow's world – is turned into a synthetized interpretation of the present. As a consequence the conceptual framework becomes self-verifying, *illustrating* its postulates with the same phenomena which at the outset were the basis of its construction. In this way theorizing begins to lose its grip on things happening 'out there', as in the process of projecting the postulated scheme onto the world it portrays a picture that is no more than a collection of illustrations of the scheme itself.

Returning to the topic of shopping, we may summarize the above argument as follows. Even though there are many good reasons for using terms like 'consumer society' and for talking about a shift of emphasis from production to consumption, one should avoid employing these as un-problematic guides or assumptions when engaged in research on shopping, for this would reduce shopping to little more than a blank sheet on which to project one's prior notions, an activity that becomes the unproblematic 'realization' of consumer society, or a practice in which the (post)modern urbanite – as a hybridization of *flâneur/flâneuse* and modern consumer – strolls through public places, thus verifying the thesis according to which shopping is the 'dominant mode of contemporary public life' (Goss, 1993: 18). There may, of course, be good grounds for such an argument. However, instead of a circular affirmation of the thesis, one should proceed by means of a more subtle and empirically based analysis of 'contemporary public life'.

Such an analysis is necessary because the change in question is not only about the increasing 'dominance' of shopping sites and practices but also about the restructuring of the relationship between public and private, individual and social, and the 'inside' and the 'outside'. All these levels of the transformation should be thematized – as is done in the following chapters – in order to avoid reducing the topic of shopping to a homogeneous thing which is then either condemned – as total commodification – or celebrated as a 'fun culture'.

The same critical points presented above apply to another related tendency in postmodern discussions, that which reduces the shopper to a mere 'subject of consumption'.[2] This is someone who is engaged in 'self-construction by a process of acquiring commodities of distinction and difference' (Bauman, 1988: 808), and hence can be judged to be 'buying' an identity for him/herself. Again, there is no reason to deny either the importance of the historically significant process of individualization in the contemporary mode of self-construction or the centrality of the world of goods as the site for this activity. Rather, the problem lies in the presentation of self-construction as a one-sided process of identity distinction. The consequence is that the selves of shoppers are reduced to mere other-related 'social identities' existing only through 'representing' themselves, in a Goffmanesque fashion, on the stage of (urban) 'public life', and thus neglecting completely the dimension of *self-relatedness* which locates the experiential (bodily) self and the reflexive (cognitive) self on one and the same continuum (Falk, 1994).

Neglecting the dimension of self-relatedness turns urban public space into little more than a huge stage upon which self-construction is realized as a combination of self-display and the acquisition of goods – the latter acting as building bricks out of which the 'persona' or mask is assembled. On the other hand, these two aspects of self-construction when taken together seem to offer the strongest argument for defining shopping as the 'dominant mode of contemporary public life' since both take place at shopping sites.

However, acknowledging the dimensions for self relatedness – from the experiential to the reflexive – opens up a perspective which goes beyond the representation of shopping as the simple 'practice' of a series of consumption actions in which choice leads to purchase, use (reduced to display) and finally to rejection (disposal). Such a perspective helps us to realize that shopping has many dimensions not included in this 'serial act' model of consumption, and that the 'interaction' with material goods ranges from a variety of sensory experiences to acts of imagination in which the self is mirrored in the potential object of acquisition with questions which are rarely formulated and hardly ever articulated: *'is that for me?'; 'Am I like that?'; 'Could that be (part of) me?'; 'Could I be like that?'; 'Would I like to be like that?'*, and so on; an endless series of questions which are acts of self-formation in themselves regardless of whether they eventually lead to the realizing phase of purchase or not.

Consequently even if this self-reflexive 'negotiating' with goods does not necessarily end up in an act of purchase – one which makes the object 'one's own', in both the juridical and practical senses of the term – it is none the less part of the process of self-formation, a process located in the realm of the imaginary.[3] From a self-construction point of view this means that reflective acts vis-à-vis goods are in a continuous relationship with other kinds of reflecting, especially other people and, of course, the whole realm of mass-mediated representations, from TV news and soap operas to movies, music videos and advertising. These experiential goods, whether distributed free or sold, may very well be consumed as 'mere experiences' but they also act as mirrors for the aforementioned self-reflexive contemplation. On the other hand, even the experiential mode of reception that does not involve too much cognitive reflection is included in the dimension of self-relatedness, for it articulates the 'feeling' of one's self – both as an emotional state and as a physical (sensory) experience. The significance of the continuum from the bodily to the cognitive or from the experiential to the reflective should be stressed in order to avoid a one-sided reduction of the 'reflexive project of the self' (Giddens, 1991: 9).

The above argument appears to have some paradoxical consequences when it comes to defining shopping as a distinctive topic of research. If the practice of shopping is not reducible to self-construction through display and acquisition, but is implemented in a wide variety of relations – including other people, material goods and representations – and involves a merging of the imaginary, experiential and reflexive dimensions, then we tend to lose touch altogether with the conventional economic definition of shopping. Certainly people do shop in shopping sites (otherwise these would not exist) but they do other things there as well, engaging in practices – ranging from various doings to just being 'where the action is' (cf. Goffman, 1967) – that cannot be reduced to the instrumental act of buying.

Doing 'other things' may still involve economic transactions, although in a specific way, that is, one that links buying and consuming in one transient moment or event at the shopping site. Whether such buying and consuming involves material or immaterial goods the act of consumption is still primarily experiential. This is obvious enough in the case of eating at a restaurant, snacking, 'grazing' around, stopping for some refreshment, going into movies, visiting an art gallery, having a massage, or perhaps even visiting a medical doctor.[4] However, when consumption does not involve such 'experiential products' (Falk, 1994, 1997) the link between experiences and goods becomes less evident and more sporadic. On the one hand, the shopping site is full of potential sources of experience which remain outside commodification. On the other hand, the whole world of goods may take on a second(ary) role, that is, as part of the stimulative environment offering both experiences and mirrors for self-reflection, which, as noted above, in many cases never forces the shopper to answer the final question – *to buy or not to buy*?

Nevertheless, even in its secondary role the goods for sale are something other than mere objects to be scrutinized and contemplated. On the one hand, there is a difference in the use of the sensory register (see Falk, Chapter 8, this volume). Art galleries and museums, as a rule, maintain a (vitrine) distance between the object and the subject, thus forcing the latter into the position of a spectator, while a shopper's relationship to goods permits close encounters, something encouraged by the 'selling party' in the hope of a purchase. On the other hand, the possibility of purchase still figures in a shopper's relationship to goods, even though it might remain no more than an unrealized potentiality (see Lehtonen and Mäenpää, Chapter 6, this volume). This is because the approach to the object is often accompanied by a self-centred reflection which involves the idea of (potential or future) possession and thus it is a relation invested with an 'interest'. Hence it is distinct from a distanced relationship – from the Kantian idea of a 'disinterested' aesthetic reflection – which might be formulated in questions like *'how do I feel about this?'* or, *'do I find this beautiful?'*

These differences are really only matters of degree.[5] Nevertheless, acknowledging them implies a redefinition of the practice of shopping in a way that emphasizes the difference between two orientations, that is, the practical and economic. These are generally equatable with shopping *for* and the recreational shopping *around*; the latter being an autonomous realm of experience and action in which the economic (instrumental) aspect has been marginalized. However, it should be noted that the distinction between the two *orientations* cannot be translated unambiguously into two different *practices* of shopping. For both orientations may be present in the same practice, as elements of a single 'shopping trip', although in an asymmetrical way. Thus shopping *around* may – and it often does – involve elements of shopping for, while the daily shopping *for* necessities rarely leaves room for a recreational orientation.[6]

What the distinctions outlined above reveal is that 'shopping' is not an easily identified research topic. If the focus is on the recreational aspect of the activity – ignoring its economic–instrumental characteristics – then this approach will give rise to two problems. The first is the difficulty of operationalization due to the fact that this autonomized shopping around is only an orientation (and motivation) and not a directly observable practice. Thus, even though contemporary shopping malls may be regarded as the primary sites of recreational shopping, the activities taking place there are not equatable with this particular orientation.

In other words, there is still a need to know what actually happens in shopping malls – otherwise these places are simply assumed to illustrate a pure, autonomized shopping orientation. Consequently, the present book contains several contributions (especially Chapters 2, 5, 6 and 7) which, by means of ethnography and empirical research, take a closer look at what is actually going on in shopping sites, thus counter-balancing the abstract and theoretical approach to shopping.

The second problem that arises if the focus is simply on recreational shopping is that it becomes indistinguishable from other modes of spending time in the city. Effectively shopping becomes indistinguishable from all those other activities (and passivities) covered by the term 'recreation', such as walking around the streets, taking in the sights in general, and effectively using public space as if it were a 'department store' of stimulative and/or relaxing experiences. This, of course, describes the life of the classic figure of the *flâneur/flâneuse*, now supplemented with the traits of the modern consumer. In contrast to his/her nineteenth-century Baudelairean predecessor, however, the modern shopper figure tends to be more interested in things than in people. Yet just like the classic figure, the updated version remains primarily a consumer of experiences, someone who enjoys the freedoms offered by urban space, especially the freedom of choice and the freedom to move around freely in the midst of the stimuli offered by people and things. The shopper's experiential focus is not primarily on 'the crowd' – experienced as 'an immense reservoir of electrical energy' by the 'perfect flâneur' (Baudelaire, 1964) – but rather on the cornucopia of goods. Nevertheless, the Baudelairean formula of the 'perfect flâneur' applies also to the contemporary shopper: 'an "I" with an insatiable appetite for the "non-I" ' (Baudelaire, 1964; cited in Bersani, 1990: 68–9).

The more the purchasing aspect of shopping is marginalized in the shopper's practice, the more he or she resembles his/her classic predecessor. Consequently, this is where 'shopping' tends to dissolve into an aspect of the urban way of life which – to echo Goffman's book titles (1963, 1972) – could be called 'behaviour in public places' or 'relations in public'. So, the next question to be posed is: on what grounds can shopping be brought back into focus as the central and paradigmatic realm of 'public behaviour'? As noted above, the self-construction-through-acquisition-and-display argument is far from satisfactory; it simply generalizes the proto-experience of modernity – which Baudelaire insightfully condensed into the formula *le transitoire, le fugitif, le contingent* in mid-nineteenth-century – and applies it, in an unproblematic manner, to the contemporary mode of self-construction.

Such an interpretation, which is frequently presented in discussions of 'post-modernity', has two interrelated consequences for understanding the fate of the self. On the one hand, there is the argument concerning the 'disappearance of the self'. Here it is assumed that subjects react to the contingency, multiplicity and polyvocality of the (post)modern condition without being able to maintain the coherence of the self and thus they face the fate of fragmentation. On the other hand, there is a more optimistic vision of the (post)modern self as being a self-reflexive and playful identity-shopper who constructs and changes his/her self either to accord with others' expectations, or to distinguish him/herself from others, or possibly just for fun.

The former argument concerning the disappearance of the self rejects the idea of a monolithic and static (core) self. This is revealed to be a straw man combining the outdated idea of an unchanging 'human nature' with a premodern 'person' whose identity is fixed by the rituals and traditions of a static social order. The core-self is a kind of synthesis of David Riesman's (1950) first two character types, the 'tradition-directed' and the 'inner-directed', and when this core-self disappears all that is left is an extreme reactive 'other-directedness', in relationship not only to others but to all external sources of stimuli. And yet, it is very difficult to find traces of such a core-self in the more serious discourses on the self, discourse which from the outset replaced such static models with (psycho)dynamic ones.

The latter version – that which presents the (post)modern self as an identity-shopper – combines the idea of the fragmented self with consumer sovereignty, that is, with the ability to make free choices and thus change one's identity at will. However, what seems to go unnoticed is that this very competence – which surely cannot be practised as freely as the idealized vision suggests – is what the dynamics of the self is actually about. The more or less developed ability *both* to stand back *and* to get involved, that is, the oscillation of detachment and attachment, of knowing and feeling, and so on, is the existential mode of the modern individual self. Certainly the (post)modern condition puts higher demands on the flexibility of the self. However, the implication of this is not the decline but rather the articulation of the coherence and continuity of the self. The pendulum-like dynamics of the self is recursive, and only if and when it stops is there an actual disappearance of the self, followed by psychosis or, in the last instance, death.

Neglecting the whole dynamics of the self, the self-as-identity-shopper model regards the variety of social identities as a series of 'selves' available to be chosen, tried on and possibly worn for a while, much like a costume, thus supporting the thesis of the disappearance of the core-self and the coming of the fragmented, multiple or optional one. Here once again we find that mode of reasoning which mixes models and metaphors in a circular way. For if the (post)modern individual self can be characterized (metaphorically) as a kind of identity-shopper, then who else could be the paradigmatic representative of this type if not the real recreational shopper, someone who spends his/her free time in the shopping sites, practising choice and building his/her self 'freestyle'? However, the latter image is already modelled on the former, and thus the circuit is completed, being condensed into the following formula: *flâneur/flâneuse* = shopper = (post)modern self.

Yet, regardless of the circular reasoning and the rhetorical acrobatics it involves, there is a sensible core to such arguments. It is obvious that the nature of consumption has changed substantially during this century and specifically since the 1950s. The boundary between the world of goods and mass culture has become more and more diffuse, not only due to expanding commodification but because of a tendency which shifts the emphasis in consumption towards the experiential. The century-long history of modern advertising both highlights this tendency and is actually a productive part of it (Falk, 1994, 1997). Mass culture transformed experiences into marketable products while advertising turned marketable products into representations, images and then, over time, into experiences once more. The consequence of all this has been that the consumption of experience and the experience of consumption have become more and more indistinguishable.

Contemporary advertisements, which 'sell goods' while being virtually autonomous experiential goods themselves, are excellent examples of this tendency. But a similar kind of dissolution takes place in contemporary shopping sites, and this time at the level of practice. Here one finds a double process – that of selling goods and being experiential freeware themselves – which is reminiscent of that characteristic of modern advertising, for a whole variety of ingredients which can serve as potential sources of experience are mixed together under the same roof (and not only figuratively). From the commercial perspective of the retailers all the experiential freeware offered (including the advertisements) should promote the sale of both the experiential goods available to be consumed on the spot and all the goods people buy and carry away. However, another process parallels this promotional pursuit. For these places also gain autonomy – in relation to their economic role – as experiential realms in themselves, as places for meeting friends, for walking around and just spending time, rather than money. And this is a tendency which is not in any simple way subsumable under the promotional aims: the

spatial practices or the 'walking rhetorics' (Certeau, 1984: 100–2) of the
urbanites – *qua flâneurs qua* shoppers – is largely self-determined, implying
a variety of ways in which these places are made 'one's own' which ignore,
or even oppose, marketing interests.

The recreational role of shopping centres is actually nothing but an
extension of the recreational role of city centres where all the commercial
and recreational facilities are located in the same streets rather than under
the same roof. If a city centre was covered by a mammoth glass roof, then
we would face a definitional problem: should we regard this simply as a city
centre turned interior space or as a shopping centre writ large? Certainly one
could find criteria for making a distinction; in terms of accessibility, control
over the space, artificiality, and so on.[7] Nevertheless, these would be rather
differences in degree. Such large-scale interiorization of city centres has not
taken place and may be considered rather unrealistic. However, the tendency
does manifest itself in more modest forms, ranging from nineteenth-century
Parisian arcades to the contemporary shopping centres. The arcades were
constructed both as 'corridors' (with shops) through a building and as glass-
covered alleys between two buildings (see Falk, Chapter 8, this volume), and
the latter applies also to some smaller shopping centres in contemporary
cityscapes.[8]

While the definitional problem presented above is primarily a speculative
thought experiment, turning the formula around takes us closer to the 'real
thing'. Should one regard contemporary shopping centres as city centres
scaled down and interiorized? And how should we then conceive of the
different relationships between the 'original' and the new miniaturized
'copy'. For example, a walk in the centre of Singapore – simply following
the crowd – turns out to be a walk through a series of air-conditioned
shopping centres and department stores. Thus the city centre is actually a
complex of shopping centres or a set of city centres writ small. To take
another example: if you walk toward the city centre in Rovaniemi – the
'capital' of Finnish Lapland – you will end up in(side) a shopping centre
which *is* actually the city centre; the utopia of the interiorized city centre
realized, or, better, a lack of scale which eliminates the difference between
the original and the copy. Yet another example, again from Finland: a
comparison of the plan of the central shopping sites of Helsinki with the
plan of East Centre Mall – the biggest shopping centre in Finland located in
the eastern suburb of Helsinki – reveals not only the difference in scale
(about 2:1) but also a certain structural similarity which makes the latter into
an approximate 'miniature' of the former (Lehtonen and Mäenpää, Chapter
6, this volume).

It is clear from this that the contemporary shopping malls and centres that
one finds throughout the Western(ized) world signify both a general change
in the structure and function of urban space and the role within it occupied
by the world of goods. The spatial differentiation of city centres and,
consequently, the concentration of both retail and recreational functions into
certain locations is not a particularly recent trend. Neither is the close

relationship between these two functions. However, the contemporary shopping centres change the configuration not only in response to the shifts in consumer 'mentality' (towards the experiential), but also as physical entities moulding both the cityscape and the spatial practices of its inhabitants. Thus, approaching shopping both as practice and as physical sites requires a double perspective; one which, on the one hand, thematizes shopping in its 'original' economic role, and, on the other, places shopping in the broader context of public behaviour and public places. The former perspective should remind us of the variety of shopping practices and sites which existed before the contemporary shopping centres and malls; and indeed still exists beside them.[9] The latter perspective should thematize the 'genealogy of the (urban) public space' (see Falk, Chapter 8, this volume), and especially those more recent historical changes which have led to the contemporary shopping sites. Both of these perspectives involve a historical dimension which features in this book in those contributions dealing with department stores (Chapters 3 and 5) and the supermarket (Chapter 4).

*   *   *

Against the background of the issues and difficulties involved in studying shopping outlined above, four main themes can be discerned in the pages that follow. First there is the claim that shopping is a more significant phenomenon than academics and intellectuals have traditionally assumed; both more significant as an experience in the lives of the men and women who undertake it, and more central as a phenomenon for an understanding of modern and postmodern society. This is the explicit theme of Miller's chapter (2), while also being very apparent in Douglas's and Nava's contributions (Chapters 1 and 3). Yet it is really a theme emphasized in one way or another by all the contributors, who are united by the view that an analysis of this apparently prosaic and mundane activity can yield major insights into the lives of contemporary men and women. Miller questions the assumption that compared with the public arena of politics shopping occupies the semi-private arena of the personal and the trivial. In a direct challenge to this view, he argues that it is increasingly the case that shopping is an activity that involves making politically and morally consequential decisions almost every day. Consequently it should be seen as an activity of the greatest importance. In a similar vein, Douglas also protests against the popular portrayal of shopping as trivial, deriding economists and market researchers for promoting an essentially derogatory image of the consumer and shopper, one in which she is presented as simply reacting either to market price or to fashion. By contrast, Douglas argues that the shopper is a rational, coherent person whose conduct is inspired by cultural considerations; essentially by consistent and repeated expressions of cultural hostility. What may appear to be a myriad of apparently unrelated consumer choices are in fact connected because they represent a consistent campaign in which cultural allegiances are announced and antipathies expressed. Time and effort are expended – and in Douglas's picture of shopping satisfaction obtained – as much by the active rejection of commodities presented to the shopper as by those that are purchased. Indeed, she goes further to argue that shopping patterns do not merely express, but are actually constitutive of, differing contemporary cultural configurations.

A second theme running through the chapters that follow is really simply a more specific version of the first. It is the claim that shopping and the retail sphere generally are important because this has been the central arena in which the drama of modernity has been acted out. This is the dominant theme in the contributions of Nava, Bowlby and Fredriksson (Chapters 3–5), each of whom identify the department store as having played a crucial innovation role in the development of a modern consumer sensibility. They certainly warrant special treatment in Bowlby's as yet unwritten history of shopping, while for Nava these 'monuments to modernity' acted as a primary channel for the introduction of a modernist ethos into industrial societies. Neatly complementing this general thesis, Fredriksson documents the way in which a more democratic version of the same institution served to teach individual shoppers of a later generation how to consume (and how not to consume) in the modern manner.

The third theme serves, once again, simply to qualify those already identified, for it emphasizes the importance of gender and, in particular, the critical role played by women as shoppers and hence as agents of modernity. For if shopping is important and crucial for an understanding of modern society, then this is largely because it is also gendered. This is the central thrust of Nava's contribution, for she argues that the comparative absence of references to women in the standard narrative of modernity stems from the self-same bias that tends to exclude shopping; the presumption that both are really features of the private rather than the public world. She convincingly disposes of this separate spheres argument, identifying the department store – as a place designed specifically for and used by women – as a 'public' urban space that was a primary setting for experiments in modernity. The suggestion that women were the primary agents of modernity is given a new twist by Campbell (Chapter 7), who suggests that women's critical role as shoppers may also mean that they are in the vanguard of any move to postmodernity.

The fourth and final theme can be seen to both encapsulate and transcend the previous three, for it focuses on the very complexity and ambiguity of the shopping experience itself, and especially on the contradictions and tensions that it contains. It is clear in the discussions that follow that investigators have repeatedly concluded that shopping is a complex and inherently ambiguous phenomenon. For example, for many people it is viewed as neither simply work nor leisure but yet partakes of both. Also, as Lehtonen and Mäenpää clearly demonstrate (Chapter 6), shopping is ambiguous in nature because it is essentially a private experience that occurs in a public setting – an activity hovering somewhere between privacy and sociability. It is also, as they argue, caught in the tension between rationality

and impulse, between a 'pleasurable social form' and 'a necessary maintenance activity'; a theme that, as Campbell demonstrates (Chapter 7), links
back directly to issues of gender. Shopping can also be said to be contradictory in that it is an experience that yields both pleasure and anxiety, a
'delightful experience' that can quickly become a 'nightmare', for there is a
dark as well as a light (or light-hearted) side to shopping. As Fredriksson
clearly shows (Chapter 5), this is closely connected to the problems of
learning to be a modern shopper; a role in which one is required both to give
in to desires and yet at the same time to curb them so that they do not exceed
one's resources. The shopping experience is the point at which the tensions
as well as the promises of modernity and postmodernity are perhaps most
apparent.

Notes

1. Probably the earliest sociological (or 'social psychological') analysis of the department
store – *Das Warenhaus* by a German scholar named Paul Göhre – was published in 1907 in a
book series entitled 'die Gesellschaft – Sammlung sozialpsychologischer Monographien'
(Society – a collection of social psychological monographs) edited by Martin Bruber. It should
be mentioned that the book series also included contributions by a number of classical German
sociologists such as Georg Simmel (on religion), Ferdinand Tönnies (on convention/custom
[*Die Sitte*]) and Werner Sombart (on the proletariat). So one could perhaps conclude that in the
German sociological tradition shopping was considered to be a relevant sociological topic even
before the emergence of a sub-field of the sociology of shopping in a more specific sense (see
Hewer and Campbell, appendix to this volume).
2. This is the subtitle of the book *Lifestyle Shopping* (Shields, 1992), in which all these
tendencies are present in a more or less articulated form.
3. This formulation is reminiscent of the Lacanian view of the self as an imaginary
construct (which does not turn the self into something 'unreal'), and is actually compatible
with it. However, in the present context the imaginary character of self-formation should be
understood both in more general terms (in distinction to the more subtle approach to the
dynamics of the human mind) and with a specific emphasis on a historical perspective which
focuses on the new aspects of self-formation that have emerged and become more and more
generalized especially from the late nineteenth century onwards. The emergence of these new
aspects of self may be summarized as a strengthening trend towards individualization which
articulates itself in a number of contextual factors linked to the rise of the urban way of life,
the coming of the 'consumer society' and the expansion of mass-media and (mass-mediated)
popular culture. In relation to these contextual (social and cultural) factors the term 'imaginary' acquires an additional meaning, referring to a subjective orientation to the world 'outside'
in which the emphasis is shifting from 'acting out' to 'inner' experiencing and reflection (Falk,
1985, 1994). Consequently there is a turning towards an imaginary reception (or consumption)
of all kinds of stimuli, impressions and images the (urban) external world provides both for
free and as commodities (from material goods to the experiential goods of mass culture). Colin
Campbell's 'romantic self' and 'modern hedonist' (Campbell, 1987) are good illustrations of
such an imaginary dimension of self-formation.
4. Visiting a doctor can hardly be characterized as consumption of experiential goods.
However, the same principle of buying and immediate consumption also applies to the various
services (medical, juridical, etc.) offered in contemporary shopping malls. Just recently a
private hospital 'Eira' advertised in *Helsingin Sanomat* – the biggest newspaper in Finland –
with the headline 'EIRA IS NOW ALSO AT STOCKMANN'S!' (the biggest department store in
Helsinki). The text under the heading reads: 'In the new Eira clinic you can consult a medical
doctor while shopping – easy and fast.'

5. In the reflexive series of questions (which runs in parallel with the shifts in sensory register: looking, touching, 'trying on') it is easy to detect a continuity from questions like '*is this beautiful?*' to those closer to a potential purchase: '*is this the one for me*', '*should I buy it?*' Then again, at a more concrete level one may construct comparative settings where the distinction between shopping and something else becomes diffuse. For example, the majority of art galleries are actually art shops where (some) people buy works of art for their private collections, for home decoration and also as investments. Actually it would be interesting to compare the visitor/buyer ratios of an average shopping mall and some (selling) art galleries. Would these ratios be closer to each other than in the comparison of shopping malls to (separate) supermarkets – especially when the 'experiential goods', consumed at the site in the former, would be excluded? On the other hand, as an example from the reverse perspective, window shopping, especially when the shops are closed, has much in common with looking into the glass cases at a museum.

6. The weekend supermarket trip – done with the spouse or family and by car, especially in areas outside the big city centres – may offer somewhat more room for the recreational aspect, even though it still accords primacy to the '*shopping for*' pattern; that is, filling up the household store with bulk goods once a week. However, in those cases where such 'semi-wholesale' shopping is done in shopping centres (which offer a considerable amount of experiential products to be consumed at the site), then we are already dealing with a shopping practice which combines the two orientations (see above). In terms of physical structure, architectural design and function such 'difference in degree' manifests itself in a certain convergence between the big supermarkets and shopping centres, especially those which are located outside big city centres: as the supermarkets grow in size they also expand their supply of services and experiential products (playgrounds for 'parked' children, cafés, restaurants, and so on), thus making them more like shopping centres.

7. Shopping centres as controlled interiors are not open around the clock like the streets, they are also controlled more efficiently than the urban exterior by means of the modern panoptical devices such as video cameras and alarm systems. In addition, a shopping centre is an especially artificial complex: an outcome of a monolithic project, planned and implemented. In the latter respect shopping centres differ from city centres, which are generally heterogeneous structures created by numerous separate projects at different times. An exception to this rule is an artificial city such as Brazilia which was basically built as one project.

8. In a certain sense the centre of Helsinki has recently (March 1997) turned into an interior. In a couple of months there will be a network of underground corridors and shopping arcades linking the central department stores and malls – together with the railway and underground stations – into one huge inner space. It is not exactly an interior but at least you can get from one shopping site to another without going outside.

9. The judgement on what constitutes shopping should be kept open, and this is why the present book is not only about shopping centres but also includes accounts on department stores and supermarkets. Furthermore, there is research conducted on such mundane retail settings as the garage sale (Soiffer and Herrmann, 1987), flea markets (Fredriksson, 1996), car boot sales and even tupperware parties (Fischer and Gainer, 1991; Rapping, 1980). These studies help to counter-balance the tendency to focus merely on the contemporary shopping centres.

References

Adburgham, Alison (1964) *Shops and Shopping, 1800–1914: Where and in What Manner the Well-dressed Englishwoman Bought her Clothes.* London: George Allen and Unwin.

Appadurai, Arjun (ed.) (1986) *The Social Life of Things: Commodities in Cultural Perspective.* Cambridge: Cambridge University Press.

Baudelaire, Charles (1964) *The Painter of Modern Life and Other Essays.* London: Phaidon Press.

Bauman, Zygmunt (1988) 'Sociology and Postmodernity', *Sociological Review*, 36(4): 790–813.

Benson, Susan Porter (1986) *Counter Cultures: Saleswomen, Managers and Customers in American Department Stores, 1890–1940*. Urbana and Chicago: University of Illinois Press.

Bersani, Leo (1990) *The Culture of Redemption*. Cambridge, MA: Harvard University Press.

Campbell, Colin (1987) *The Romantic Ethic and the Spirit of Modern Consumerism*. Oxford: Basil Blackwell.

Certeau, Michel de (1984) *The Practice of Everyday Life*. Berkeley and Los Angeles: University of California Press.

Csikszentmihályi, Mihály and Rochberg-Halton, Eugene (1987) *The Meaning of Things: Domestic Symbols and the Self*. Cambridge: Cambridge University Press.

Dittmar, Helga (1992) *The Social Psychology of Material Possessions*. Hemel Hempstead: Harvester Wheatsheaf.

Falk, Pasi (1985) 'Corporeality and Its Fates in History', *Acta Sociologica*, 28(2): 115–36.

Falk, Pasi (1994) *The Consuming Body*. London: Sage.

Falk, Pasi (1997) 'The Benetton–Toscani Effect: Testing the Limits of Conventional Advertising', in Mica Nava, Andrew Blake, Iain MacRury and Barry Richards (eds), *Buy This Book: Contemporary Issues in Advertising and Consumption*. London: Routledge. pp. 64–83.

Fischer, Eileen and Gainer, Brenda (1991) 'I Shop Therefore I Am: The Role of Shopping in the Social Construction of Women's Identities', in Janeen Arnold Costa (ed.), *Gender and Consumer Behavior*. Salt Lake City, UT: Association for Consumer Research. pp. 350–7.

Fredriksson, Cecilia (1996) 'Loppmarknader och ruiner. Om loppmarknadens estetik [Flea Markets and Ruins: On the Aesthetics of Flea Markets]', in I. Nordström and R. Valerie (eds), *Tyche och Smak [Living and Taste]*. Lund: Carlssons. pp. 17–46.

Giddens, Anthony (1991) *Modernity and Self-Identity*. Cambridge: Polity Press.

Goffman, Erving (1963) *Behavior in Public Places*. New York: Free Press.

Goffman, Erving (1967) *Interaction Ritual: Essays on Face-to-Face Behavior*. New York: Allen Lane & The Penguin Press.

Goffman, Erving (1972) *Relations in Public: Microstudies of the Public Order*. New York: Harper & Row.

Göhre, Paul (1907) *Das Warenhaus*. Frankfurt am Main: Rütten & Loening.

Goss, Jon (1993) ' "The Magic of the Mall": An Analysis of Form, Function, and Meaning in the Contemporary Retail Built Environment', *Annuals of the Association of American Geographers*, 83(1): 18–47.

Jackson, Peter and Thrift, Nigel (1995) 'Geographies of Consumption', in Daniel Miller (ed.), *Acknowledging Consumption: A Review of New Studies*. London: Routledge. pp. 204–37.

Leach, William (1993) *Land of Desire*. New York: Pantheon Books.

Miller, Daniel (ed.) (1995) *Acknowledging Consumption: A Review of New Studies*. London: Routledge.

Miller, Michael B. (1981) *The Bon Marché: Bourgeois Culture and the Department Store, 1869–1920*. London: George Allen and Unwin.

Nava, Mica and O'Shea, Alan (eds) (1996) *Modern Times: Reflections on a Century of English Modernity*. London: Routledge.

Rapping, Elaine (1980) 'Tupperware and Women', *Radical America*, 14(6): 39–49.

Riesman, David (1950) *The Lonely Crowd*. New Haven: Yale University Press.

Sack, Robert D. (1992) *Place, Modernity, and the Consumer's World: A Relational Framework for Geographical Analysis*. Baltimore: Johns Hopkins University Press.

Shields, Rob (ed.) (1992) *Lifestyle Shopping: The Subject of Consumption*. London: Routledge.

Soiffer, Stephen S. and Herrmann, Gretchen, M. (1987) 'Visions of Power: Ideology and Practice in the American Garage Sale', *Sociological Review*, 35: 48–83.

Williams, Rosalind (1982) *Dream Worlds: Mass Consumption in Late Nineteenth-Century France*. Berkeley and Los Angeles: University of California Press.

Zukin, Sharon (1991) *Landscapes of Power: From Detroit to Disney World*. Berkeley: University of California Press.

1

IN DEFENCE OF SHOPPING

Mary Douglas

Shopping

This is a defence of shopping. Particularly, it is a defence of women's shopping, of the time they take over it, and the amount of money they spend on it. It is meant to rebut the ideas that men have about shopping as an activity and to indict a consumer theory that demeans consumer choice. To make the counter-attack I will mention some well-known weaknesses of consumer theory, which is, after all, a one-sided theoretical approach to shopping with crashingly obvious limitations.

Economics and market research are good at explaining the influence of the market on consumers' choices. The basis for that achievement was laid in the nineteenth century with the theory of utility. But nowadays the really difficult problem is the other way round. We need to understand the influence of the consumer on the market. To approach the current question, the effect of the consumers' tastes on markets, the idea of the consumer has to be re-examined. How homogeneous is the consumer's choice? Or how superficial? How episodic and disconnected from her deeper interests? Why do we suppose that she has any deeper interests than shopping? The very questions, as formulated within the current psychological paradigms, are surprisingly insulting to the intelligence of the shopper, who is, after all, the sovereign rational consumer.

One popular explanation presents the shopper as essentially reactive: she reacts to swings in fashion even more than she reacts to market prices. Swings and prices are the two explanations of shopping; by implication, if the shopper's actions are determined by market or fashion, the decisions are mechanical, not worth further examination. There is a respectable literature on hem-lines in this vein. Let us turn to the historical case of Edwardian trouser legs, getting narrower and narrower and then suddenly widening. An apocryphal story favoured in the retail market is that the Prince of Wales, before he became King Edward VII, fell one day into a pond and ruined his trousers; he was forced for the only time in his life to buy a ready-made pair. This did not fit the royal leg so well as those produced by the Court tailor. The politeness of courtiers made loose trousers the height of fashion. The prince's mishap provided the occasion for a swing that was bound to happen anyway. The tube-like Edwardian fashion was facing a point of no return as the tube got narrower and narrower. Eventually the boundary between trousers and hosiery would have to go under (to the professional loss of tailors), or trousers would have to get wider. 'Never trust a man in baggy trousers', my father was warned by his aged Cambridge tutor. If he thought to arrest a trend, the tutor was wildly optimistic, Oxford bags were to win the day.

If there is a pendulum, it is going to swing first one way and then another. But what kind of explanation is it that predicts change but cannot say when or what the change will be? Not everything changes; some fashions stay stable for many generations. Swings of the pendulum have not affected the design of standard knives and forks, used on standard tables on standard plates. It takes an antiquarian expertise to date them. Other civilizations – Ethiopian, Indian – eat elegantly without either knives or forks. Why has their pendulum not swung our way in the matter of forks, or why have we not swung into an anti-fork mode? The fact is that the swings theory explains very little.

Its supporters qualify it by claiming that only certain choices are subject to swings. The explanation works with an implicit division between purchases based on rational choice, and an optional element, for example everyone might need a coat, but the colour is optional and liable to swings toward the colour of the year. The implication is that some choices are central and steady, others are peripheral and transient, some have to do with internal, others with external matters, some are about necessaries, others about luxuries or surface decoration. Without some such division between choices, the swings model of the consumer would be absurd.

Style

A contrast of intrinsic/extrinsic features saves the swings theory and is congenial to a widely accepted idea of style as to how a work is done, as distinct from what it is. This theory of style implies some essence which can be separated from its appearance; the style is the external surface of a work of art, the polished smoothness or the rough graininess, the surface, extrinsic to the work itself. The theory stops further analysis by the implicit notion that everything has a hidden essence. There is always a reality which the appearance of the thing does not immediately reveal, something inaccessible. This aesthetic philosophy has been thoroughly denounced by Nelson Goodman (1978). If it is misleading in art history, it is pernicious in the theory of consumption. It encourages us to wave away possible reasons for consumer behaviour as inherently unknowable. Always be wary of a model of the human mind which brackets off large areas as irrational or unknowable; the conversation-stopper is also a thought-stopper. Ask instead the common-sense question: Why should people adopt a style that has nothing to do with their innermost being? Or, how could a person reserve his or her innermost being from influencing his or her regular choices? Or, ask what determines the part of human behaviour that belongs to the irrational periphery? What is the part that belongs to the ineffable inner centre? Consumer theory needs either to answer these questions, or to improve its idea of the human being. This improvement, I suggest, can be made by taking seriously culture as the arbiter of taste.

Market forces go some way to reinforce the swings model by identifying certain parts of consumer behaviour as more responsive to prices than free to follow styles. Changes in technology, new openings for labour, changes in production, these all produce price changes to which the consumer is more sensitive than to fashion. The postal zip code, for example, reveals the lifestyle of the consumer because choice of location responds to a set of market constraints. A given locality affords multiple opportunities connected with the engagement of the householder in the labour market. On the consumption side, if an urban area is so densely populated that there are no gardens, then there will be no call for lawn-mowers, pesticides, garden furniture, hoses or sprinklers. A huge bundle of choices tied to the postal zip code are made coherent by reference to market forces. But there are ups and downs of taste which cannot be accounted for by market changes. Even swings theory cannot explain a recent change in attitude to pesticides. It is part of a cultural change, whatever that is.

We have identified some things that are wrong with present paradigms of consumption. It is wrong to suppose that some choices, because they are not obviously responsive to the market, are trivial. It is equally wrong not to take account of the responsiveness of market forces to consumer choice. Above all, it is wrong to consider the consumer as an incoherent, fragmentary being, a person divided in her purposes and barely responsible for her decisions, dominated by reaction to prices, on the one hand, and to fashionable swings, on the other. Does she have no integrating purposes of her own?

Protest

I argue that protest is the aspect of consumption which reveals the consumer as a coherent, rational being. Though intergenerational hostility is important, consumption is not governed by a pattern of swings between generations. Even between generations, consumption is governed by protest in a much more profound and interesting way. Protest is a fundamental cultural stance. One culture accuses others, at all times. Instead of the weak notion that some choices among consumer goods are acts of defiance, I would maintain much more strongly that consumption behaviour is continuously and pervasively inspired by cultural hostility. This argument will reinstate the good sense and integrity of the consumer.

We have to make a radical shift away from thinking about consumption as a manifestation of individual choices. Culture itself is the result of myriads of individual choices, not primarily between commodities but between kinds of relationships. The basic choice that a rational individual has to make is the choice about what kind of society to live in. According to that choice, the rest follows. Artefacts are selected to demonstrate the choice. Food is eaten, clothes are worn, cinema, books, music, holidays, all the rest are choices that conform with the initial choice for a form of society. Commodities are chosen because they are not neutral; they are chosen because they would not be tolerated in the rejected forms of society and are therefore permissible in the preferred form. Hostility is implicit in their selection:

'I can't stand that ghastly orange colour on the walls,' says the unhappy tenant of a public housing unit (Miller, 1991). She knows perfectly well that a neighbour appreciates that vivid orange colour for its brightness. The colour is implicated in her neighbour's lifestyle. Why does she not paint it over in a decent creamy beige? The anthropologist thinks that she does nothing to remove the thing she hates because she is alienated from the council estate she lives in. Yes, and it might be a positive value for her to have a colour on the wall that she considers ghastly, a reminder of the war against the others and their despised way of life, on behalf of herself and hers. What colours did she wear? No shopper himself, the anthropologist does not report on her other antipathies.

'I wouldn't be seen dead in it,' says a shopper, rejecting a garment that someone else would choose for the very reason that she dislikes it. The hated garment, like the hairstyle and the shoes, like the cosmetics, the soap and toothpaste and the colours, signals cultural affiliation. Because some would choose, others must reject. Shopping is reactive, true, but at the same time it is positive. It is assertive, it announces allegiance. That is why it takes so much deliberation and so much time, and why women have to be so conscientious about it, and why it gives them so much satisfaction. That is why men are wise to leave shopping to their wives. Anyway, men's clothing and hairstyle is much more highly prescribed by the occupational structures in which they spend so much of their lives; they are not sensitized to such a wide diversity of signals. And the fact that men stand outside these arenas of cultural contest explains why they are surprised that things are so costly and why it is difficult to explain to them that so much is at stake. At the beginning of utility theory there were alleged preferences, then there was the indifference schedule. What has been missing all along is a scale of hostility between cultures. Inquiries about consumption patterns have focused on wants. The questions have been about why people want what they buy, whereas, most shoppers will agree, people do not know what they want, but they are very clear about what they do not want. Men, as well as women, are adamant about what they do not want. To understand shopping practices we need to trace standardized hates, which are much more constant and more revealing than desires.

Four cultural types

Cultural theory can explain how hates get to be standardized. It assumes four distinctive ways of organizing; four cultures which are each in conflict with the others. Choosing commodities is choosing between cultures, choosing one and rejecting the others. The four types are as follows. One is an *individualist* lifestyle, driving in the fast lane, as the advertisements say. It is a choice for a competitive, wide-flung, open network, enjoying high tech instruments, sporty, arty, risky styles of entertainment, and freedom to change commitments. In choosing this, the individualists reject the three other styles. One of these is the *hierarchical* lifestyle, formal, adhering to established traditions and established institutions; maintaining a defined network of family and old friends. (This is definitely driving in the slow lane: it only seems to be a thriftier lifestyle; it costs a lot to maintain the family network, so there is not much cash left for the high tech, travel, entertainment, and so on.) The other lifestyle rejected both by the in-dividualists and by the hierarchs is egalitarian, *enclavist*, against formality, pomp and artifice, rejecting authoritarian institutions, preferring simplicity, frankness, intimate friendship and spiritual values. Finally, there is a fourth type of culture recognized by cultural theory, the eclectic, withdrawn but unpredictable lifestyle of the *isolate*. Whatever form it takes, it escapes the chores of friendship and the costs imposed by the other types of culture. The isolate is not imposed upon by friends, his time is not wasted by ceremony, he is not hassled by competition; he is not burdened by the obligatory gifts required in the other lifestyles, nor irked by tight scheduling: he is free. Or you could say, in another frame of reference, that he is alienated.

Anthropologists have been interested in cultural strategies as a defence against the possibility of alienation.[1] This argument is on the same lines: there is a defensive element, also an element of attack, not against alienation necessarily, but against the rejected cultural forms. Alienation from one culture does not necessarily leave a person stranded; there are other cultural options. The option for punk culture is a rejection of the mainstream cultures, true enough, but rather than an opting out of culture as such, it is a creative cultural strategy in its own right. An isolate is not necessarily alienated in a general way; he can be quite benign in his attitudes to the cultures he does not want to adopt.

None of these four lifestyles (individualist, hierarchical, enclavist, iso-lated) is new to students of consumer behaviour. What may be new and unacceptable is the point that these are the only four distinctive lifestyles to be taken into account, and the other point, that each is set up in competition with the others. Mutual hostility is the force that accounts for their stability. These four distinct lifestyles persist because they rest on incompatible organizational principles. Each culture is a way of organizing; each is predatory on the others for time and space and resources. It is hard for them to co-exist peacefully, and yet they must, for the survival of each is the guarantee of the survival of the others. Hostility keeps them going.

Let me pause to illustrate the inherent conflict between cultures. Con-sumption has been defined by the image of the household shopping basket. Whatever comes home from the shops is designated for use in specific spaces and times. The fast-lane individualist culture is driven by the principle that each person should expand his/her network of alliances. It is hard to do this in a hierarchical household without tearing up the fences and intruding into the reserved times and spaces needful for the hierarchist's lifestyle. The hierarchical and individualist principles are at war, each contemptuous of the other, each seizing a victory where it can. This basic incompatibility lies behind the conflict between generations, and specially between mother-in-law and daughter-in-law, since there is a movement towards hierarchy with advancing age. It would not suit either the hierarchist or the individualist to have the household turned into an egalitarian commune. The isolate tries to avoid alignment, and in doing so gives offence to all, for it is difficult to back out of the cultural conflict going on in any home.

The myths of nature

Anyone reading this can recognize it, and anyone can see that if there is a constant pressure to define allegiance to one or another of these four conflicting cultures, it will go a long way to explain shopping. But so far it sounds didactic and a priori. The theory is that cultural allegiance pervades all behaviour, including shopping. The consumer wandering round the shops is actualizing a philosophy of life, or, rather, one of four philosophies, or four cultures. The cultural bias brings politics and religion into its embrace, aesthetics, morals, friendship, food and hygiene. According to the theory in its strongest version, the idea of the consumer as weak-minded and easily prevailed upon is absurd. Only consider the turning away from pesticides, and the turning away from aerosols, artificial fertilizers and carnivorous diets, and consider the great interest shown in the source of energy, whether powered by nuclear or solar energy or by fossil fuels. These examples of consumer preferences are not responses to market conditions. Quite the contrary: they bid fair to change markets profoundly. The consumer has become interested in the environment. But this interest is not uniform. The consumers are found in all four cultural corners: some are in favour of cheap fuel, including nuclear power; others are against it and focus more upon conservation of energy; others simply do not care.

Michael Thompson has led the way in applying cultural theory to the confused and stormy debates on environmental policy (Schwartz and Thompson, 1990; Thompson, 1988; Thompson et al., 1986). In what follows I attempt to apply his method to consumer theory. Thompson's method is to hearken attentively to the debates on the environment and to extract the basic assumptions from their arguments. Infinite regress reaches no conclusion. Eventually explanations must come to an end. Thompson hears the different strands in the environmental debates making appeal to the way that nature is. Nature, being this way or that, can only support this policy or that, and ruin will follow inexorably on failure to recognize what nature is like. He tracks down four distinctive myths of nature (Thompson et al., 1990). Each is the account of the world that will justify the way of life to which the speaker is committed. The commitment is not a private intention. It is part of

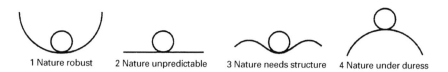

1 Nature robust   2 Nature unpredictable   3 Nature needs structure   4 Nature under duress

Figure 1.1   *Myths of nature (Schwartz and Thompson, 1990)*

the culture with which the speaker has chosen to be aligned. Thompson illustrates the four myths of nature with four diagrams from equilibrium mechanics (see Figure 1.1).

1 *Nature is robust.* This version justifies the entrepreneur who will not brook his plans being blocked by warnings that carbon dioxide pollution or soil erosion may cause irreversible damage. His cultural alignment is to a way of life based on free bidding and bargaining. He needs nature to be robust to refute the arguments of those who are against the trans-actions he has in mind.
2 *Nature is unpredictable.* There is no telling how events may turn out. This version justifies the non-alignment of the isolate. He uses it as his answer to attempts to recruit him to any cause.
3 *Nature is robust, but only within limits.* This is the version that issues from the hierarchists' platform, their justification for instituting controls and planned projects. The hierarchist wants to manage the environment. To justify imposing regulation on the entrepreneur's projects, he needs nature to be not completely robust.
4 *Nature is fragile and pollution can be lethal.* This position is entered in fundamental disagreement with the policies of development entrepre-neurs and with organizing hierarchists, and with the fatalism of the isolate. It is the version that justifies the anxiety of the green lobbies.

Cultural theory starts by identifying the context of appeals to nature, then it uncovers the strategies of debate, and shows the foundation myth as the final clinching argument. In fact, the base-line does not clinch anything, because there is no way of demonstrating that one or the other myth of nature is the right one. At some point the summoning of evidence becomes unnecessary; more evidence will not settle the divergence of opinion. Somewhere along the line the debaters realize that they are facing infinite regress, more explanations calling forth more counter-explanations, and when this happens, theorizing has to end. In a debate about what to do with the environment, explanations come to rest on their appropriate myths of nature. The task of cultural theory is to decompose the elements of the argument, and to show how each vision of nature derives from a distinctive vision of society, individualist, isolated, hierarchical or egalitarian. If the debaters were to take up their issues from the vision of society, instead of from its justification, they would confront the choice between organizing principles, instead of vilifying one another for moral obloquy. Between

visions of society there is no moral judgement. We are dealing in preferences, assessments of the outside conditions, aptitudes for achieving different kinds of results.

Myths of persons

With a little ingenuity this cultural analysis can he turned around so as to
apply to consumption. First, the field of shopping is not the global scene of
disappearing forests, eroded soils or large-scale desertification. The field is
defined by the shopping basket. The arguments are not about how to
persuade governments or control multinational companies, but how to
organize the household. We will hear an argument going on, and there will
be recurring clinching phrases, and regular appeals to nature. But of course
these foundation myths do not refer to the nature of the physical environment. In the contest about shopping, the threat of infinite regress is blocked
by reference to the nature of the person. The choices relate again to
regulation and control, but this time to regulation of persons, not of the
environment. Let us take each of the myths of nature in turn and extrapolate
from them what the corresponding myths of the person would be (replacing
the balls with persons in Figure 1.1 above).

Whoever wants to claim that nature is robust enough to take any amount
of knocking about is using nature to defend the entrepreneurs' claim to do
the knocking about. We would expect that claim to be reversed in the case of
the person on whom that householder wishes to put constraints. The
entrepreneur householder will claim that the nature of the person is very
robust so long as it is not put under stifling controls; the person's true nature
is to be free and will suffer damage if constrained.

As to the isolate, with no reason for sustaining any particular view of the
natural environment, neither would he have reasons for a sustained view of
the nature of the person. The way of life of the household isolate is
maintained by an uninvolved eclecticism. On the other hand, the hierarchist,
whose way of life is to organize and be organized, and whose justification is
that the environment can only be safe if it is regulated, will argue that it is
the nature of the person to thrive within organizations. Structure is a –
necessary – support for the person. Lastly, whoever disagrees with all of
those outlooks because of commitment to an egalitarian social order will
have the same argument for the nature of the person as for the nature of the
biosphere. The same corrupt, unequal structures that have caused the
pollution of the environment will also contaminate the child.

The source of foundation myths of nature also produces foundational
models of persons justifying or rejecting claims of authority from other
persons. If these four models of the person are sound they deliver the
consumer from the reproach of superficial fashion-proneness. It is cultural
competition that causes the underlying coherence of consumption choices.
Cultural competition is a matter of conscience. Looking for coherence from
the point of view of individual psychology will never reveal the con-

scientious shopper defending a cultural outpost. Psychology has no idea of what she might be protesting against. But according to cultural theory, when she chooses a commodity she chooses a flag to wave and she knows whom she is waving it against. Her front doorstep is a public show, to encourage fainthearted followers: she may want them to stay loyal and keep cleaning, or to break out of the chains and leave the step alone – either way, the step is a sign. The choices are acts of defiance, intimidation and persuasion. Buying groceries or cosmetics is buying weapons. Tables and chairs, detergents and polishes are badges of allegiance. Choosing pots and pans or pharmaceuticals is declaring dogma. So far from being mindless, shopping demands infinite attention. Pressed hard by enemy forces, it calls for constant vigilance, subtlety and resource.

Occupation opportunities

The argument about cultural hostility has, until recently, lacked facts to support it. The statistics of consumption have been collected within an interpretative framework based on individualist psychology. For a long time no empirical research was designed to test cultural theory. Now, however, that has changed. First there was the work of Gerald and Valerie Mars (no date) on the cultural alignment of London households. Then there was the reanalysis of survey data by Karl Dake and Aaron Wildavsky (1990) which successfully connected attitudes to risk to political preferences. Now there is the new research being conducted by Karl Dake, Aaron Wildavsky and Michael Thompson on 'energy futures' and consumption patterns.

The upshot is that cultural alignment is the strongest predictor of preferences in a wide variety of fields. The shopper's sanity has been vindicated. Her integrity is no more in doubt. She shows far more coherence and steadfastness than under the reigning idea of consumers reacting to market opportunities and fashion swings. She is revealed in her power, the main arbiter of the demand to which the market responds, before whose sovereign judgement the market stands in awe.

In *Cheats at Work* (1982), a study of occupational crime, Gerald Mars has identified different cultural types in the workplaces of modern industrial society. The social environment, being dominated by large-scale hierarchical organizations, exemplifies distant authority, centralized and delegated. Within its interstices there is scope for workers bonding together in ranked hierarchical units working for their own interest, also scope for egalitarian groups bonded for the sharing of some common booty, and scope for isolates and entrepreneurs working on their own. Systematizing, Mars finds the four types indicated by cultural theory:

1   Individualists can be recognized as lone operators working for themselves; specially favourable conditions are prepared for them by remote hierarchical control. Where incentives have been sucked out of institutions, leaving them blocked by bottle necks and redtape, the lone

entrepreneur can move in with not quite legitimate proposals, make profitable arrangements, help everybody, and get things moving, to their and his advantage. For example, lawyers, management consultants, small businessmen, chefs, taxi drivers, can slip the yoke of the system they work in.

2   Isolates are working where the institution gives little scope for autonomy or exercise of authority. They may be found in large numbers in the industrial scene. Bus conductors, supermarket check-out girls and others with practically no autonomy on the job can find ways of asserting themselves. Their typical response to a system which denies their dignity is to sabotage it.

3   Hierarchists are implementing a division of labour in an organization with ranked levels, responsibility located at each level. Where there is delegation of the work, resulting in remote and weak control, and a requirement for specialization, they can make up a pilfering gang. Dockers or airport baggage handlers can make a handsome penny on the side if they organize well and remain loyal to their gang.

4   Among egalitarian groups, with a strong external boundary, and weak ranking between members, are roundsmen and hotel workers, who flourish at the edges where, the hierarchy's writ having run out, they have scope to make a shared profit.

This framework of opportunism and evasion of control reveals a systematic picture of occupational crime. When Mars turns to another aspect of modern industrial society, the household, his method needs only to be inverted. Research on occupational crime has given him a practised eye for classifying organizations according to the amount of autonomy allowed to each member, the incentives for banding together, and the resort to ranking on the job. The object of that research was to assess individuals' self-assertion against a structure that is already in place.

Households

Gerald and Valerie Mars have now turned their expertise to household structure. For this research the objective is to assess individuals' efforts to build their own organization. The same practised eye can recognize the implications of spatial and temporal divisions and budgetary constraints, but this time they are not being imposed on the subjects. The household organization is created by its members. This approach runs so counter to the usual assumptions and methods of consumer research that it is impossible not to accuse social scientist researchers of 'cultural innocence'. Usual work on consumption behaviour works within the frame of inquiry generated by acknowledged administrative problems. Do we need more hospitals? Do we need more schools? Or prisons? How much public assistance, or public medicine, can we afford? For such questions the social categories developed by the Registrar General are the most accurate to be had. The population has demographic features, it is classified by ages, by sex, by education, by income, by nationality, religion. There is always argument as to whether it is well classified, and the boundaries of the classifications are regularly adjusted. But just as the categories are culturally innocent, so are the arguments. Cultural innocence characterizes a discourse about local politics that takes values as given even while arguing normatively about them; a discourse that seeks to persuade and justify action.

Cultural innocence is a dead hand on free inquiry in the social sciences. If all the information we have about household consumption has been collected for these practical purposes, it is unsuited to the profound questions about the motives and intelligence of the shopper that we started with. In those culturally innocent arguments the shopper is a cypher, nothing more. But the attack on the dignity of the shopper that is implied by swings theories has to be answered at another level. The question raised is not 'Why do these particular people buy these things now?', which is a question located in some culturally defined site. It is 'Why do people ever buy what they buy? Not now, but always?' Interest in their choice has been escalated to a meta-cultural level, beyond any local reference. The answers that we have surveyed (which imply a passive shopper responding to swings of fashion or following the market) have to be taken to a different level. Therefore we need information that has been collected specially with intent to test the hypothesis of cultural competition.

The first task is to get some imaginative grip on the idea that family organizations differ culturally. We are used to thinking (in cultural in-nocence) that the only significant differences between households depends on that very same set of demographic variables that is collected by the census: number of members, age of members, dependent children, other dependants, work of the bread-winner, single parent or not, income, educa-tion, employment. There is an implicit idea that if it were not for these differences, families would all be run the same way. To discount such factors, the Marses' research chose households that were as alike as possible for all these characteristics. They only examined households that belonged to the same social class; the householders had the same educational level, same numbers and ages – a husband and wife and two children of school age – living in the same kind of locality, suburban duplex units, with the same level of incomes. The differences that they found in organization could not be attributed to these usual explanations because all the demographic variables were held constant. With the practised eye they looked for use of space and objects and divisions of time, and for division of labour in the home. They carefully checked points in which common budgetary control would be strong or felt not at all. When they had established their index of cultural bias, they revealed four archetypal ways of organizing, linked to four distinct sets of values, attitudes and cosmology.

Once they had found extreme examples of each type, they studied them in detail. They studied the choice of toiletry, choice of foods and choice of methods of preparing them. Gender recognition (as in the choice of colours, towels, wallpapers, newspapers and weeklies) turned out to be an infallible indicator of cultural allegiance, positive in the case of individualist and hierarchical households, and negative in the case of the egalitarian households, as one would expect. Some households made a point of playing up gender difference, organizing chores by the sexual division of labour, and developing gender as a prime distinguisher for other choices, as between drinks, say, or soap, toothpaste, shampoo, hair oil, and so on. Other households played down gender distinctions, whether for allocating tasks in the home or for any other distributions whatever. It is a pity that this research is not yet published, for the early drafts hinted that when the method was perfected, a quick look in the drinks cupboard would predict the contents of the bathroom cupboard, or vice versa, and if both of these cupboards were read correctly, they would support a good guess at the range of friends who came into the house and the occasions for their coming. By the time they had finished their fieldwork, the Gerald and Valerie Mars had found the clues about time to be so revealing that they could almost identify the cultural allegiance of the household by the response to the request for an appointment.

Hierarchy against the rest

Obviously this was bound to be path-breaking work. Though the detailed consumption patterns were local to the time and place of the fieldwork, the principles on which it had been designed were general. Questions about how time is distributed, about space, work, gender roles, attitudes to authority and equality, could be framed for any part of the world. The principles on which distinct cultures come into conflict over resources are clear enough to generate new questions.[2] For example, it was outside the brief for the Marses' household study to follow up the pattern of relations and friends who were admitted to a given household's celebrations. But presumably hierarchists would spend a lot more time and trouble with inherited friends and less with work-related friends. One would predict that the hierarchists could be recognized by the number of their parents' friends' children they still see. Funerals and weddings would make another contrast between the two cultural types: hierarchists should be expected to attend relatively more funerals of old family friends, and individualists more weddings of new friends. The individualist household is much more dependent on workplace as a source of friends. Attitudes to sickness and health would be expected to vary along this division.

The existence of distinctive household cultures in itself demonstrates that the different acts of shopping that furnish the different parts of the house are not haphazard responses to particular needs. Some overall pattern is being used. It is not a static, rigid pattern. Cultural theory argues that it emerges afresh in new kinds of commodities every year, every month, every week, because of the opposition between cultures. The array of consumer goods in a house are the surface symptoms of an effort to realize a more or less coherent world-view about how a home should be organized. We also realize that shopping is not an exclusively feminine task. The right expression is that the woman 'does the shopping'. She may go to the shops, but the choices she applies are already made in joint choices about what kind of marriage and what kind of home not to have. As far as vindicating the integrity of the shopper, the research goes a long way, but not far enough. That household shopping is a joint affair makes it all the more important to reach into politics, ethics, religion. Nothing said so far shows a link between the organization of the home in terms of age and gender, on the one hand, and in terms of attitudes to pesticides, capital punishment, political parties and ideas about the dangers of modern technology, on the other.

The question is: do hierarchical rankings between sexes and generations apply beyond the range of the home? Is it unreasonable to expect that the hierarchical family is readier than the individualist family to accept inequality in the larger arena? Does cultural theory predict some homogeneity between the way the domestic scene is constructed and the construction of the rest of the universe? We who are working on cultural theory are divided on this issue. What follows is my own extreme position, which I doubt if any one else shares completely. I put it as forcibly as I can, with a simple comparison between hierarchy and individualism.

In the hierarchical home there is a strict division of labour: the man does the work labelled 'heavy', such as carpentry, work labelled 'emergency', such as unblocking the drains, and work labelled 'technical', such as mending the fuse. He is content that his wife should do regular chores that are not labelled 'heavy', 'emergency' or 'technical', so she cooks and washes the dishes, cleans the house and makes the beds, and, of course, she shops. This is the traditional division of labour. It seems reasonable that this background should predispose the man to divisions of labour in general. He can be expected to combine with his wife in setting up what Bernstein (1971) has called 'the positional family', a structure of relations in which everyone has an alloted place. His children are dealt with according to gender and age. The chores they are allotted follow the same principles as followed for the parents. Their bed-times reflect the age differentials: eldest has privileges in virtue of being first born. Thus there is a rooted expectation of inequality between the sexes and between ages. To me it seems obvious that this would be carried forward from the confines of the home to the rest of life. Is it not this same man who makes 'Yorkshire jokes' in the pub with his mates? Yorkshire jokes are affectionate stories about how odd it is for women to want to go out to work, and how the wife's work costs more than she earns, and how funny women are about shopping. With good luck, the wife in this home has her circle of cronies with whom she makes the equivalent jokes about how funny men are.

For contrast, take the individualist at home: this husband does the shopping and shares the washing up; he is not going to be able to laugh in the pub with the men who don't. But then he is not very likely to be drinking with them anyway and he can laugh at them somewhere else. Industrial society has its own division of labour: some occupations provide an all-male workplace, which would be congruent with the sexual division of labour in the home. At this point we need to face our own preferences.

Hierarchy, individualism and enclave egalitarianism are incompatible organizing principles. We are each bound to prefer one type of culture to the others. It is inevitable and right to have a preference. But cultural innocence should not obscure our professional judgement. One type of culture is not ineluctably, eternally better than another. There is currently a general prejudice in favour of the egalitarian home, in favour of the individualist home, or of attempted compromise combinations of the two, and a strong prejudice among social science professionals against the hierarchical home. Is this antipathy for hierarchy culturally innocent? The division of labour generally gives expectations of more prestige and higher lifetime income to those employed in the service industries than to those in manufacturing and extraction industries. It is in the latter that sexual segregation is strongest and where we are most likely to find the hierarchical domestic culture. It is possible that the current rejection of the hierarchical home is partly simple snobbism, partly opportunism, a conforming preference for an elite lifestyle. The child brought up in the individualist regime has a chance of profiting well from the opportunities of contemporary life. But there are costs. The hierarchical culture is destructive in some ways, the individualist culture is destructive in others. The hierarchical household is less likely than the individualist household to fall apart when calamity strikes. If the wife is struck with a crippling disease, if a child is severely handicapped, if the husband becomes permanently unemployed, the hierarchical home has more resources for dealing with the tragedy. For one thing, at least if either of the parents is incapacitated, it is an advantage to have friends who are not based on the workplace.

New research

A complex and subtle interlacing connects the domestic cultural bias with that of the occupational structure. Though religious affiliation might be the same, or education, or income level, the Marses' research suggests that the jokes will not be the same. Nor will the politics. We would expect that caring for the environment, caring for equality, and worrying about risks of technology would all go together. Respect for the established professions, suspicion of alternative medicine, worrying about the influx of foreigners would be another bundle of concerns. It is not daring to predict a connection, but, in fact, it has not been revealed by the surveys of lifestyles and values. The empirical data to support this argument have been hard to assemble. The reason is that domestic cultural bias has been ignored.

So consumer studies are left with the surprising possibility that a man has one attitude to his wife in the home and another attitude to women in general. It is still possible to believe, against intuition, that no connections hold regularly between home life and life at work. Since the idea of the hierarchical home has not been the object of study, we cannot tell whether it generates a desire for a new social order with greater concern for the environment – I would expect not. Does domestic hierarchy support egalitarian politics? I would say no, impossible, or most unlikely. Does domestic hierarchy go with green politics? Does domestic individualism support green politics? I would expect not. We will never know, so long as the market researchers are convinced that the significant differences between homes are registered in the census. If the market researchers believe that cultural bias in national politics is independent of domestic politics, crucial information about the noble art of shopping will never be collected and we will all be left with our prejudices.

Fortunately for the strong version of cultural theory, research to test it is now being developed. Given their professional training, it is natural that psychologists should look for individual personality differences to explain attitudes to dangers from technology. The change of direction comes from work on perception of risk. It was difficult to get acceptance for the first work on this subject (Douglas and Wildavsky, 1982). The breakthrough started with a survey that asked respondents about their attitudes to risks from specific technologies and at the same time sought to link their answers with one of two world-views (Buss et al., 1985). Contemporary World-View A offers a high-growth, high-technology, free-enterprise society, with a pro-business stance on goals and governance. Contemporary World-View B offers a future in which material and technical growth will level off, and in which governments will be concerned for social and environmental welfare, redistribution of wealth from richer to poorer nations, participative decision making and non-materialistic values. In terms of cultural theory, the survey asked about political preferences between two cultural types, individualist (World-View A) and egalitarian enclavist (World-View B). The result of the survey showed strong correlations between political world-view and perceptions of danger from technology. Since then more empirical results have connected attitudes to risk with cultural bias (Dake and Wildavsky, 1990).

We are on the track of the connection between the choice among pesticides and the differential bed-times of children, if there is one. We will soon know whether the preference for artificial fertilizers versus organic gardening is linked to Yorkshire jokes and the rules for washing the dishes. When the results of new surveys which are now being designed have appeared, we will discover whether the principles that run the home normally stay within the home. My predilection is for expecting the connection to be very close. If the new data now being collected by Karl Dake, Aaron Wildavsky and Michael Thompson support the strong hypothesis, then we are on the way to a comprehensive cultural theory that will connect preferences among commodities to preferred lifestyles, and these to the economic structure of the society.

Though this programme sounds familiar enough to make sense of it, we have not been able to exploit it theoretically because empirical support was lacking. The assumption that shopping is the expression of individual wants has misdirected all our inquiries. Consumer research had succeeded in turning round the normal everyday expectation. Most people generally assume that these cultural and occupational connections are there and that shopping is a fully rational activity, but consumer theory introduced utterly implausible limitations on that rationality. All we have to do now is to go back to common sense and take account of cultural bias. The idea of consumer sovereignty in economic theory will be honoured in market research because it will be abundantly clear that the shopper sets the trends, and that new technology and new prices are adjuncts to achieving the shopper's goal. The shopper is not expecting to develop a personal identity by choice of commodities; that would be too difficult. Shopping is agonistic, a struggle to define not what one is, but what one is not. When we include not one cultural bias, but four, and when we allow that each is bringing its critique against the others, and when we see that the shopper is adopting postures of cultural defiance, then it all makes sense.

Notes

1. Miller (1991) gives a summary of the writings in this vein.
2. Michael Thompson and Karl Dake are developing Gerald Mars's pilot study for a large-scale test, but this is not ready to publish.

References

Bernstein, Basil (1971) *Class, Codes and Control: Vol.1. Theoretical Studies Towards a Sociology of Language*. London: Routledge and Kegan Paul.

Buss, David M., Craik, Kenneth H. and Dake Karl M. (1985) 'Perception of Decision Procedures for Managing and Regulating Hazards', in Frank Homberger (ed.), *Safety Evaluation and Regulation*. New York: Karger. pp. 199–208.

Dake, Karl and Wildavsky, Aaron (1990) 'Theories of Risk Perception, Who Fears What and Why?', *Daedalus* (Special Issue on 'Risk'), 119(4): 41–60.

Douglas, Mary and Wildavsky, Aaron (1982) *Risk and Culture: An Essay on the Selection of Technical and Environmental Dangers*. Berkeley: University of California Press.

Goodman, Nelson (1978) *Ways of Worldmaking*. Indianapolis: Hackett.

Mars, Gerald (1982) *Cheats at Work: An Anthropology of Workplace Crime*. London: Allen and Unwin.

Mars, Gerald and Mars, Valerie (no date) *The Creation of Household Cultures* (originally commissioned as a report for Unilever, now being developed with new empirical inquiries).

Miller, Daniel (1991) 'Appropriating the State on the Council Estate', *Man*, 23: 352–72.

Schwartz, Michiel and Thompson, Michael (1990) *Divided We Stand: Redefining Politics, Technology and Social Choice*. Brighton: Harvester Wheatsheaf.

Thompson, Michael (1988) 'Socially Viable Ideas of Nature', in Erik Baark and Uno Svedin (eds), *Nature, Culture, Technology: Towards a New Conceptual Framework*. London: Macmillan.

Thompson, Michael, Warburton, Mark and Hately, Thomas (1986) *Uncertainty on a Himalayan Scale: An Institutional Theory of Environmental Perception and a Strategic Framework for a Sustainable Development of the Himalaya*. London: Milton Ash Editions Ethnographica.

Thompson, Michael, Ellis, Richard and Wildavsky, Aaron (1990) *Cultural Theory*. Boulder, CO: Westview Press.

2

COULD SHOPPING EVER REALLY MATTER?

Daniel Miller

In recent years the term 'politics' has expanded its semantic reference as almost all acts are 'politicized' or considered potentially political, while consumption has also become a rather general term for the use or reception of goods and services. As a result we could all too easily talk of an articulation between politics and consumption in a manner which would be vague and banal. My hope is that this would be less likely when one starts from the more specific activity of shopping. Shopping is particularly apposite because it is still commonly used to form a polarity which provides a rather narrower sense of the meaning of the term 'political'. In British popular culture we commonly denigrate a political pretension by suggesting they are concerned merely with shopping. Thus a satirical television show (*Spitting Image*) parodied charity pop concerts as having run out of real 'concerns' by suggesting they become involved in decisions as to whether a kind of soft cheese (fromage frais) should be placed in supermarket shelves next to the yoghurts or next to the cheeses. In the *Guardian* newspaper (on the day I am writing) the British prime minister is being 'put-down' in a satirical cartoon strip ('If . . .' by Steve Bell) by being said to be concerned with motorway toilets rather than some real 'political' issue.

I believe these satirists accurately reflect a popular conceptual opposition which defines shopping and politics as non-overlapping terrain. This is particularly the case for what might be called left-leaning politics, which seems to maintain a general distaste for what otherwise might be termed the 'vulgarity' of mere shopping decisions. It would seem that shopping has become about the only area of social action which is defined as clearly not politicized. This derives, I would argue, from a long tradition of development of the fundamental ideologies of politics as left and right, a structure of thought which today appears highly conservative and resilient against any attempt to rethink political possibilities at a time when many people feel we desperately require some new realignment of political ideology. In Britain it is generally recognized that it was the journal *Marxism Today* which attempted over several years to force through a transformation in political attitudes towards consumption, and it was probably this aspect of that journal which was most subject to ridicule by entrenched ideologists.

In a sense, then, shopping acts as one of Goffman's frames – it defines the importance of true or real political discussion by its opposition. There is a kind of logic of inversion which may in part account for this. In democratic politics the vote for government is a single act that stands symbolically for a vast range of choices about which the political parties as potential governments are presumed to differ. The degree of delegation of future micro-choice is encapsulated in the tense seriousness of this single act of choice. By contrast, individual shopping choices consist of constant, often repetitious acts, mainly directed to small, in themselves relatively inconsequential, actions. Choice, then, is as much a symbol of lack of consequence for shopping as it is a symbol for supposed consequence for politics.

I suspect it is important to the institution of politics for people to believe that the overall consequence of the single vote is of far greater import than the accumulated consequence of the micro-choices of shopping. Yet for the particular household or individual it is quite possible to subvert this supposed seriousness by arguing that the multitude of shopping choices have in practice far greater cumulative consequence than the political vote. Shopping brings decision-making down to the level of the consumer, who remains active; politics, outside of this one, some might say tokenistic, involvement, tends to rise quickly to a level where the individual appears passive in relation to decision-making. It could well be, then, that it is necessary for those (and I suspect this includes most of us) who wish to preserve the seriousness and esteem of political action to maintain this constant denigration of shopping by repudiating its relatively populist and anarchistic decision-making processes. We thereby retain the ideological underpinnings of politics as action.

This denigration of shopping is much assisted by the well-established legacy of its gendered nature. Cartoons such as 'Blondie' and 'The Gambols' have for decades sneered at the inconsequential nature of women by detailing their involvement and concern with shopping. In turn this ideology resides also in the relative expectations of political interest associated with each gender.

There are other reasons why politics may well require some such protection of its seriousness by opposition to mere taste. One of the most interesting chapters in Bourdieu's (1984: 397–465) book *Distinction* focuses upon political opinions. The emphasis is not on right versus left in political opinion but on the separation between the large group that tend to answer 'don't know' when asked for political opinions and the rest of the population. These are the people who don't have an opinion on the situation in Bosnia, who don't have firm political allegiances, who read newspapers that say more about the doings of soap opera stars than events in Latin America.

Bourdieu suggests that having political opinions, indeed the belief that politics matters, is itself one of the strongest elements of taste in modern life. It is a particularly strong marker of class difference and the lack of political knowledge and opinion is a strong disparagement of lower class status.

Politics as a matter of taste acts alongside other consumption arenas to assist in choosing compatible friends, partners, and so forth. One of the strong points of some Woody Allen films (for example, *Manhattan*) is their foregrounding this sense of political opinion as taste.

It seems that we start with a rather strange ideology which implies that the arena in which consumers have relative power is inconsequential as compared to that in which they are relatively powerless. This suggests that any exploration of the articulation between shopping and power has to include a critical appraisal of the semantic and connotative implications of terms such as 'politics'. Of course I am not arguing that only one of these phenomena is in fact important. Political decisions may have radical effects on people's lives, saving or condemning whole peoples, or alternatively bear on little other than slight changes in taxes, degree of control over big business, and so on. Shopping may range from people in near poverty saving months for some special item, to trivial choices over gifts masking insincere relationships. The important point is that there are overarching ideologies which prevent us seeing the seriousness in one or the lack of importance in the other.

This legacy of a politics–shopping polarity may explain why so few political theorists have devoted much time to the topic of shopping. In this chapter I will start with a critique of perhaps the most influential theorist on this topic – Walter Benjamin. I will then attempt to articulate the findings of an ethnographic examination of shopping in Trinidad with the major political and economic forces that bear on that island at present. This will provide further evidence for the negative consequence of the polarity between shopping and politics and lead to a final consideration of the possibility of a shopping that matters.

Shopping with Walter Benjamin[1]

Outside of what might be called the consumer studies devoted to commercial considerations, the social science literature on shopping is not extensive. The main recent burst of writings has been directed towards the spread of shopping malls and in particular the most spectacular malls such as the one at West Edmonton (for example, Chaney, 1991; Hopkins, 1990; Shields, 1992). I think it is fair to say that most such writings remain strongly influenced by Walter Benjamin, either directly or indirectly. For Benjamin's own ideas I am gratefully reliant on the book *The Dialectics of Seeing* by Buck-Morss (1989), and in particular her highly empathetic reconstruction of the Arcades Project, which is that section of Benjamin's writings (Benjamin, 1973a) most clearly directed to the political significance of shopping.

The Arcades Project was itself historical, rather than ethnographic, in conception, and Benjamin seems to have been convinced that the Parisian arcades represented a vital period in the proto-history of capitalism. This was important since, as Buck-Morss makes clear, Benjamin's aim in this study was not to analyse shopping per se but to identify a key manifestation of what he regarded as the essence of capitalism, and also socialism, in their historical evolution. Benjamin sees himself as sifting through some key historical debris, from which as archaeologist he then constructs two theoretical insights. The first is the arcades as a revelation of the awfulness of capitalist practice. Buck-Morss notes the constant allusion to the arcades as hell. This diabolical aspect of shopping is centred on its fetishistic purpose, its sundering of the population from consciousness of reality. Writing in the Hegelian tradition, there was no worse crime than such a systematic deprivation of consciousness. The shopper in the arcades is deluged with fantastic images that have as their purpose the mystification of the shopper, a dream world of mass culture that hides the failure of political progress in the image of progress as material abundance. All the shopper could obtain was a stupefied sense of anomie within a world of fantasies one could imagine but that proved merely elusive and unretainable promises if one attempted to take hold of them through purchase. The significance of such historical materials was precisely that they revealed the mere transience of these fashionable dream worlds, and for these European thinkers transience is almost synonymous with superficiality. There would be nothing more dead that the last generation's high fashion.

The complexity of Benjamin's vision lies in his idea that the arcades simultaneously provide evidence for another unseen development. To quote Buck-Morss, 'This fetishized phantasmagoria is also the form in which the human, socialist potential of industrial nature lies frozen, awaiting the collective political action that could awaken it' (1989: 211). As with his well-known essay on the reproduction of art, Benjamin was unusual in perceiving a true democratic potential in this new industrial capacity, but with regard to the arcades this is perceived to be merely a frozen embryonic form. The arcades provided, in a kind of grotesque parody, an image of what a genuine expansion of material and technical progress might provide for a population. As a result this imagery is important as a resource for the imagination of a future which was an important political tool within the present. The purpose of the Arcades Project for Benjamin was a bringing into consciousness of these hidden truths for the sake of the contemporary generation. This was achieved by showing that they were not what they claimed to be: 'The discarded props of the parental dreamworld were material evidence that the phantasmagoria of progress had been a staged spectacle and not reality' (Buck-Morss, 1989: 286). Thus the radical potential could only be allowed as embryonic, to be realized when society woke up from its trance condition, a catatonic state induced by an overdose of commodity spectacles.

It seems to me that most of the recent work on shopping and especially on the shopping mall has continued this tradition of analysis. The term 'staged spectacle' seems to echo through the decades to remain the conclusion of most current attempts to analyse current shopping displays as, on the one hand, achieving a distance from the reality within which we actually live, and, on the other hand, providing clues to the able semiotician as to some essence of capitalism which needs to be excavated through symbolic or cultural analysis.

I believe that if one is concerned about the political implications of shopping in the modern world, then the continued influence of this work of Walter Benjamin has been little short of disastrous. Even within the corpus of Benjamin's own work the problems involved in adopting his perspective are evident. Buck-Morss goes to some length to develop an analysis of Benjamin's complex philosophy and his understanding of concepts such as reality. Benjamin appeals to the aesthetically inclined not only because of his brilliance of style, but also because he maintained a deep – indeed mystical – sense of essence. Fundamental to the Arcades Project is the idea of an essence of capitalism and socialism and the superficial nature of the appearance of things which might or might not be cajoled into an experience of revelation. What Benjamin could not allow for, indeed what would have been his ultimate nightmare, is the acceptance of this world of shopping as mere reality. In Benjamin's notes there seems to be no attempt to understand the practice of those who used the arcades, and we are almost always confronted by two rather hollow figures: the bourgeois and the worker, for whom the arcades are supposed to have evoked this or that possibility or, more commonly, illusion.

This same refusal to acknowledge the 'reality' of commodity worlds, through the retention of this spatial model of the superficial façade against some inner 'real' core, remains the 'conclusion' of even the most vanguard theorizing of today. The debate over postmodernism began in architecture, which saw the liberating effects of pluralism against the hegemonic claims of a certain form of modernism, but this was quickly swamped by a pessimistic rendition of the triumph of sign over referent. Most writers associated with this tradition continue to inhabit a metaphysic where there is a hidden reality, both a pre-modern authentic subjectivity of the person and a global capitalist motivation or hidden logic. Both of these are mystified in the enchanted brilliance of refracting lights and colours of commodity imagery. In most recent literature, therefore, shops act merely to symbolize some generic sense of capitalism. This stance is enhanced in that branch of cultural studies which relies on semiotic decoding as its methodology. It is most clearly challenged by an alternative tendency in cultural studies towards ethnography.

If, however, one does not start with Benjamin's metaphysics, then it is possible to perceive much of his work in a very different light. I want to note another example of Benjamin's work which has not, as far as I know, been regarded as being a key work on the topic of shopping, and yet which I believe provides a pointer to this experience in a manner that Benjamin himself could not have conceded. Reprinted in the book *Illuminations* (Benjamin, 1973b: 59–67) is a piece called 'Unpacking my Library', subtitled 'A Talk about Book Collecting'. This actually provides one of the most sympathetic and eloquent accounts of shopping that we have available, although Benjamin attempts explicitly to distance his sense of the grandeur of book collecting from what he describes as merely 'the student getting a textbook, a man of the world buying a present for his lady'. This is, however, merely (intellectualized) elite presumption on Benjamin's part. In this piece Benjamin discusses the various means, what he calls the highways and byways, by which books might be acquired, the ability to seize the opportunity when a find, one might say a bargain, unexpectedly comes one's way, or the exhilaration of the auction. Benjamin recognizes what we might call the art of shopping as he notes 'The acquisition of books is by no means a matter of money or expert knowledge alone. . . . Anyone who buys from catalogues must have flair in addition to the qualities I have mentioned' (Benjamin, 1973b: 63).

In regard to buying books, Benjamin – the arch critic of fetishism – is able to make statements that could have come out of Hegel's *Philosophy of Right* (1952), such as: 'ownership is the most intimate relationship that one can have to objects. Not that they come alive in him; it is he who lives in them' (Benjamin, 1973b: 67). Because he regards himself not as shopper but as collector, Benjamin does not seem to have considered that the shoppers within the arcades might be in any sense comparable. The desire to valorize acquisition as collection is, however, by no means unusual. Belk and others (Belk et al., 1992) have carried out extensive studies of modern collecting and demonstrate the pervasive extent of this activity from at least Victorian times to today. This suggests that most consumers have had available, for quite some time, at least one strategy which Benjamin himself regards as an overcoming of alienation. Book collecting represents that vision of intimate and proper living which Benjamin, unlike his colleagues, was prepared to grant us as a possible future.

This piece by Benjamin is important to us as academics, since while most of us are not collectors as such, if there is one activity which might lead us to empathy with shopping more generally then it would be book purchasing. There must be academics who do not find pleasure browsing in bookshops, but I have never met them. Indeed in relation to books many academics will admit to just those 'pathologies' which are noted with concern in discussion of other kinds of shopping. There is the academic who feels the only thing that can alleviate a temporary depression is to go out and buy a book, or the academic who feels buying is tantamount to reading and does much more of the former than the latter. There is also the academic (and student) who steals books but not other objects because of the distance between what they feel they can afford and what they feel they have to have in their possession. The problem is that Benjamin brings his own poetic qualities to the sense of wandering the streets looking through the second-hand bookshops, and the atmosphere and sensuality of the activity. The problem is whether academics can break through this aesthetic barrier and grant poetic achievement and perspicacity to individuals considering the balance between the washing machine whose façade integrates into fake wood panelling as against the traditional aggressive modernism of white wares. Finally even if we romanticize such acts as on a par with Benjamin's own habits of acquisition, can these in any sense be regarded as of political significance?

Benjamin's legacy to shopping studies has, however, been through the Arcades Project rather than this article on book collecting. In his main work he more often resorted to the fragmentary aphorisms of the modernist, and their premise of unseen totalities. Benjamin was influenced by the boredom that the sophisticated intellectuals of Berlin and Paris felt about mundane provisioning. He and other intellectuals of his time were trying to evoke a spirit of increasing aloofness to the development of the modern world, to what they saw as mere opulence. But their figures were *flâneurs* – wealthy middle-class posers, full of angst and self-consciousness, their key influences were the modernist avant-garde keen to *épate* the bourgeoisie because that was central to their own acceptance.

These writings are no more true to the experience of the bourgeoisie as to that of any other group. Far from an inability to understand their own conditions as reification, current studies (for example, Nigel Thrift personal communication) show an increasing willingness on the part of bourgeoisie to put their sophistication to use. The modern middle class trained in institutions of higher education are a highly self-conscious and in some ways self-critical class watching Woody Allen films and advertising full of pastiche and irony; they exude scepticism, cynicism and even on occasion anti-materialism. They utilize commercial images constantly but with considerable nuanced and complex strategies and performances which are increasingly informed by relativism, structuralism, post-structuralism and the other resources supplied them by academics. The hip bourgeoisie of today would sooner betray ignorance of a designer shoe than admit to having never read Derrida or indeed Walter Benjamin.

If Benjamin and his intellectual friends failed to predict the trajectory of the bourgeoisie, they are still less relevant to the working-class shoppers of Chaguanas, the small town in central Trinidad where I carried out my study of shopping. By contrast to the Berliners of the 1930s, most of the people of Chaguanas experience modern shopping as the antithesis of their recent experience of sugar-cane estates and village life. For them the past is a kind of dark age of repetitive mundane daily tasks with few opportunities and few rewards. Enchantment must precede disenchantment and for the present at any rate shopping in Chaguanas is probably the most delightful experience available to most people in the town. But, contra Benjamin, it was not the appearance per se of the new commodity world that seems to have had this effect; rather I want to suggest it is the ability to appropriate such goods in the display of the person.

An ethnography of shopping[2]

The following account of shopping formed part of a more general ethnography which attempts to articulate the analysis of business, advertising and retail with that of mass consumption (Miller, 1997). There are many problems with ethnography in turn, about which anthropology as a discipline is currently exercised (possible over-exercised), but there may be advantages over the semiotician who merely projects this or that quality onto supposed but never encountered shoppers.

Not surprisingly the ethnographic encounter immediately fragments even the category 'display' into a variety of possibilities. The display forms favoured by retailers in Chaguanas are usually distinct from those most evident in the capital city Port of Spain. This stems in part from the particular position of Chaguanas within the retailing structure of the country, where it is generally regarded as the cheapest place in Trinidad to buy a range of goods. Local shopkeepers keen to retain this reputation tend to avoid the more spectacular forms of window display, and prefer a kind of 'pile them high and sell them cheap' aesthetic, which fits the expectations of the shoppers in the area. The shopper is faced with an impression of quantity of goods almost spilling out through the plate glass frontage onto the pavements or mall ways, with a clear message that the primary concern is not to waste money and thereby put up prices by a concern for the aesthetic of presentation. There are of course many exceptions and alternative strategies, but this one dominates the town.

By contrast, in districts in the capital where style rather than thrift is of greater consequence, the local shopping malls do indeed have the concern for eye-catching display modes which resonate with a desire for aesthetic pretension. Much of this is based around the particular ways in which Trinidadians envisage possession of and appearance with the objects concerned. This suggests that displays may speak to the 'promise' of capitalism but often by isolating particular claimed attributes such as cheapness or diversity and fitting these into particular shopper imperatives.

What does not follow, however, is that the intentions and strategies of retailers necessarily capture the actual concerns of shoppers. I spent some time trying out different theories as to how the shopper might consume the display, especially where this was a prominent feature, and to look for any relation between this and some general attitude to capitalism. I was forced to conclude, however, that there is actually relatively little attempt to appraise the appearances of the shops themselves, and my expectations with regard to trying on clothes and items and integrating oneself with the atmosphere of the shops as a form of display were only partially confirmed.

Even in Chaguanas there are examples of shops which have attempted elaborate façades and decorative elements which are intended to create a spectacular and dazzling effect. A pizzeria attempts the transformation of its interior through fake brick facing to that vague American/Italianicity which is common to pizzerias worldwide. A shop selling costume jewellery uses the displays of its merchandise to create a kind of Aladdin's cave. A mall at Christmas will be festooned with decorations and seasonal images so that entering it is made into an experience comparable with a child coming into a fantasy grotto.

There are also occasions when the ambience of a shop acts as a kind of frame intended to alter a shopper's behaviour in order to be appropriate to it. In a sense the shopper may 'dress' in the shop, trying out a persona or style of behaviour. Just as there are the larger categories of 'dressy' as against 'casual' in clothing, there are different expectations of how one behaves in a record shop as compared to a parlour. A certain way of walking and talking may emerge, as one tends to 'pose' using clothes held against one as props in an up-market clothes shop, while one's voice and posture signal how relaxed and 'cool' one is feeling within a bar. Often the nuances come from the slight ways in which the body moves in relation to and thereby acknowledges the music coming from the surroundings. Although I have not heard anyone express the relationship in this way, it is clear that many Trinidadians dress themselves above all in music and it is commonly music rather than visual display that is central to the sense of ambience.

It follows that shoppers may utilize display to reflect on themselves in relation to larger aspects of modernity. The clearest example of this relates the emergent concept of class to the use of supermarkets. Despite this, in terms of my more general concern to study the consumption of display, I as ethnographer suffered the same humiliation as the retailer. After a while it became clear that despite my and the retailers choosing to focus upon display, in the main this is of limited consequence to shoppers.

The only display that receives continual attention is that of the fellow shopper. Trinidadians while shopping constantly dwell upon the appraisal of other shoppers. They comment often volubly upon their dress, their bearing, their body and their language. What shopping provides above all is an excuse to encounter other people. It is commodities once appropriated and expressive of the person that are of concern; neither the promise nor the premise of future acquisition can rival this interest despite all the blandishments of retailers. This is true not only for shoppers but also for groups of men who 'lime', that is, hang around, in shopping districts and constantly make comments upon the appearance of shoppers as they pass by. This is a fiercely critical audience and there are many local terms such as *cosquel* and *moksi* to denigrate a lack of style which may be thrown out at the passing shopper. Public Man in Richard Sennett's (1977) terms, is not fallen, these are not mere *flâneurs*; rather one finds public appraisal and perhaps surprisingly public insult as a highly developed form of sociability.

The irony of this finding is perhaps best expressed in the words of the Trinidadian dialect poet Paul Keens-Douglas, who provides a humorous variant on this cliché about dressing to go to a dress shop, here with reference to the new fashion for keep-fit gyms:

Is at dat point Dorothy drop in de shop, she dress-up in one fancy jogging outfit wit' a sweat band roun' she head, an' ah towel over she shoulder. She tell Lal, 'Lal boy is only water ah drinkin' today, ah have to make three rounds roun' de savannah [an open space within the capital, Port of Spain]. Ah have to lose weight before ah go an' lose weight up in de exercise club. Is only nice man dey have up

dey an' yu girl cannot go up dey lookin' out ah shape, so ah have to get in shape
before ah go an' get in shape!' (1984: 87)

In the same way the clearest evidence for the importance of the shopper as
the key display item in shopping is the considerable time shoppers spent
dressing for the event of shopping. As in many other instances, retailing and
malls become largely a new form of public space which is quickly
appropriated for forms of social interaction whose logic and experiential
consequences are by no means a mere effort of the retailing institutions
themselves. Goods are of interest as display mainly when they provide social
information about others, especially people one knows.

I acknowledge that the above example is limited and 'vulgar' with respect
to the breadth and depth of Walter Benjamin's writings, but I believe the
ethnographer of shopping will find few worthwhile insights in the work of
Walter Benjamin. Benjamin promised to find philosophy in the mundane
object, but he was too infected by avant-garde modernism to ever really
attempt to evoke the experience of mundane people in mundane objects. But
at this point the implications of the ethnography may broaden out from the
agenda established by Benjamin to consider other possible relations between
shopping and politics. I will start with the immediacy of the experience of
shopping and the pleasure and anxiety associated with it, before examining
how far the Trinidadian study confirms the more general assumptions often
made about the implications of shopping in the modern world.

Shopping – pleasure and anxiety

The experience of shopping will matter to a varying degree to those who
participate in it. Apart from the sense of social occasion referred to above,
much of the importance of this activity derives from the sense of pleasure,
on the one hand, and of anxiety, on the other, and it is these which I will
briefly examine to construct a foundation for what might be called the
micro-politics of shopping.

Shopping as desire in Trinidad is complex and varied. To simplify this
complexity into two main tendencies, the first is the pleasure experienced
from spending itself. For many Trinidadians there is a bravado in the
'spending out' of money as quickly as possible as an act which demonstrates
one's commitment to a network of peers with an ethos of generalized
reciprocity and maximum sociability, as opposed to the individual retention
of resources. Such money is spent mainly on alcohol, frequent changes of
stylish clothing and liming (for a fictional example, see Lovelace, 1981).
Shopkeepers tend to assume that such people are relatively easy to exploit,
since part of the bravado is competitive, spending on conspicuously expensive things, where price is an important element. The shopkeepers claim
that the shopper won't buy unless a high price is charged and that they raise
prices to match the expectations. The constantly reiterated example of such
forms of spending is whisky in the oil boom and the desire to find

increasingly expensive labels (for example, Johnnie Walker Black Label) in order to demonstrate one's generosity.

Such spending out has strong metaphorical links with the realm of sexual experience, which seems to provide the dominant idiom. Spending out has therefore its own sensuality as exhilarating, exhausting and relaxing. As with sexual activity, many women regard spending as having powerful capacity to 'ease the tension' (the title of a popular calypso). This same group tend to oppose window shopping as something which simply builds up pressure. There were many comments such as 'I don't like window shopping. If I see something I like I must buy it straight away. It really digs me when I see something I like but I can't buy it, so I rather not see.' This may be associated with descriptions of pressure building up through money that is unspent and the sense of release when it is spent. Men will less readily associate these ideas with shopping as a generic activity, but there are domains of goods such as alcohol and clothes, and the external decoration of cars (for example, stripes or car wheel hubs), which do seem to provide a comparable sense of excitement.

There is, however, a quite different (indeed opposed) attitude to pleasure which is based around shopping rather than spending. Here it is the social activity, the escape from the confinement of the house and the investment in a gradual accumulation of possessions (which are often cheap and small in themselves but gradually fill up the house interior) which is key. The dominant idiom here comes from a sense of property and descent rather than sexuality, and storage is the goal rather than the threat. Shopping can be reconciled to thrift since the goal is accumulation as investment rather than spending. There is considerable comparative shopping in order to locate the cheapest example of the product. This distinction between the pleasure of spending and shopping may apply to different people but is also a temporal distinction with spending out associated with the period around Carnival and shopping as accumulation and investment associated with the period before Christmas.

In opposition to both sources of pleasure comes the sense of anxiety which is most often associated with the mundane shopping for daily groceries and household objects. Although such shopping may seem rather utilitarian and mechanical, as with provisioning in other societies it has its own complex rituals, skills and moralities. To take one example in brief, the decisions made with regard to a common type of household cleaner/ disinfectant were based on discussion around smell, colour and effectiveness, as well as comparative price. This was quite enough to provide considerable potential for rivalry in knowing trends, achieving bargains, having taste, and so forth. The atmosphere reflects the gamut of social relations. In one case a daughter-in-law may exact revenge on a dominating mother-in-law by her superior knowledge of changes in the market and constantly implying that her rival's products and choices are out of date or inappropriate. In another context two housewives freely exchange experiences of consumption in order that both should be protected against critical comments from what is regarded as the ignorant but malevolent world of men. The conversion of shopping knowledge into social relations was most evident in intra-female discussion, but may become highly emotive when it is others (especially children) of the household complaining that their expectations have been thwarted. What emerges is the moral responsibility of objectifying family values through maintaining the constancy of familiar products with a particular emphasis upon routine. When there is change it is crucial that this be perceived as progressive – an achievement – rather than merely a failure of routine or lacuna in daily life.

Mundane shopping, then, is an activity which is resonant with what has recently been termed 'the moral economy of the household' (Silverstone et al., 1992). In Britain the evidence of my own fieldwork on kitchen fitments (Miller, 1988) certainly supported that of other research on housewifery, which suggested that a prime cause of depression lay not in activities such as shopping and cooking in themselves, but in their subsequent lack of valorization. Depression arose from the fact that this key responsibility was trivialized, as was the material culture that flowed through the household. It is interesting to contrast this with areas of the world where the basic ideology that undervalues shopping does not seem to operate in the same way. Ursula Sharma's (1986: 63–74) analysis of women migrants to the town of Simla in northern India is interesting in this regard. Here a woman's work in creating networks of support for her husband's position in wage labour, as also her finding the right schools for the children, seems to be more highly regarded. Indeed the fact that there is as much concern for the rupee she saves by thrifty shopping as for the rupee her husband earns by gaining promotion is only striking because this is so rarely met with in the literature on domesticity.

The situation in Trinidad seemed to be between that of the Indian and the British case. There was in Trinidad little valorization of women's responsi-bilities. The point was rather clearly made in a typical wedding speech joke which tells how the wife will make all the little decisions like the children's education, where they will live and what they will eat, while the groom will make the big decisions like who will win the next election. I would not, however, confirm that this necessarily has the same consequences in Trinidad as in Britain since in Trinidad gender conceptions and roles seemed much more autonomous and, in a sense, self-valorized as against the close complementarity by gender definition found in Britain. Nevertheless this joke clearly exposes the ideologies of what might be called 'mattering'.

Observations which arise from the immediacy of the experience of shopping tend to be relegated to a domestic world of household relations. The term 'politics' may be used here as in the relations of power which exist in household structures, but our tendency is to see this as metaphorical, merely analogous with the 'real' world of politics which belongs to the public sphere. Making the linkage between these issues of the experience of shopping and more formal politics is made difficult because this articulation passes through a whole series of clichés and assumptions about the nature of shopping and consumption more generally. We are constantly being told both colloquially and by academics that shopping relates to say capitalism or the postmodern world because it is assumed to be intrinsically 'individualizing', 'competitive', and so forth. In the next section I want to directly address such claims to the larger social effects of consumption, since as long as they remain, it is very difficult to give serious consideration to the actual implications of shopping in any given situation. The next section is therefore at one level an aside, but I believe a necessary brief clearing of space to allow for a more sustained debate on the politics of consumption.

Shopping: relativism and assumed political effect

It is not only the legacy of Benjamin that has resulted in generalized clichés about consumer society. The literature on this topic is replete with attempts to derive a single explanatory account of this activity. Though more circumspect and less generalized in their original form, particularly influential have been Veblen's (1970) work emphasizing emulation and conspicuous consumption, Campbell's (1987) focus upon the legacy of romanticism in individual fantasy and lack of fulfilment, and Bourdieu's (1984) focus on the use of taste discrimination to reproduce class distinction emanating from habitus. In Trinidad I certainly encountered most of these traits, but also met with many social and symbolic uses of goods which contradict or qualify such generalizations. Here I will address just a sample of these assumptions, those of: increasing global homogenization; emulation; competition; individualism; irrationalism; superficiality; and Americanization.

Over the last decade, as historical and ethnographic studies of consumption have become more precise and the persistence of diversity clearer, earlier assumptions about global homogenization have been re-examined. On the whole the stress has been on relative continuity for prior social and economic structures. The anthropologist Marshall Sahlins (1988) has discussed the varied cosmologies of capitalism that result from different encounters with, for example, China as opposed to Hawaii. The historian Lizbeth Cohen (1990: 99–158) shows how the development of mass consumption in Chicago in the 1920s was much affected by the various class and ethnic differences that became the context for its further development.

In Trinidad, also, the new facilities and institutions of retail tend to be localized in relation to particular and often precedented concerns. For example, the appropriation of shopping malls as public space could hardly be more distinct than from Britain. In Trinidad they are utilized for a wide variety of social activities apart from shopping, of which the most important is liming. The small shops known as parlours become the focus of an ambivalent attitude to gossip related to the local concept of bacchanal. Similarly consumption attitudes that I took at first to derive from recent capitalist imperatives such as the tremendous capacity to absorb new clothing again turned out to be largely a completion of a cultural project which long predates the oil-boom and can be related to the use of clothing as style in village life in earlier decades.

Less stressed than such structural continuity but perhaps even more important is what might be called the 'a posteriori' source of difference. One of the main conclusions of my Trinidadian work is that mass consumption is not merely affected by prior structures but also gives potential for new unprecedented forms of cultural diversity and heterogeneity, which eliminate the presupposition of global homogeneity even as a future prospect. An example of this was the intense relationship between Christmas and shopping, which clearly contradicted the second common generalization about consumption leading to greater emulation and competition.

Emulation and competition may certainly be found, especially in relation to style-oriented modes of appearance. By contrast a study of 160 home interiors revealed quite the opposite: an intensely normative and non-competitive arena of consumption which is used to promote values of commonality and equality rather than individualism and competition. This is an observation which could be repeated in several other studies of home interiors such as McCracken's (1989) analysis of the material culture of 'homeyness' as a value in Canadian house interiors (or see Gullestad, 1984, for Norway). These ideals of normative and non-competitive consumption dominate the shopping associated with Christmas, which becomes in turn the primary means by which an idealized homogeneous community is formed/imagined out of what is historically a community constructed in rupture and creolization. This represents a far cry from the assumptions about the destruction of community that is the supposed intrinsic effect of the rise of competitive and individualistic mass consumption. Incidently Christmas, which dominates the shopping year, may (contrary to most assumptions) be primarily anti-materialistic in the values it expresses and embodies (for details of these arguments, see Miller, 1993).

One of the most bizarre clichés about shopping and modern mass consumption is the assumed unprecedented nature of those irrationalist and fantastic desires associated with it. I would not for a moment deny that shopping is an enchanted domain, but the discourse appears to imply that this is to be held against some other or some previous relation to material culture which was strictly functionalist. It is as though our interest in material culture would be pragmatic and related to some concept of basic needs (use-value) and true interests were it not for the blandishments of capitalism. But whether we recall Melanesian cultivation of long yams or seventeenth-century Netherlanders' concern with tulips, an abstract principle of use-value and basic need is something of a cultural rarity. If anything it is the abstraction of pure function which is unprecedented.

Trinidadian shopping provides considerable material for discussing an equally absurd supposition that the world of shopping is more superficial than a world without. This legacy of a strange mixture of Marxism with elite criticism of low culture (for example, Hebdige, 1988: 45–76) vulgarized as a debate on postmodernism informs us that objects have increasingly replaced people as vehicles of symbolic value (see especially the trajectory from Baudrillard, 1981, through Jameson, 1991). There are two related problems here, first that of the commoditization of symbolism, and second the concept of increasing superficiality. Trinidad, born in conditions of extreme rupture, demonstrates many of these traits of modernity with particular clarity but also suggests that their consequences are poorly understood. It may well be that within modernity there is a much clearer distinction between persons and objects as symbolic vehicles (assuming that Mauss [1954] was correct in his assertion that in gift societies the two are in effect entirely commensurable). It could then be argued that there has been a recent shift towards commodities rather than persons as the core expressive media.

In Trinidad there would be important advantages to such a transformation. Previously peoples had been generally essentialized in order that they could be expressive of key cultural values. For example, those of African descent were said to have no thought for tomorrow and were bound to the event, while those of South Asian descent were said to care only for accumulation and descent with no sense of freedom. Today, however, this dualism is increasingly evolving into attitudes towards goods such as those described above in association with shopping at Carnival and Christmas respectively. To some extent the achieved symbolism of goods is reducing the ascribed symbolism of peoples. Possibly as a result the prejudices surrounding ethnicity show some signs of loosening their grip. I am anyway somewhat sceptical that the writers on postmodernism really would prefer the kind of Maussian world where it is persons (mainly children and women) who circulate as primary valuables in the circulation of property.

A further advantage of commoditized symbolic value, pointed out by Wilk (1990) with respect to Belize, is that goods are increasingly utilized as the primary mode of objectification for plural political possibilities in the developing world. For example, with respect to identity, whether people should become more Americanized, more nationalistically Belizian, relate more to localized, for example Amerindian identity, or become creolized are increasingly both envisaged and then argued through the symbolic qualities of alternative goods such as Coca-Cola or reinvented 'crafts' which can stand unambiguously for these various alternatives. It is through consumption that political values may be formulated in such a manner that populations are at least able to appropriate the images of the possible worlds they seek to create. Through this objectification they come to consider who they might be in relation to the gamut of potential political identities.

Evidence may also be found in Trinidad, which would support the idea of a superficial element in modernity's sense of being, but once again the consequences of this are simply presumed. Most respected European and North American philosophical traditions and the more colloquial ideologies associated with them assume what might be called a 'depth' ontology. This implies that 'being' is some unchanging deep interior, often associated with roots. It is held against and opposed to the sense of surface or façade. This ideology clearly infects debates about modernism in the opposition to façade, but most especially the debate over postmodernism where lack of depth and constancy is the principal accusation held against modern life. But there is no reason why important issues of identity and indeed of ontology should not be conceptually located in both more transient and more surface-oriented modes. For at least one group of Trinidadians the concern with style is quite evidently profound precisely because there is a very different relationship between surface and being. Indeed their most common accusation against other Trinidadians is precisely that they are given to storage and interiorization, which is regarded as the primary source of their anti-social nature. Henry Louis Gates (1988) provides just one recent argument for such a critique of the connotations of the term 'superficial', and there are others more particular to the circumstance of Trinidad (for details see Miller, 1994: 219–31).

These relativistic critiques are important, since if we merely accepted the given generalities about the effects of mass consumption, then there would be little point to a debate on its relation to politics. As atomized passive symbolic vehicles for globally homogenized capitalist lifestyles our debates could only be rhetorical, never consequential. It is quite possible that many of these traits are found in association with consumption – indeed I will affirm the importance of fetishism in shopping below – but they are particular effects which arise in specific conditions and cannot be assumed as merely synonyms of consumption itself.

The political impact

Hopefully the space is now cleared for assessing an example of the relationship between shopping and macro-economic and -political forces, before attempting to dissolve their 'distance' from the experiential side of this activity. In politics it is likely to be the legitimation criteria that people bring to their activities as much as the activity itself which is of significance. Irrespective of the nuances of mundane shopping as expressive of social relations, shoppers in Trinidad are constantly expected to legitimate or rationalize their purchases in terms of value and thrift. In Britain as well as in Trinidad retailers stress the appeal of goods which claim to be on sale precisely because the shopper can in turn make claims to virtue in accounting for their activities and their expenditure within the home. This combines, of course, with the actual close relationship between available monetary resources and their ability to provision the home.

It is I believe this striving for cheapness and value, together with the notions of availability and variety, which subsumes many of the wider interests of shoppers and in turn provides the principal point of articulation between shopping as a domestic act and an expression of cultural values, on the one hand, and the macro-world of the political economy, on the other. I now want to come back to this relationship by examining the other end that is the political economy of Trinidad. Debates about contemporary economics and politics in Trinidad are dominated by a concern with the same bodies which today control not only small or peripheral states but increasingly even larger states, that is, the IMF and the World Bank. Trinidad has recently followed many other countries in being prescribed a period of what has come to be called 'structural adjustment'. I would not pretend to any training in economics but it does seem that these institutions and the whole outcome of the Bretton Woods conference do provide an unusually clear example of an economic vision developing as the pressure towards particular political practice.

In general I share with many Trinidadians a sense of disgust as to what these bodies represent and the effects they are likely to have. The Trinidadian economist Dennis Pantin (1989) has described the IMF as analogous to bringing in the receivers. In effect countries resort to these bodies when they can no longer pay accumulated debts, often the result of inequalities in trade between costs of raw materials and finished goods, on the one hand, and the over-eager lending by first world and borrowing by third world countries in the past, on the other. The IMF first and later the World Bank seem to do little more than secure the continued credit rating of a nation such that it can continue to borrow in order to in effect reschedule previous debts. But in order to secure this credit rating the country is forced through structural adjustment to become the epitome of a particular ideology emanating from the discipline of economics itself, which argues for purity of exchange controls and purity of free trade. As a result, irrespective of whether countries such as the United States or Japan retain protectionism and control of their exchange rates, states such as Trinidad are forced to abandon the protection of nascent manufacturing or control over their currency exchange (McAfee, 1991: 67–82).

The legitimation behind this activity given by the institutions is that from the perspective of the global economy the net result will be that goods will always be produced by that country which is most efficient in production and will therefore come on to the global market at the cheapest possible, that is, most competitive, price. It is argued to be better for all if countries only work at that in which they are judged through free competition to be exceptionally efficient. In Trinidad there is considerable unease at the likely effect of these measures. The IMF ideologists insist on the kind of balance of payments concerns which often result in huge cuts in social welfare, and which in a number of countries, including neighbouring Venezuela, have thereby caused understandable social unrest. Even big business in Trinidad has some ambivalence about the likely impact of free trade measures over the next few years. Beyond these effects the IMF is also a powerful symbol of post-colonial dependency. It demonstrates in truth that it would make little difference at this point of time which government was in power in Trinidad because the key decisions as to the political and economic programmes to be taken in this country will increasingly be dictated by outside economic bodies. It is clear to most Trinidadians, however, that what purports to be merely the dictates of an economic logic is in fact the instrumental arm of what is in effect a powerful political programme. In the global economy it is the IMF and World Bank far more than personalized Thatcherism and Reaganomics which is pushing for the world to be remoulded into the image of, perhaps not capitalism per se, but that most extraordinary institution, the modern academic discipline of economics.

What has all this to do with shopping? Well the resistance to the IMF in Trinidad, as in many countries, comes from a wide range of protectionist strategies that insist that local production under control of local forces may have many advantages even if the result is lower quality goods at higher prices than would be the case in a pure open market. Such a policy lessens dependency, it promotes local employment and the production of items with local symbolic significance as against the mere homogenization of commodities which derives from the global marketplace.

I suspect many shoppers in Trinidad would ascribe to the values and sentiments of the anti-IMF lobby, but their collective actions as shoppers may do far more to undermine that lobby than support it. As a collectivity Trinidadian shoppers are most often looking for the best value they can find. Certainly in legitimating their purchases they would most often claim that they spend considerable time looking for the cheapest prices for any given object and the best quality. Overall they see themselves as the arbiters of good value. This means that when, thanks to economies of scale, high capital investment, advertising and unequal terms of trade, a Canadian company, for example, can produce a higher quality (which here means preferred image not functional advantage) example of a soap powder or breakfast cereal than a local company, the shopper generally buys the Canadian product. In this Trinidad remains what might be called a sophisticated market. An importer of peanuts, for example, informed me that he can successfully outcompete a rival because his Chinese-derived peanuts are just that little bit glossier than those imported from the United States, and overall this gives him dominance in the market. I figure glossy peanuts are as good a definition as any of what we might mean by the term 'sophisticated market'.

The anti-local effects should not be exaggerated. Trinidadian products have improved in quality by leaps and bounds over the last two decades and in many cases can rival imported goods. Much to my surprise I found that by 1993 it is a Trinidadian conglomerate (Neil and Massey) that has become the dominant multinational company in the Caribbean as against the likes of Nestlé or Lever Brothers. Moreover, there are many areas where local products do appeal over and above imported goods or are simply not available as imports, reflecting a specific local demand for say pigeon peas or sorrel-flavoured drinks.

Nevertheless it is probably true to say that most Trinidadians are far less sentimental when it comes to the actual practice of shopping than in abstract discussions about national interests, and 'buy Trinidadian campaigns' are on the whole pretty fruitless. As such there seems to be at least some affiliation between the collective pressure exercised by shopping as an activity, insofar as this is governed by thrift and the search for what might be called good value, and the ideology of those bodies such as the IMF that look for economies of local scale and competition on a global scale in order to promote (they would argue) the cheapest and best value commodities possible. There is, then, an association in this case between shopping and what would usually be characterized as extreme right-wing pressures. Furthermore the political centrality of these questions about the availability of foreign goods and relative prices in the shops becomes evident when it comes to electioneering. These issues of the accessibility of goods then become tokens of future poverty and wealth whose political importance is evident.

Before, however, coming to a conclusion from this case alone, it may be worth taking one comparative case which might help assess this apparent linkage. There have been a number of accounts in recent years about the imperative to shop in the communist regimes of Eastern Europe prior to the recent collapse of those regimes. One of the most poignant is the book *How We Survived Communism and Even Laughed* by Slavenka Drakulić (1992). This attempts to communicate the feelings of ordinary women about the experience of shopping during the 1980s. What she portrays is a culture of shortages in which she implies that the degree of state control resulted in a particular neglect of priorities of concern to women. The humiliation felt at the inability of the regimes to produce sanitary napkins is argued to be as corrosive as ideological disagreements to long-term political support. There is the exhaustion of housework exacerbated by the sheer time involved in obtaining goods when shops are controlled by what happens to be available rather than by what people want. The less that is available in the shops, the more enticing become the images of the goods and magazines obtained from the West that seemed to make a mockery of everyday experience. Others have documented the emphasis on black market supplies or systems of barter felt to be forms of resistance to the current regime. Indeed this desire for goods may have been only second to the search for political freedoms in undermining established political systems.

In the Trinidad case the effect of shopping is to support the hegemonic transnational establishment against nationalist political concerns, which is exactly opposite to the political effect in Eastern Europe where it promoted the rise of nationalistic politics against the hegemonic transnational establishment. Nevertheless there are aspects in common to the political impact of shopping. I obviously do not want to proclaim intrinsic properties to shopping. The Japanese cooperative movement, for example, is intended to restrict the available range of goods and to pay more for goods which are seen as having certain moral qualities. This has, however, been rare in shopping as against the demand for as wide a range of goods as possible and for the lowest prices in a search which sees the source of goods as of little or no consequence. Where the latter position is true, then it would seem that the pressure emanating from the mass world of shoppers is towards a sympathetic reception for the claims by capitalism that it provides precisely the greatest choice at the least expense.

Towards a shopping that matters

The text so far has moved from a polarity between shopping and politics, to that between micro-experience and macro-economics, to, finally, the conventional political distinctions between left and right. I want to suggest that there is indeed a close relationship between all three and it is this which makes the challenge to our original polarity of such importance. To begin with the third dichotomy, the evidence from Trinidad and Eastern Europe suggested that in general the imperatives of the consumer as shopper have tended to be denigrated by the left and utilized by the right. Drakulić suggests that the obsession with equality in production was directly responsible for an extreme neglect of consumption concerns. There was, however, a wider asceticism in the left outside the communist bloc which tended to denigrate the desire for goods per se except as the removal of poverty. The right, by contrast, has tended to emphasize choice as a genuine consumer concern and promote laissez-faire capitalism as the most efficient agency for the fulfilment of the demand for cheap and varied goods. I recognize that this situation has certainly changed over the last decade but there is a legacy to be faced.

To dissolve this dichotomy we should start to positively value the concerns of consumption, but then realign these alongside, instead of against, the more general welfare concerns promoted most commonly by the left. To promote consumption interests means first recognizing that the desire for equal access to goods in terms of their variety, cheapness and quality seems entirely reasonable in its own right. Second, there are grounds for seeing the process of consumption as properly a key adjudicator of politics. The left–right dichotomy we seek to transcend is still burdened with obsessive arguments about the relative merits of state and private ownership per se. There seem good grounds for forcing these arguments to regroup around a realization that of greater importance is the subsequent quality of service for the consumer. Third, shopping is also a key moment of negation of the largely alienatory scale of both business and the state, and this sense of appropriation through consumption is closely related to the possibilities of actual empowerment and moral responsibility being experienced in consumption just as they are presently taken away from the population in conventional politics (Miller, 1987). To conclude, there has been a recent reaction in cultural studies against a tendency to romanticize consumption as always 'positive' or consumer choices as though they were inevitably politically 'correct' (see Morley, 1992: 20–32). But this was never necessary if one merely wishes to sustain the assertion that we need to realign our sense of politics to respect the imperatives behind consumer demands.

Breaking down the conventional divisions between right and left politics also implicates the tendency to separate off the micro-world of domestic experience as a pseudo politics of experience against a macro-world of true economic and political significance (Morley, 1992: 270–89). The problem here is directly pivoted on the overall dichotomy between shopping and politics, because it rests not on the lack of importance of ordinary shopping to politics but on our failure to give regard to this relationship – our division into separate private and public spheres. There is surely a close connection between the lack of 'mattering' which trivialized the perspective of women as the gender most commonly responsible for shopping and the lack of 'mattering' which refuses to perceive the direct consequences of shopping for debates about the IMF and major political changes.

It could be argued that this lies behind what is perhaps the most important cause of inequality in the world today. This is the relationship between the low prices paid for raw materials in the third world and the cheapness of goods in the first world. This situation persists in part because voting within first world democracies includes all the relevant consumers but only a fraction of the relevant producers. The net effect has been a fetishism of commodities on a much vaster scale even than that described by Marx, since here the global disparity of third world worker and first world consumer enlarges upon the original problem for the proletarian within the first world.

What one can only describe as this crime is then closely related to a reasonable desire for cheap, varied and good-value goods. It can therefore only be addressed when this imperative behind first world consumption is also directly addressed. This is why Benjamin's quick aestheticized route to fetishism is of no help, nor are those recent critics of consumption studies, who see us as merely reducing politics to the trivial and self-indulgent choices of the middle class as though these were of little consequence. Consumption is not an alternative to or rejection of the political economy. Rather it has become today the hidden key to the political economy! This is equally evident within first world economies in which the trend is towards backwards integration, where manufacturing is increasingly dominated by retail. In addition there is the development of post-Fordist production which constitutes a massive shift in the forms and organization of production in order to create greater sensitivity to the complex and nuanced local cultures of demand (Mort, 1989; Murray, 1989). As in so many other areas, we are having to acknowledge that the global questions of future economic and political development actually manifest themselves as much in the emotional significance of mundane household responsibilities as in the computer screens of world stock markets. The significance of consumption is that it represents a simultaneity between, on the one hand, a demand for value and an empowerment of the individual or household and, on the other hand, a negation of both state and commerce. In short it is where the politics of empowerment and the politics of equality meet.

I do not want to end, however, with merely rhetorical demands and no consideration of how they might be accomplished. I will therefore briefly consider three movements which appear to address these issues. Perhaps the most obvious response is that associated with the consumer cooperative. I would certainly not deny their contemporary significance in areas such as Japan where one recent source suggested up to a third of all consumer choices are made through such cooperatives (Clammer, 1992: 203). The cooperative represents perhaps the ideal in the politicization of consumption. But with respect to the particular issues of this chapter there are also limitations. I am working on a comparison between consumer cooperatives in Trinidad, Britain, Sweden and Japan which suggests that the relationship to politics is extremely diverse – a point insisted upon by Charles Gide in his original work on the topic (1921: 3). I suspect that future growth may well come rather more from an area not considered by Gide, that is, mediation in the consumption of goods and services provided by the state. At the risk of over-generalization, the political developments of the last few decades suggest that the relative monopolistic control of the state has tended to make it less suspectible to consumer demand than market competition in many areas. Indeed this may be the major cause for the decline of state involvement as in explicitly socialist states, even where there are a number of other clear social advantages to state rather than market distribution. A development of collective forms of appropriation that act to filter consumer concerns to the state may be most effective in extracting what are politically constituted as rights and ameliorating through protest what are seen as negative consequences of state provision. Such institutions might help swing consumer preference back to a preference for the state over the market as the primary provider of a wide range of services.

The final point with regard to such cooperatives is that they represent an ideal, but one based on the involvement of the consumer as, in effect, political activist. Since one might be excused some pessimism as to the likelihood of this being sustained in many regions and times, it is necessary also to consider other ways in which shopping might come to matter which rely less on shopping becoming politicized and more on breaking down the polarity between shopping and politics. From this perspective, while I feel more sympathy with Gide than with Benjamin, there remain grounds for seeing his contribution as the Charybdis to Benjamin's Scylla with respect to the larger articulation between shopping and politics. This is because the solution depends on the subsumption of consumption within politics rather than a challenge to the basic antinomy between them.

There is, however, a second-level version of this de-fetishizing of goods, which is possibly more subversive of the conceptual distinction between shopping and politics and which has been particularly prominent in the green movement. Despite a period of political success the green movement (when looked at with hindsight) seems to have been rather more successful to date as a shift in consumption than in politics, but this may be precisely its strength as a movement. It has focused upon an arena where most people feel they retain responsibility for decision-making. Recently, we have seen the rise of an alternative branding such as organic goods, free range eggs, environmentally friendly cleaning, animal friendly cosmetics and people-friendly catalogues of goods from third world cooperatives.

This remains a specific case, often associated with a particular (middle) class. There is no automatic switch which would turn green consumption into red consumption, dolphin-friendly into worker-friendly, though this has happened in the Japanese cooperative movement. The possibilities of such a shift are, however, of considerable interest. Once carpets have to carry labels asserting that they are not made by child-labour in India, once business has to make claims about the environmental consequences of particular products, then all sorts of new possibilities for shopping arise. Such information radically shifts the political participation of the population, complementing the tokenism of occasional elections with politically consequential decision-making on a daily basis. Once sufficient numbers of goods become moral, then by definition the choice of all other goods becomes a refusal of this alternative option. As with the cooperative, however, this remains at present perhaps only a straw in the wind.

The third potential transformation of the current alignments of shopping would require movement within the political realm to match these movements in consumption. Politics would be wise to be in the vanguard of such changes rather than resisting pressures from popular culture which not only are evident in shopping but can also be discerned in the wider demand to invade public space in anything from public access television to the rise of audience participatory chat shows. A sensible left at this stage might leapfrog the right and reform as the consumer's party, a stance which would include the reinscription of morality onto goods and affirm the links between an affirmation of the importance of consumer demands and more conventional welfare demands. Indeed state bureaucracy is essential to any such political programme since it is the only institution that could be expected to attest the veracity of consumer information by prosecuting clearly fraudulent claims to, for example, environmental concerns. The result would be more bureaucracy rather than laissez-faire economics. The appeal of such politics must also lie in state support for the self-interest of consumers through bodies of consumer information and protection services. This effective conjoining of altruism and self-interest is evident in the current green consumption which seems to comprise in equal measure a concern about pesticides as a threat to the world and pesticides as a threat to one own health.

A focus upon consumption may have certain advantages over current trends stressing a new politics of citizenship and rights. In many respects these latter are relatively abstract phenomena defined by legal forces rather than by those who make the claims, and retain a dualism whereby people encounter politics and have to prise rights out of it. By contrast, consumption is relatively anarchic and dispersed down to the level at which most people already feel a sense of both freedom and responsibility insofar as their consumer decisions are already part of the 'politics' of domestic life. It also starts to break down the ideological polarity between politics and shopping which continues to provide the principal barrier to the valorizing of the moral responsibilities of the ordinary shopper.

To conclude – the polarization between shopping and politics lies deep in contemporary ideology. It will not be threatened either by the approach to shopping which followed Benjamin's semiotic aphorisms or by Gide's emphasis on shopping as political activism. Rather we require first the ethnography of mundane shopping that may relativize the phenomena and detach it from the clichés that supposedly describe its intrinsic attributes. A subsequent reconsideration of shopping could challenge given divisions between private and public spheres and conventional notions of right versus left in politics by highlighting the relationship between the profundity of consumers' involvement and their political and economic effect. It is the principal assertion of this chapter that the ideological dichotomy between politics and shopping is a major barrier to the badly needed transcendence of these other dichotomies. What is required is both a realignment between the imperatives of consumption and political goals, and an acknowledgement of the centrality of consumption to politics. So in answer to my original question as to whether shopping could ever really matter, it seems that shopping can only matter more if politics were to matter less. There are at least some grounds for suggesting that such an act of political humility might well serve certain political purposes surprisingly effectively.

Notes

1. The following section on Benjamin was subject to a powerful critique by both Stuart Hall and Michael Taussig when I presented this chapter as a paper at a workshop at Rutgers University. Both of these scholars are far more knowledgable on this topic than I would claim to be, and I am convinced that my treatment of Benjamin is superficial and in part a misrepresentation. My only defence is that I was concerned not so much with Benjamin himself as with an abiding influence on what I regard as a problematic tendency in the study of shopping. Rather than withdraw this section I would therefore suggest that it be read as a vulgar critique of a vulgar use of a profound thinker!

2. This section is based on fieldwork in Trinidad.

References

Baudrillard, Jean (1981) *For a Critique of the Political Economy of the Sign.* St Louis, MO: Telos Press.

Belk, Russell, Wallendorf, Melanie, Sherry, Jr., John F. and Holbrook, Morris B. (1992) 'Collecting in a Consumer Culture', in Russell Belk (ed.), *Highways and Buyways.* Provo, UT: Association for Consumer Research. pp. 178–215.

Benjamin, Walter (1973a) *Charles Baudelaire: A Lyric Poet in the Era of High Capitalism.* London: New Left Books.

Benjamin, Walter (1973b) *Illuminations.* London: Fontana.

Bourdieu, Pierre (1984) *Distinction: A Social Critique of the Judgement of Taste.* London: Routledge and Kegan Paul.

Buck-Morss, Susan (1989) *The Dialectics of Seeing: Walter Benjamin and the Arcades Project.* Cambridge, MA: MIT Press.

Campbell, Colin (1987) *The Romantic Ethic and the Spirit of Modern Consumerism.* Oxford: Basil Blackwell.

Chaney, David (1991) 'Subtopia in Gateshead: The Metrocentre as a Cultural Form', *Theory, Culture & Society*, 7(4): 49–68.

Clammer, John (1992) 'Aesthetics of the Self: Shopping and Social Being in Contemporary Urban Japan', in Rob Shields (ed.), *Lifestyle Shopping.* London: Routledge, pp. 195–215.

Cohen, Lizbeth (1990) *Making a New Deal*. Cambridge: Cambridge University Press.
Drakulić, Slavenka (1992) *How We Survived Communism and Even Laughed*. London: Hutchinson.
Gates, Henry (1988) *The Signifying Monkey*. Oxford: Oxford University Press.
Gide, C. (1921) *Consumers' Co-operative Societies*. New York: Haskell House.
Gullestad, Marianne (1984) *Kitchen-Table Society*. Oslo: Universitetsforlaget.
Hebdige, Dick (1988) 'Towards a Cartography of Taste 1935–1962', in his *Hiding in the Light: On Images and Things*. London: Routledge.
Hegel, Georg (1952) *Philosophy of Right*. Oxford: Clarendon Press.
Hopkins, Jeffrey (1990) 'West Edmonton Mall: Landscape of Myths and Elsewhereness', *The Canadian Geographer*, 34: 2–17.
Jameson, Frederic (1991) *Postmodernism or the Cultural Logic of Late Capitalism*. London: Verso.
Keens-Douglas, Paul (1984) *Lal Shop*. Port of Spain: College Press.
Lovelace, Earl (1981) *The Dragon Can't Dance*. London: Longman.
McAfee, Kathy (1991) *Storm Signals: Structural Adjustment and Development Alternatives in the Caribbean*. London: Zed.
McCracken, Grant (1989) ' "Homeyness": A Cultural Account of One Constellation of Consumer Goods and Meanings', in Elizabeth Hirschman (ed.), *Interpretive Consumer Research*. Provo, UT: Assocation for Consumer Research, pp. 168–83.
Mauss, Marcel (1954) *The Gift*. London: Cohen and West.
Miller, Daniel (1987) *Material Culture and Mass Consumption*. Oxford: Basil Blackwell.
Miller, Daniel (1988) 'Appropriating the State on the Council Estate', *Man*, 23: 353–72.
Miller, Daniel (1993) 'Christmas against Materialism in Trinidad', in Daniel Miller (ed.), *Unwrapping Christmas*. Oxford: Oxford University Press. pp. 134–53.
Miller, Daniel (1994) *Modernity – An Ethnographic Approach*. Oxford: Berg.
Miller, Daniel (1997) *Capitalism – An Ethnographic Approach*. Oxford: Berg.
Morley, David (1992) *Television Audiences and Cultural Studies*. London: Routledge.
Mort, Frank (1989) 'The Politics of Consumption', in Stuart Hall and Martin Jacques (eds), *New Times*. London: Lawrence and Wishart. pp. 160–72.
Murray, R. (1989) 'Benetton Britain', in Stuart Hall and Martin Jacques (eds), *New Times*. London: Lawrence and Wishart. pp. 54–64.
Pantin, David (1989) *Into the Valley of Debt*. Trinidad: Gloria V. Ferguson. Ltd.
Sahlins, Marshall (1988) 'Cosmologies of Capitalism', *Proceedings of the British Academy*, LXXIV: 1–51.
Sennett, Richard (1977) *The Fall of Public Man: On the Social Psychology of Capitalism*. New York: Alfred A. Knopf.
Sharma, Ursula (1986) *Women's Work, Class and the Urban Household*. London: Tavistock.
Shields, Rob (1989) 'Social Spatialization and the Built Environment: The Case of the West Edmonton Mall', *Environment and Planning D: Society and Space*, 7(2): 147–64.
Shields, Rob (ed.) (1992) *Lifestyle Shopping: The Subject of Consumption*. London: Routledge.
Silverstone, Roger, Hirsch, Eric and Morley, David (1992) 'Information and Communication Technologies and the Moral Economy of the Household', in Roger Silverstone and Eric Hirsch (eds), *Consuming Technologies*. London: Routledge. pp. 15–31.
Veblen, Thorstein (1970) *The Theory of the Leisure Class*. London: Unwin.
Wilk, Richard (1990) 'Consumer Goods as Dialogue about Development', *Culture and History*, 7: 79–100.

3

MODERNITY'S DISAVOWAL: WOMEN, THE CITY AND THE DEPARTMENT STORE

Mica Nava

Introduction: a genealogy of absence

This project started out as an investigation of the position of women in modernity. By focusing on shopping and the emergence of the department store as key iconic aspects of modern urban society my intention was to argue against those theorists who defined modernity of the late nineteenth and early twentieth centuries as a public stage from which women were excluded. However, my attempt to integrate conceptualizations of modernity with questions raised by feminism and the culture of consumption revealed a surprising paucity of theoretical and historical work – a phenomenon which itself required explanation. Increasingly, therefore, my project was transformed into a genealogy of absence. It became, in addition to an engagement with existing debates and histories, an investigation into the often unconscious motives and priorities that operate in the production of intellectual work and that in this instance have led, I will argue, to the disavowal of a major narrative of twentieth-century life.

Modernity and women

The argument for deploying the concept of modernity in order to make sense of the cultural and material changes which were accelerated in the major cities of the Western world towards the end of the nineteenth century and the early decades of the twentieth century has been elaborated elsewhere (O'Shea, 1996).[1] My particular focus is on the experience and representation of women, and in this context, on the emergence of new forms of social interaction and perception and on the development of a new consciousness about the possibilities that modern urban life was able to offer. Modernity as I use it here – and I have produced a composite account for the purpose of this argument by selecting pertinent features from a range of contributions, both contemporary and more recent[2] – highlights the complexity and danger, as well as the richness and excitement, of everyday life in the modern city.

It draws attention to the texture of commonplace experiences in the metropolis, to an environment characterized by continuous flux and frequent encounters with strangers, in which signs and appearances acquire a new importance and substitute increasingly for traditional narratives of social and geographical belonging. There is a new stress on display and the visual – on looking. Modern urban existence, with its transience and uncertainty, demands new morals as well as new fashions. It produces new aspirations. It generates new enterprises, new languages and cultural forms. But modernity is not only about renewal. As a concept it also emphasizes disintegration and fragmentation. It signals the destabilizing of many nineteenth-century con-ventions and highlights the pessimism as well as boldness of the modern imagination. And yet throughout it suggests a kind of *forward-lookingness* and a way, as Marshall Berman (1984) has put it, of making oneself at home in the chaos – 'the maelstrom' – of modern life, of becoming the subjects as well as the objects of modernization.

Modernity of course is a constructed narrative, and, like any other, offers us a *version* of events and the past in that it singles out certain phenomena for investigation or emphasis and ignores others. It is perhaps unsurprising to note, therefore, that despite the wide range of appropriations of the concept and its fertility in epistemological terms, it has failed on the whole to address the experience of women. In some of the classic accounts the prostitute or actress-entertainer is depicted as the characteristic female figure in the iconography of the urban landscape, in this way shoring up nineteenth-century dualistic thought about virtuous and fallen women as well as mythologies of the sexually licentious city (Buci-Glucksmann, 1987; Wilson, 1991) and at the same time ignoring ordinary women. Some of the more recent accounts have been even more neglectful, astonishingly so given the critical climate of the last two decades: Frisby (1985), for example, refers not at all to sexual difference in his study of Simmel, Benjamin and Kracauer as key commenta-tors on modernity, far less even than the authors did themselves when they wrote at the beginning of this century (van Vucht Tijssen, 1991).

The project of academic feminism has been to prise open this sort of narrative and make sense of the marginalization of women both theoretically and historically wherever possible. Janet Wolff's influential 'The Invisible Flâneuse: Women in the Literature of Modernity' (1985) has been the seminal piece on this intellectual issue[3] and the argument I develop here was generated in the first instance in response to hers. Wolff's thesis is that women are absent from the critical literature of modernity because its focus is largely upon the public sphere, on the crowded city street and the experience of the *flâneur*, on the world of politics and work – on areas from which, according to her, women were excluded. Hence their neglect by the theorists of modernity. Women's increasing confinement to the domestic sphere during the nineteenth century coincides with the development of the new discipline of sociology, which is concerned to classify and explain the changing phenomena of the modern *public* world. The more literary con-tributions also understand modernity as uniquely associated with the city and public life. Thus women's activities and labour, even where these are not confined to the home, are largely invisible. 'The literature of modernity ignores the private sphere and to that extent is silent on the subject of women's primary domain' (Wolff, 1985: 44). Although Wolff acknowledges, though almost as an aside, that women are provided with a new public arena as a consequence of the emergence of the department store,[4] her argument is that the characteristics of modernity identified by authors like Baudelaire and Benjamin – 'the fleeting anonymous encounter and the purposeless strolling' – do not apply to activities of women. In sum Wolff's argument is that women were not only excluded from the literature of modernity but, confined as they were to the domestic sphere and the suburbs, women were also excluded from the *experience* of modernity. No female equivalent of the *flâneur* can be invented.

Although this article has made a valuable contribution by opening up the debate, there are nevertheless certain key assumptions in it with which I disagree. My argument will be that women were *not* excluded from the experience of modernity in the public sphere: that, on the contrary, they participated quite crucially in its formation. Indeed women's experience can be interpreted as a quintessential constituent of modernity. So we must look elsewhere if we are to understand the exclusion of women from the literature.

The reason that Wolff has argued otherwise is in part a consequence of her periodization. The historical focus of her essay is on conditions during the second half of the nineteenth century, on those roughly contemporaneous with the 'early modernity' of Baudelaire, the period which Benjamin called 'the prehistory of modernity'.[5] If she had periodized modernity differently and linked it to the drama of high modernism, the expansion of mass culture and consumption and the socio-political instability of the late nineteenth and early twentieth centuries, her investigation would have encompassed the moment when women's appropriation of public spaces, in both symbolic and material ways, was growing rapidly. In this case, her argument about women's lack of participation in the experience of modernity would have been harder to sustain.

Another difficulty with Wolff's argument is that she depicts the '*flâneur*' as the archetype of modernity. Here she reproduces the tendency in much of the literature to single out the artist-observer – 'the botaniser on the asphalt' (usually the author himself) – as *the* representative of the modern urban experience. In fact Baudelaire's *flâneur* – 'the painter of modern life' – was an observer and recorder of modernity, he did not exemplify it. Wolff's *flâneur* is, moreover, always a man, because according to her argument only men have the freedom to wander at will and 'take visual possession of the city'.[6] My argument will be that Wolff's concept of the *flâneur*, although productive for its emphasis on the ephemeral and the ocular – on looking – is limited insofar as it excludes the everyday spectatorship of ordinary people, and especially ordinary women.

In general Wolff's conclusions are representative of a rich but often pessimistic tradition in feminist historiography which tends to focus on the subordination of women and their marginalization in mainstream historical accounts.[7] Although these readings have had their political and theoretical importance, they have also inhibited the excavation of other 'truths'. Berman's emphasis on making the world your own, on the heroism as well as the despair of everyday life, offers the possibility of a different kind of interpretation of women's relationship to modernity, despite his own relative neglect of the issues. If Janet Wolff had been readier to focus on the expansion of women's cultural experiences in the city rather than on the constraints, then, paradoxically, she would have been in a position to advance more forcefully the second part of her argument, where she points to the invisibility of women in the *literature* of modernity.

But Wolff's process of deconstruction is not taken far enough. The absence from the literature is read as evidence of a 'real' absence rather than evidence of itself. A different reading of women's participation in modernity would have emphasized the constructedness of this literature. It would have highlighted the *intellectual* exclusion of women and the ambivalence of the authors about cultural change – the androcentrism of most of the texts about modernity. Janet Wolff's own argument about women's invisibility would have been rendered at once more complex and more persuasive.

These are the issues that are going to be developed in this chapter. The focus will be mainly on the department store and shopping in the urban context as an example of the way in which women engaged with the maelstrom of modern life. An exploration of this history will expand our understanding not only of the process of modernity but also, quite crucially, of the way it has been represented to us. In this sense it will be, as I suggested earlier, a kind of genealogy of absence. The question is: how can we make sense of the failure to acknowledge women's participation in the making of modern urban consumer culture – of the disavowal of this pivotal aspect of early twentieth-century life?

One way of addressing this – even if not resolving it – is to look also at some of the formative popular and critical responses to consumerism and mass culture during the first decades of this century and to consider the ways in which the psychic and historical formations of authors inflect the texts that they produce.

Women and the city

It is important first to explore the symbolic resonance of the city in modernity and register its significance in relation to our objects of concern, to women, the department store and mass culture. More than any other social force of the nineteenth century, the city evoked the freedom as well as the menace that characterized the modern experience. Throughout this period it grew as a territory not only spatially but also in terms of its cultural significations, in the way in which it was understood and represented. The city was increasingly mythologized – albeit in contradictory ways. The British version of this imagined geography tended to stress the disturbing aspects of the urban environment, the chaos and pollution, moral and sexual dissolution and the erosion of traditional order.[8] In this narrative the threatening nature of the city regularly operated as a counterpoint to the ideal of a virtuous and harmonious rural or suburban domestic existence.[9]

This kind of polarization (splitting and projection, in psychoanalytical terms) can be understood as an attempt to impose a moral and cognitive order on a highly volatile and incomprehensible geo-political context. It is also linked to the sexualization of the symbolic register of the city. The position of women in nineteenth-century urban mythologies was particularly charged (Nava, 1984; Walkowitz, 1980, 1992; Wilson, 1991). Here, too, classifications of opposition and exclusion operated to maintain order. Disreputable women were associated with the immorality of public life in the city, with the despised prostitute and the unruly and often feminized urban mob (Davidoff et al., 1976; Huyssen, 1986; Sennett, 1986).[10] Respectable and virtuous women were connected to the home, and the ideal home was situated outside the city, in the leafy suburbs or village community. The sexual prohibitions and incitement elaborated in these discourses were marked by a deeply rooted conceptual and emotional adherence to the immutability of divisions – the fortified nature of boundaries – between women of different social classes and physical locations, and between the 'naturally ordained' spheres of men and women.

It has already been pointed out that much influential feminist historical research of the last decades (including Wolff's) has been concerned to trace the development of an ideology of separate spheres among the Victorian middle classes and has attempted to show how the cultural entrenchment of such ideas resulted in the social and material exclusion of women from public life and urban areas. This has undoubtedly been the dominant tendency in feminist historiography.[11] However, there have also been some dissenting interpretations. Amanda Vickery in her discussion of such positions has suggested 'the stress on the proper female sphere in Victorian discourse signalled concern that more women were active outside the home rather than proof that they were so confined' (1993b: 6). Elizabeth Wilson (1992) has also argued that women were not easily banished from public places, and Judith Walkowitz (1992) and others have drawn attention to the large numbers of middle-class women philanthropists who moved freely around the city streets.

These conflicting versions are evidence not only of current academic debate, they also suggest a much more uneven and contradictory picture of women's experience of city life than can be deduced from a face-value analysis of dominant discourses. Vickery's comment implies (though doesn't develop in this context) a reading against the grain, a reading which hints that the continuous reiteration of certain ideas might be evidence of anxiety and attempted denial rather than 'reality'. Moreover there is evidence that, during the closing decades of the century, there occurred increasingly in ideas about

femininity and in women's circumstances precisely the instability and unfix-
ing of parameters of difference that the concept of modernity as it has been
used here seems to encapsulate so well.

One of the most significant changes that took place during this period was
a rapid expansion of what counted as respectable, or at least acceptable,
public space for unaccompanied women (Abelson, 1989; Greenhalgh, 1988;
Walkowitz, 1992; Wilson, 1991). The category included the great exhibitions, galleries, libraries, restaurants, tearooms, hotels and department stores
(which will be returned to in more detail in the next section) – 'public–
private liminal spaces', as Zukin (1988) has called them, associated in part
with a more general promotion of buildings and events as cultural commodities and in part with the clear demands made by women themselves. A
growing number of authors (but still a minority in the context of feminist
debate) have described in detail the growth of these places and the ways in
which they catered specifically to women visitors and clients. A significant
but neglected consequence of this expansion was that middle-class women
travelled with increasing freedom through the streets and open public spaces
of the city. They took advantage of all available forms of travel: some had
their own carriages, others travelled by public transport – on trains, buses
and tubes – some rode their bicycles (during the 1890s there was a cycling
craze for women) and yet others travelled on foot.[12] Lynne Walker's
research on this subject has shown how the private and public spaces that
middle-class women frequented were often also within walking distance of
each other and movement between them necessarily entailed mingling with
the crowd and encountering strangers – possibly disreputable strangers – at
close proximity. These forays were conducted on a daily basis for very many
women. Several authors have drawn on diaries and correspondence to show
the frequency and normality of such excursions, despite in some instances
familial opposition and harassment on the streets.[13] So what begins to
emerge is a picture in which middle-class women were much closer to the
dangers and the excitement of city life than the notion of separate spheres
would lead us to anticipate.

In fact middle-class women laid increasing claim not only to 'respectable'
public places. Large numbers also visited less salubrious neighbourhoods as
part of the proliferation of philanthropic schemes that emerged during the
late nineteenth century in order to cope with the perceived crisis of the city
– with the threat of social disorder, disease, destitution and inadequate
housing. Middle-class women, as bearers of a particular kind of knowledge,
were involved on a huge scale in the process of disseminating information
about morality, domestic economy, hygiene and child care to women of the
working class. In 1893 it was estimated that 20,000 women were paid
officials and an astonishing half-million were voluntary workers engaged in
philanthropic projects dedicated to improving the lives of the urban poor
(Hollis, 1979: 226).[14]

So it is clear that middle-class urban women were not confined to their
homes all the time. Indeed in their pursuit of 'adventure, self-discovery and

meaningful work' (Walkowitz, 1992: 53) many would have ventured into slum territory unfamiliar even to their husbands and brothers. These journeys – which involved travel on public transport and on foot along unknown streets, and encounters in insanitary overcrowded housing with strangers possessing quite different life experiences – demanded from these urban explorers a quite extraordinary degree of intrepidity and yielded a rich store of personal and social discoveries. Women charity workers were engaged as much in a mapping of the new social relations of the city as were the more esteemed and recognized historians and poets of the moment. The visionary element in their activities was perhaps somewhat compromised by the fact that their personal freedom from the constraints of late Victorian domesticity was gained in the process of attempting to enforce them elsewhere, on the women of the poorer classes. But this contradiction need not undermine the *modernity* of their consciousness and experience any more than the contradictions of Faust's grand modern project as described by Berman (1983).

The women who travelled in this capacity, purposefully and relatively freely through the notorious streets of London, were unlikely to have lingered in parks and other public places to observe the ephemera of urban life – especially feminine life – in quite the voyeuristic style attributed to Baudelaire's *flâneur*.[15] Nevertheless, charity work established for these women the right to look. It authorized the observation and classification of the homes, lives and even marital relationships of the poor. Middle-class women involved in the philanthropic enterprise were not obliged to conduct their affairs with lowered gaze. They could indulge the pleasures of urban spectatorship – of the voyeur – with a sense of entitlement which is not so easily distinguishable from that of the male *flâneur*. Moreover, their participation in increasingly professionalized 'social' work also implicated them in the project of the regulation of populations – in the observation, correction and improvement of the social body – which is the central feature of Foucault's rather differently defined and periodized 'modernity' (Foucault, 1980).[16]

Philanthropy is just one instance of the way in which the Victorian ideal of separate spheres was undermined, if somewhat contradictorily, and in the years around the turn of the century the numbers of women refusing to stay within the confines of the domestic sphere expanded rapidly. Modern women were increasingly, if unevenly, engaged in the public world, in work, in financial transactions, in education and the dissemination of knowledge, and in political action. The movement for women's suffrage represented, perhaps more than any other activity, the spectacular high point of the early twentieth-century challenge to Victorian conventions of femininity. During the years preceding the First World War many thousands of women from all social backgrounds took to the city streets in flamboyant, public and sometimes quite astonishingly violent protest against the injustice of disenfranchisement based on sexual difference (Robins, 1980; Strachey, 1978; Tickner, 1987). In 1908 it is estimated that as many as half a million people converged in Hyde Park to support (or observe) the struggle. The striking impact of enormously long columns of militant women marchers, progressing from all corners of London, dressed in the suffragette colours of white, green and purple and bearing thousands of boldly designed banners, is described by Lisa Tickner (1987), who argues that the campaign marked a significant turning point in the modern use of visual imagery and publicity. Moreover, in their articulation of a modernist imagination with political consciousness and a will to change, the protest marches for women's suffrage exemplify with extraordinary vividness the evocative concept of 'primal modern scene' developed by Marshall Berman (1983: 63) to describe the archetypal or determining events of modernity in which the city streets become the stage for great moments of mass action and social transformation. Berman, however, does not include the suffrage demonstrations among the historical events he selects to validate his category. So the campaign for votes for women is yet one more instance which demonstrates both the precariousness of nineteenth-century codes of femininity and the narrowness of a notion of modernity which ignores the experience of women.

This period also saw a destabilization of Victorian sexual mores. There is a rich literature which situates the challenge to sexual conventions within the broader framework of the new woman's pursuit of fresh opportunities and greater social freedom. This challenge was posed not only in relation to choice of partner, courtship patterns and independence of movement. 'Free love' and the idea of sexual pleasure as an entitlement for women as well as men were gradually put on the agenda, albeit mainly in urban Bohemian and intellectual circles, and argued for alongside the need for sexual reforms like contraception and abortion. Despite the dangers of social ostracism and the continuing influence of social purity movements, the old sexual order was increasingly defied (Brandon, 1990; Sackville West, 1983; Showalter, 1992; Trimberger, 1984; Weeks, 1981). Ideas about 'modern relationships' and new ways of living were slowly disseminated and popularized. Women's magazines and later the cinema were to be among the main sources of information about many of these questions for ordinary women. It was in these fora that women readers and spectators encountered representations of the new femininities, of vamps and independent women (Ewen and Ewen, 1982). It was here that public discussion took place about the appropriate constituents of women's behaviour.

This section has set out some of the contradictory and unstable elements in city life and women's circumstances during the years around the turn of the century in order to provide a context for the ensuing study of early twentieth-century cultural responses to women as consumers. What has emerged in this account is a dissonance between women's lived experience and the discourse of their seclusion in the domestic sphere. One way of making sense of this discourse is to see it as a form of denial, as a way of attempting to hold back the modern, of resisting – or at the very least of regulating – the encroachment of women, and the 'new woman' in particular. (We will see later that a similar process of denial operated in the public and critical responses to women's involvement in mass culture, particularly to shopping and cinema-going.) The turn of the century did indeed see an accelerating challenge to the rhetorical conventions of public and private spheres and to the distinctions between respectable and disreputable – to some of the major symbolic markers of sex and sexual identity. Insofar as modernity signals a permeability of boundaries and the blurring of categories and difference it seems untenable to argue that women were excluded from it. Furthermore, the women described here, in negotiating urban and political turbulence and challenging social orthodoxies, were engaged in the project of making themselves at home in the maelstrom of modern life, of becoming the subjects as well as the objects of modernization, however contradictory, painful and uneven the process.

Modernity and the department store

Alongside these developments in personal mobility, urban spectatorship, political consciousness and social freedoms – and complexly related to them – was women's massive participation in the exploding culture of consumption and spectacle. It is here, in this arena, that the everyday lives of large numbers of ordinary women were most deeply affected by the process of modernity. The department store was from the late nineteenth century central to the iconography of consumer culture; it exemplified the ubiquity of the visual in the new 'scopic regime', and should be read as one of the archetypal sites of modernity which both produced and was produced by the experience of women (Falk, Chapter 8, this volume; Jay, 1992). Émile Zola, in his carefully researched novel about late nineteenth-century Paris, *The Ladies' Paradise*, described such stores as a 'triumph of modern activity' (Ross, 1992; Zola, 1992).[17]

Shopping in fashionable city centres as a pleasurable social activity was already established among the upper classes prior to this period, as was the enhancement of social status and identity which derived from the consumption of intricately coded possessions and styles (Adburgham, 1979; Campbell, 1987; McKendrick et al., 1982; Veblen, 1979; Vickery, 1993a). In the late eighteenth century Oxford Street had already been described as a 'dazzling spectacle' of 'splendidly lit shop fronts' and 'alluring' and 'handsome' displays. In 1807 Robert Southey wrote of their opulence and social importance:

> Shops are become exhibitions of fashion. . . . When persons of distinction are in town, the usual employment of the ladies is to go a-shopping. This they do without actually wanting to purchase anything. (cited in Adburgham 1979: 71, 93)

As the century proceeded a number of factors combined to make the experience of fashionable shopping even more agreeable and to extend it to women of the middle classes, to 'democratize luxury', as Zola (1992) put it.[18] The expansion of shops and shopping during the latter decades of the nineteenth century and early years of the twentieth was due in part to a general growth in the economy and more specifically to developments in public transport, which benefited manufacturers as well as consumers and altered the spatial relations of the city. New forms of mass production of non-essential 'consumer' goods and ready-to-wear clothing also made a crucial contribution, as did the ambitions of individual entrepreneurs. The most significant factor, however, was probably growing demand. The aspirations of an expanding and increasingly socially and geographically mobile urban population were inextricably bound up with the emergence and consolidation of modern forms of retailing, and the department store in particular (Campbell, 1987; Davis, 1966).

Department stores were established in all the major cities of the Western world and reached their 'zenith' (Adburgham, 1979) during the period identified at the beginning of this chapter as the high point of modernity. Zola depicts the department store at the centre of his novel as a modern machine which devours the small outdated commercial enterprises surrounding it. According to him, department stores symbolize the 'forward momentum of the age: the bold new forms of capitalism' (Ross, 1992). Their precursors, the covered shopping arcades of the mid-nineteenth century whose small specialty shops were unable to compete with mass-produced commodities, are described by Walter Benjamin in his Arcades Project as an earlier form of capitalism: part of the 'ur-landscape of consumption'(Buck-Morss, 1989: 83). The new stores modernized retailing not only by offering a wide range of cheaper, mass-produced fashionable clothes and other commodities, but also by rationalizing the use of space, making economies of scale, introducing clear pricing systems, and displaying goods in a safe and pleasant environment so that customers could look and compare without obligation to buy (Chaney, 1983).

Linked inextricably to these commercial developments – and also a crucial component of the concept of modernity – was the growing importance of external appearances, of surface impressions. This concern for what Ewen (1988) has called 'armour for city life' was a feature of the specific historical conjuncture under review, which was characterized by an escalating instability of class and geographical boundaries. This increasing social fluidity is what fuelled Simmel's (1971) preoccupation with the meaning of modern fashions. The period also witnessed the growing influence of a more open American culture, brought to Britain by developments in shipping and the mutual benefits of alliances between New World wealth and European 'distinction'. At such a socially precarious time, new signs were required as emblems of status and individuality. Dreiser's heroine Carrie (who at the beginning of the novel *Sister Carrie*, published in 1900, seeks a job in a department store) exemplifies this in her meticulous acquisition and display of the codes of social position. Leonore Davidoff (1973) has shown how those aspiring to become part of society in nineteenth-century Britain paid scrupulous attention to dress and comportment. During this period the fashioning of the home also gained significance as a visible indicator not only of rank but increasingly also of choice and 'identity' (Dreiser, 1981; Ewen, 1988; Featherstone, 1983; Forty, 1986).

Women played a crucial part in the development of these taxonomies of signification – in the acquisition of goods which conveyed symbolic meanings about their owners – since it was women who went to the department stores and did the shopping. From their inception the department stores provided a particularly welcoming space for women and numerous contemporary accounts indicate that visits to them took place frequently, sometimes several times a week (Abelson, 1989; Leach, 1984; Walkowitz, 1992).[19] As institutions the stores made a major contribution to the twentieth-century consolidation of women as consumers and to consumption and consumer expertise as activities that were as gendered as production.[20] During the period we are looking at women were confirmed as arbiters of taste and interpreters of the new – the modern. It was women who first of all encountered new fashions and domestic novelties and decided whether they were worth adopting. As those most literate in the complex signifiers of social hierarchy – a literacy acquired largely from magazines and the stores themselves (Breward, 1994) – it was women who decoded and encoded the changing images of class. Within two or three decades these lessons were to be learned mainly from the movies – indeed Hollywood was to become a major inspiration for shop design (Eckert, 1990) – but before the First World War, the principal source of information about the meaning of how others lived and dressed was found in the stores.

So clearly, department stores were more than just places where merchandise was bought and sold. In addition to facilitating the acquisition of 'cultural capital' (Bourdieu, 1986), they formed part of the huge expansion of public space and spectacle which included the great international exhibitions, museums, galleries, leisure gardens and, a little later, the cinema, and they provided an extraordinary range of facilities, entertainments and visual pleasures. People visited them as tourist attractions – as monuments to modernity – for the interest and pleasure they afforded in themselves.

The historians of the most renowned department stores[21] describe them as fantasy palaces. Increasingly purpose-built in the most luxurious styles with the most modern as well as traditional indigenous and imported materials, many had grand open staircases and galleries, ornate iron work, huge areas of glass in domed roofs and display windows, mirrored and marble walls,[22] parquet floors covered with eastern carpets, and furniture upholstered in silk and leather. These emporia were among the very first public spaces to be heated and use electric light not only for illumination but also for effect. In their display of goods and use of colour, they often drew on the conventions of theatre and exhibitions, continually innovating to produce new, vivid and seductive environments, with *mises-en-scènes* which combined, or offered in sequence, modernist, traditional and exotic decors (anticipating, or perhaps undermining, late twentieth-century postmodernism). Rosalind Williams (1982) describes this constant renewal disdainfully as a 'hodge-podge of visual themes'. However, Zola's enthusiastic account of the exhibition of parasols in his (fictional) department store suggests a scenario which has been carefully designed:

Wide-open, rounded off like shields, [the parasols] covered the whole hall, from the glazed roof to the varnished oak mouldings below. They described festoons round the semi-circular arches of the upper storeys; they descended in garlands along the slender columns; they ran along in close lines on the balustrades of the galleries and the staircases; and everywhere, ranged symmetrically, speckling the walls with red, green and yellow, they looked like great Venetian lanterns, lighted up for some colossal entertainment. In the corners were more complicated patterns, stars composed of parasols at thirty-nine sous, the light shades of which, pale-blue, cream-white and blush-rose, seemed to burn with the sweetness of a night light; whilst up above, immense Japanese parasols, on which golden-coloured cranes soared in a purple sky, blazed forth with the reflections of a great conflagration. (Zola, 1992: 215)

These magnificent stage sets also served as backdrop to live entertainment, which was provided on a regular basis. There were live orchestras in the restaurants and tearooms – and even, occasionally, in the grocery departments. Dress shows and pageants were regular occurrences. 'Spectacular oriental extravaganzas', which included live tableaux of Turkish harems, Cairo markets or Hindu temples, with live performers, dance, music and of course oriental products, were also frequent events. It is interesting to note that during this period these exoticized yet commercial representations of 'oriental' imagery and narratives were a major source of popular knowledge about Empire, other cultures and other aesthetic formations. Liberty's, which from 1875 specialized in Indian, Persian and Arabic merchandise and themes, was a pioneer in the development of this tradition. An example of Selfridges' 'cosmopolitanism', in which it took great pride, can be seen in Figure 3.1.[23] Another recurring feature in the entertainment provided by the stores was the exhibition and deployment of the most advanced technologies. Rosalind Williams (1982) describes how in France new photographic techniques were used for cineoramas, mareoramas and dioramas to create the illusion of travelling not only in exotic places but also by balloon above the sea and to the surface of the moon.

In addition to these visual experiences the department stores provided a vast range of facilities that enhanced the convenience, comfort and pleasure of shopping. These included supervised children's areas, toilets and powder rooms, hairdressing courts, ladies' and gentlemen's clubs and writing rooms, restaurants and tearooms, roof gardens with pergolas, zoos and ice rinks, libraries, picture galleries, banks, ticket and travel agencies, grocery provision and delivery services. Standards of service were high and customers were made to feel welcome by obliging liveried doormen and deferential yet astute assistants. Alison Adburgham cites an article written by Lady Jeune in 1896 in which she comments on contemporary developments and in particular on the significance of the increase in *women* shopworkers:

two very important changes have contributed to the temptation of spending money nowadays. One is the gathering under one roof of all kinds of goods – clothing, millinery, groceries, furniture, in fact all the necessities of life. Nearly all the great shops in London are becoming vast stores. Many more people now come to London to shop and they prefer to make their purchases where they can concentrate their forces and diminish fatigue. The other is the large number of women now employed. Women are so much quicker than men, and they understand so much more readily what other women want. They can fathom the agony of despair as to the arrangement of colours, the alternative trimmings, the duration of a fashion and the depth of a woman's purse. (Adburgham, 1979: 159)

So the department stores provided a source of employment for women as well as a welcoming place for them to shop.

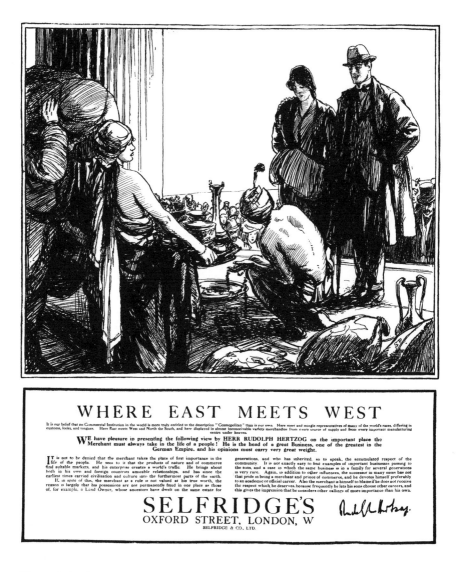

Figure 3.1   *From 'The Spirit of Modern Commerce', 1914, one of the 'cosmopolitan' posters in the souvenir collection published by Selfridge's to celebrate its fifth anniversary (Selfridges archive)*

The physical scale of these socio-commercial enterprises was huge. In 1903, Macy's restaurant in New York could accommodate 2,500 in one sitting. Harrods of Knightsbridge, which prided itself on being 'the most elegant and commodious emporium in the world' and 'a recognized social rendez-vous for members of Society' where it is 'perfectly proper for a lady to meet a gentleman', had at the turn of the century 6,000 employees and thirty-six acres of shopping space organized into eighty different departments (Adburgham, 1989; Callery, 1991). Selfridges, launched by the American entrepreneur Gordon Selfridge in 1909, was the first purpose-built store in Britain and was even larger than Harrods. It distinguished itself from Harrods by targeting a more middle- and lower-middle-class clientele and offered 'bargain basements' from early on (Honeycombe, 1984). Yet it, too, was designed to be a social meeting place and the public was encouraged to come and look without obligation to buy. The publicity slogans invited people to 'spend the day at Selfridges', and they did. 'It's so much brighter than their own homes. This is not a shop – it's a community centre', Mr Selfridge is alleged to have said, and kept the doors open till eight or later and the window-displays illuminated until midnight. The store was considered one of the great show sights of London, like Westminster Abbey, which all visitors from the provinces and abroad would expect to see. In the period prior to the First World War, there was a relative scarcity of forms of public entertainment (cinema and radio were to take off later) and partly because the stores were open so far into the evening they did indeed become the entertainment centres and meeting points their founders envisaged. (see Figure 3.2).[24] Some anxiety was expressed by social observers and customers alike about the mingling of social classes within the confines of the stores and there were worries about the difficulties of 'placing' some young women shoppers and shopworkers because of their respectable and fashionable appearances.[25] Concern was also voiced about the possibilities of illicit encounters between men and women. Whiteley's of Bayswater had a 'reputation' in this respect, though what this signified in commercial terms is open to question. It is clear from Selfridge's inaugural publicity that the possibility of 'pleasure' and 'recreation' in the company of a gentleman was deliberately presented as part of the allure of the store (Figure 3.3). So, in general, the blurring of class divisions and the relaxation of socio-sexual prohibitions, though in some respects risky, were considered necessary for the social appeal and commercial success of the stores and were likely to have been justified insofar as they were modern.

Visiting the stores during this period became, then, an excursion, an exciting adventure in the phantasmagoria of the urban landscape. The department store was an anonymous yet acceptable public space and it opened up for women a range of new opportunities and pleasures – for independence, fantasy, unsupervised social encounters, even transgression, as well as, at the same time, for rationality, expertise and financial control. Shopping trips, sanctioned by domestic and familial obligations, justified, as

Figure 3.2   *One of a series of advertisements which appeared in the London daily press promoting the launch of Selfridge's in March 1909 (see note 24 for a transcription of the text) (Selfridges archive)*

did the philanthropic expeditions referred to earlier, relatively free movement around the city and travel on public transport in the proximity of strangers. The inspection of the merchandise on display in the shop windows was a necessary part of the activity so the streets and pavements in the main

SHOPPING at SELFRIDGE'S

A Pleasure—A Pastime—A Recreation

WE aim to make the shopping at "Selfridge's" something more than merely shopping. We would like to think that everyone who spends an hour or day beneath our roof is better for the experience, has seen many "things different," has gathered some new point of knowledge, has discovered a way to do something better and revealed the thought to us.

Such suggestions we will welcome very gratefully and act on to the best of our ability, for by this friendly criticism we can more readily accomplish the work that we have set ourselves, that is, to do every day some one thing better than we did the day before.

This is part of our ambition, and what we know will come about by cordial "entente" between Customers and ourselves.

SELFRIDGE & CO.
OXFORD STREET, LONDON, W.

Figure 3.3 *Another of the alluring advertisements in Selfridge's promotional campaign, 1909 (Selfridge's archive)*

shopping centres were monopolized by women, ordinary middle-class women, part of the ebb and flow of the urban crowd, going about their business, or indulging their dreams, sometimes alone, sometimes with family or friends. The department store, together with the proliferating women's household and fashion magazines and the popular story papers of that period, contributed to the creation of modern female identities (Breward, 1994; Melman, 1988; Stein, 1985). It facilitated the acquisition of consumer knowledge and enabled women to make informed and independent decisions about shopping. It also offered a language to imagine a different and better future, one in which the injuries and wants of everyday existence could be soothed and family lives enhanced. And in addition it provided a spectacular environment in which to stroll aimlessly, to be a *flâneuse*, to observe people, to admire and parade new fashions. This was a context which legitimized the desire of women to look as well as be looked at – it enabled them to be both subject and object of the gaze, to appropriate, at one go, the pleasure/power of both the voyeur and the narcissist.

To draw attention to the exciting and empowering aspects of women's visits to the stores is not to deny that shopping can also be arduous; that anonymity and desire can be reread more negatively as loneliness and dissatisfaction. It is nevertheless to insist that the stores and shopping be recognized as one of the main contexts in which women developed a new consciousness of the possibilities and entitlements that modern life was able to offer. William Leach in his study of American department stores concludes thus:

> In those early . . . euphoric days of consumer capitalism, textured so much by the department store, many women thought they had discovered a more exciting . . . life. Their participation in consumer experience challenged and subverted that complex of qualities traditionally known as feminine – dependence, passivity . . . domestic inwardness and sexual purity. Mass consumer culture presented to women a new definition of gender that carved out a space for individual expression similar to men's. (Leach, 1984: 342)[26]

Leach's article also elaborates on the connections between the department stores and early feminist organizations. In England, as in the United States, the high point of the department store coincided with the peak years of suffragette militancy. The owners of the department stores were well aware of the importance of the movement and several manufactured, displayed and supplied a wide range of goods – from tea services to outer garments – in purple, white and green, the symbolic colours of the struggle (Lancaster, 1995; Leach, 1984; Tickner, 1987). They perceived their innovations in retailing as part of the same modernising process as women's emancipation and saw no conflict of interest between women's growing independence and the economic success of the stores. Harley Granville Barker's play *The Madras House*, originally published in 1911, includes among its characters an American department store magnate, Eustace Perrin State, who is an avowed supporter of what he refers to as 'the great modern women's movement'. 'A man who is not consciously in that movement is outside history,' declares State. Having made a careful study of the issues involved in 'the women's question', he concludes that political claims for the vote constitute only a small part of it. In his opinion 'the women's movement is [about] woman expressing herself'. His interest is not unrelated to his position as a store owner because, as he also points out, 'the economic independence of women is the next step [after their political freedom] in the march of civilization' (Granville Barker, 1977: 83–8).[27] There are plenty of 'real' as well as fictional instances of support, or at least acknowledgement, by the stores for the demands of feminism. Most overt was that of Wanamaker's, the American store which gave all women employees time off during working hours to march in suffrage parades (Leach, 1984). Restaurants in a number of stores in England became the meeting places of suffragettes during the period we are looking at. Fenwick's in Newcastle was apparently particularly well known for this.[28] Mr Selfridge was another example of a store owner who claimed to give support to the emancipation of women: 'I came along just when they wanted to step out on their own. They came to the store and realized some of their dreams,' he is supposed to have said (Honeycombe, 1984: 24).

But consumption of course is about more than emancipation or the realization of dreams or even politics. It is also crucially about work. Effective retailing is an absolutely integral aspect of modern capitalism. Without efficient marketing, which includes shopping, the production of goods ceases to be profitable. Yet despite the absolute centrality of consumption to modern Western economic life, and despite the cultural and social resonance that I describe in this chapter, consumption as labour – unlike production – has until recently been remarkably neglected, both theoretically and politically. Shopping has been overlooked or trivialized by economists, sociologists, the left and cultural theorists. As Grant McCracken has put it: 'The history of consumption has no history, no community of scholars, no tradition of scholarship' (1990: 28). Shopping is also theoretically insignificant in the literature of modernity. Why should this be?[29]

Shopping, the cinema and public anxieties

In order to make sense of this historical neglect we must look at the broader context, at the ways in which shopping and a range of associated mass-cultural activities were perceived during this critical period. What emerges is a complex discursive formation composed of different strands – popular and intellectual – held together nevertheless by certain common anxieties which seem inextricably linked to the gendered nature of shopping. This is the context from which the seminal theoretical approaches develop and which goes on to shape the ways these processes have been more recently understood.

First of all it must be noted that the expansion of women's social and economic activity in the public sphere as consumers came at the moment not only of growing suffragette militancy, but also when men's work as producers was increasingly subject to new forms of discipline and rational-ization, particularly in the United States though increasingly in Europe. This was the period of the emergence of 'Fordism', the assembly line, mass production and Frederick Taylor's theories about 'scientific management' which were designed to increase productivity by systematic observation and standardization of human behaviour in the workplace. The implementation of Taylorism, which entailed a deskilling process as work became more routinized, inflexible and required less thought, was not confined to factories. It was applied increasingly to office work, retailing and the service industries, so rationalization also affected the middle classes. The new systematized work processes were often resisted but the resulting increases in productivity and economic surplus led to higher wages for workers which enabled them to pay for the range of new commodities now available at lower prices on the market (Ewen, 1976, 1988; Gramsci, 1973; Schwarz, 1991; Wollen, 1993). This increased ability to consume acted in effect as compensation for the greater monotony and duress of the workplace (Bauman, 1983). Yet in its turn this compensation was undermined by the contradiction between men's work experiences and those of women, because precisely at the moment that many men were experiencing constraints in their places of employment, women were stepping out. The work that women were doing as consumers, unlike men's, continued to require substantial levels of skill and expertise and remained the one sector of the modern production–retailing cycle that was un-Taylorized and self-regulated. Moreover, this loose, undisciplined activity, although essential in terms of its economic productivity, often took place in the luxurious and symbolically resonant environment that I have already described.

The imagined freedoms and pleasures that these unsupervised excursions to the department stores offered, the ambiguous position of shopping as an activity which was neither clearly work nor leisure, and the financial control and social powers accruing to shoppers together combined to generate a range of anxieties not only among the 'public' but also among those intellectuals whose ideas contributed to the formation of ideas about modernity and mass culture. Some of the anxieties to which I am referring surface and are easily identifiable in the contemporary accounts excavated by the historians of the stores. Others are more elusive and require different tools of analysis in order to make sense of them. The argument here is that all are associated in one way or another with the feminization of consumption, with the fact that it was mainly women who did the shopping, and that the modern form of consumption was consolidated during a period in which earlier social conventions and boundaries appeared to be rapidly dissolving.

A number of authors have produced work which contributes to the development of a sharper, more textured picture of the nature of the unease that seemed so pervasive and of the way it might have operated to deflect attention away from this particular aspect of commerce. The envy of men confined to routine Taylorized jobs in the face of the expanding liberty and responsibility that the new consumption entailed has already been argued for. Another less historicized way of explaining this envy can be developed by drawing on psychoanalysis. This is the approach of Rosalind Minsky, who has explored the unconscious dynamic processes involved in the formation of envy provoked by the fantasized indulgence of desire and has argued that the sense of threat is constituted through the unconscious interpretation of the woman shopper as the pre-Oedipal phallic mother (Minsky, 1994). This kind of account, which draws attention to the fear of dependence as well as greed, goes some way towards explaining the continuing ambivalence of many men, including academics, to the processes involved in shopping. A more historically grounded version (but not one which focuses on gender) is offered by Daniel Horowitz, who investigates the shifts in the nature of the anxieties expressed about consumption in the United States between the late nineteenth century and the 1920s. During the earlier period, concern is oriented towards the dangers of profligacy, particularly among workers and immigrants. Subsequently the emphasis is on the dangers – the vacuity – of mass culture. Underlying both phases, he argues, is the fear of loss of self-control in the pursuit of commodities and pleasures; this, however, sits uneasily with the recognition, current in the same moral discourse, that self-denial is not compatible with the imperatives of economic growth (Horowitz, 1985).

Anxiety about the loss of moral and financial control generated by consumption is confirmed by Elaine Abelson (1989), who documents the increase in shoplifting by respectable middle-class women from the department stores during the same period. Losses incurred thus were not inconsiderable: in 1905 in New York alone they were estimated to reach thousands of dollars a day. Yet prosecutions were often not carried out since many of the women were also valued customers, wives or daughters of men quite able to afford the price of goods that had been stolen. The inevitable publicity of legal action in such cases was considered counterproductive. The stores had to be careful to maintain their attractive image, to encourage desire, yet at the same time not permit uncontrolled illegal consumption. Men, not surprisingly, were anxious in case their womenfolk succumbed to the temptations of theft or unconsidered buying in the course of their socially sanctioned shopping trips. This is the context from which emerged the construct of kleptomania, considered from its inception to be an illness of middle-class women and associated specifically with department stores (Abelson, 1989; M. Miller, 1981; Zola, 1992). Interestingly, a popular film of the period entitled *The Kleptomaniac* (dir. Edwin S. Porter, 1905) addresses precisely this issue. It is about a wealthy woman guilty of stealing a decorative item from a store who is not prosecuted and a poor woman, guilty of stealing a loaf of bread, who is (Ewen and Ewen, 1982: 89). The contradiction inherent in the commercial practices of the department stores which on the one hand endorsed the creation of desire and on the other refused to prosecute 'respectable' customers guilty of theft is an example of the disavowal consumption seems to produce. It is also there in the contradiction highlighted by Horowitz between self-denial and spending.

Yet another reading of the ubiquitous anxieties associated with consumption can be elicited from the work of Stuart Ewen, who emphasizes the declining authority of fathers and husbands in the early decades of the century as women gradually enter the labour market and as their managerial status in the home is raised. Ewen (1976; Ewen and Ewen, 1982) understands this as a welcome diminution of patriarchal power. Less positive readings of the phenomenon are made by Christopher Lasch (1979) and members of the Frankfurt School and will be returned to in the next section.

Expressions of concern about the erosion of men's control over spending and money merge into much more overtly sexualized narratives. Elements of sexual fearfulness and rivalry surface in most of the accounts about women and shopping during this period. The department stores are accused of 'unleashing passions'. 'Temptation' and 'gullibility' become growing preoccupations. Anxieties are voiced about the 'intoxication' caused by the 'sensuous' display of goods. Zola talks about the 'longing covetous gaze' of women customers and the danger of being devoured by the 'erotic' and 'seductive' world of the store. Miller (1981: 204) in his account of *Le Bon Marché* in Paris, tells us of a woman who was alleged to obtain more 'voluptuous sensations' from the feel of silk than from her lover. A few decades later women shoppers in the United States are represented as capricious and emotional, craving glamour and romance (Marchand, 1986). Interestingly these sexual metaphors contain elements of both passivity and activity. On the one hand, they seem to suggest the fear that innocent women will be seduced and ravished. On the other, that the stores will release an unbridled sexuality, an ominous transgressiveness. Zola represents his women sale-shoppers in this way, as part of an aggressive and sexually voracious mob:

> The women reigned supreme. They had taken the whole place by storm, camping there, as in a conquered country, like an invading horde. . . . (Zola, 1992: 236)

> They advanced slowly . . . kept upright by the shoulders and bellies of those around them, of which they felt the close heat; and their satisfied desire enjoyed the painful entrance which incited still further their curiousity. There was a pell-mell of ladies arrayed in silk, of poorly dressed middle-class women, and of bare-headed girls, all excited and carried away by the same passion. A few men buried beneath the overflow of bosoms were casting anxious glances around them. . . . (Zola, 1992: 214)

> The furs were scattered over the flooring, the readymade clothes were heaped up like the great coats of wounded soldiers, the lace and underlinen, unfolded, crumpled, thrown about everywhere, made one think of an army of women who had disrobed there in the disorder of some sudden desire. (Zola cited by Ross, 1992: xvii).

These descriptions not only refer us back to the fears of uncontainable sexuality that the urban context itself seemed to mobilize during that period (and that are alluded to in the section of this chapter on the city),[30] they also evoke the way in which the crowd – the mob – has been recurringly feminized. Andreas Huyssen makes this point in the following way:

Male fears of an engulfing femininity are . . . projected onto the metropolitan masses, who did indeed represent a threat to the rational bourgeois order. . . . The fear of the masses in this age of declining liberalism is almost always also a fear of woman, a fear of nature out of control, a fear of the unconscious, of sexuality, of the loss of identity and stable ego boundaries in the mass. (1986: 52–3)

It seems therefore that the loss of authority over women shoppers cannot be dissociated from the semi-conscious fear of their untrammelled sexual desire and of the potential eruption of social forces. And in fact some of these connections were fairly explicitly made. The desire of ordinary women for 'finery' in the late Victorian period was perceived as not only an indication of sexual immorality but also as an attempt to rise above their station (Valverde, 1989). The decomposition of the visible signs of class distinction that the department store offered, the continuous incitement of desire to possess commodities, the associated discontent and the promulgation of aspirations for a better life, did indeed represent a threat to the social order as well as, at the same time, a modernizing force. Berman (1983) has pointed to the energy with which the bourgeoisie disrupted the earlier regimes. In this instance the increasing and disturbing disintegration of social boundaries was produced by a contradictory alliance between modern capitalist methods of retailing and women consumers.

The anxieties about consumption and women shoppers that are outlined here have been deduced from a sparse literature. Commerce has not been considered worthy of much intellectual attention, as I have already pointed out, and so is not able to yield a theoretical commentary on the issues which is as extensive as that on other comparable aspects of mass culture. Cinema has produced the richest archive of comment and debate and it is from this source that it is possible to infer further evidence of anxiety about shopping as well as denial of its theoretical significance. Shopping, where it was referred to at all, was quite often associated with cinema-going in the period we are looking at. During the early decades of the century the cinema – like the department store – experienced a remarkable expansion. By 1909 there were over 340 movie houses and nickleodeons in New York City with an estimated two million visits per week. Paris had two cinemas in 1907 and by 1913 it had 160. In Germany the number of cinemas rose from two in 1900 to 2,446 in 1914. In Britain in the same year the number of cinemas was estimated at 4,000 with a weekly audience of seven to eight million (Ewen and Ewen, 1982; Kuhn, 1988; Mast, 1982; O'Shea, 1996; Ward, 1991). The audiences who attended these movie houses – or 'dream palaces' as the agreeable new public social spaces were quickly to be called, echoing the language used about the stores – were composed predominantly of women, young people and children. Seebohm Rowntree estimated in the 1930s that 87.5 per cent of all cinema-goers fell into these categories (Richards, 1984).[31] During the daytime, audiences would have been almost exclusively made up of women and the young and women often combined their visits to the cinema with their shopping trips on their day excursions to the city centres.

The literature about this period of cinema-going indicates that there was widespread concern about the moral and physical consequences – particularly for the working class and the young – of the content of films and the social and physical environment in which they were shown (Kuhn, 1988; Mast, 1982; Ward, 1991). Concern about the specific influence of cinema-going on women has been less documented but is also likely to have been extensive, and indeed Miriam Hansen has argued, in relation to this conjunctural moment in Germany, that the resistance to cinema's cultural respectability was a consequence of the threat posed to the organization of public space by the high proportion of women cinema-goers (Hansen, 1983: 73–5). Furthermore, women not only went to the cinema unaccompanied by men, but once there they were not easily differentiated from each other in social terms: housewives, shopworkers and prostitutes sat as spectators in close proximity, blurring physically and metaphorically the boundaries between the respectable and the unrespectable.

It is certainly the case that 'passivity' and 'excessive excitation' appear as recurring preoccupations in much of the contemporary social comment about movie-going and that these personal attributes contain some of the same gendered and sexualized connotations that are repeated in the discussions about women's visits to the department stores. Some of these connections between shopping and cinema-going are quite explicitly made; others remain more coded, to be uncovered in the course of a closer examination of critical responses to mass culture more generally. The explicit links, made here and there, are what enable us to make the leap into another discourse and assume that the structures of feeling displayed by some of the most influential commentators on cinema and mass culture during the first half of this century have something to reveal to us about how shopping was understood then, and continues to be understood today, in relation to modernity. A few examples from a small selection of key thinkers will trace this chain of cultural associations.

Intellectuals, consumption and mass culture

Louis Haugmard was among the first cultural critics to concern himself with the new form of cinema. In 1913, in his *Aesthetics of Cinema* (cited by Rosalind Williams, [1982]), he analyses the specific complexities of film as a medium and elaborates his condemnation of its social ramifications, its escapism and its ability to deceive the naïve public. He is among those commentators who consider the movies emotionally over-stimulating and intellectually pacifying and he refers repeatedly to the 'excitation' and 'passivity' of cinema spectators. Moreover, and this is why his views are pertinent here, he makes a quite explicit connection between shopping and the cinema:

> the passive solitude of the moviegoer resembles the behaviour of department store shoppers who also submit to the reign of imagery with a strange combination of

intellectual and physical passivity and emotional hyperactivity. (cited in Williams, 1982: 80)

Siegfried Kracauer is another cultural critic who, over a decade later, echoes the approach of Haugmard in his piece entitled 'The Little Shopgirls go to the Cinema' and expresses similar fears about emotionality, passivity and receptivity and similarly connects the spheres of shopping and movie-going – not only materially but also symbolically in the very title of his work (Hake, 1987; Hansen, 1983; Kracauer, 1987; Petro, 1987).

Kracauer was part of a circle of intellectuals, often loosely referred to as the Frankfurt School, which during the 1930s generated a number of seminal critiques of cultural and social issues. Over the last fifteen years, in the context of the emergence of cultural studies as an academic discipline, and with the translation and (re)publication of well-known and more obscure essays, the influence of the analytical approaches and concerns of those associated with the Frankfurt School has been consolidated and is now extensive. In this section I want to sketch out some of the suggestive connections and omissions which appear in this work and which support my general thesis about the anxieties of influential cultural thinkers about consumption. This method will inevitably be deductive, since questions of consumption and shopping are simply not raised in most of the debates about mass culture. So, in order to unravel what might have been thought, consciously or unconsciously, it will be necessary to read texts against the apparent intentions of their authors, to pursue insights across arguments and moments and refocus so that the historical and psychic context from which ideas emerge is scrutinized with as much attention as the ideas themselves.

A useful starting-off point is Theodor Adorno and Max Horkheimer's (1973) critique of the culture industry, partly because of its status as a classic, almost iconic, piece of socio-political comment. Adorno and Horkheimer, drawing on both American and German cultural examples, are deeply disturbed and angered by what they see as the banality of most mass culture – its dissipating amorphousness and triviality – and they too condemn the 'passivity' and lack of discrimination of the consumer. One way of making sense of what emerges from this text (sometimes only in quite coded form) as a virulent denigration of ordinary audiences is to turn to the authors' work on the family, much of it written in the preceding decade while they were still in Germany (Held, 1980; Horkheimer, 1972a; Jay, 1984; Poster, 1978). What emerges from this writing is a surprising nostalgia about an idealized family of the past and a sense of loss about the declining authority of the modern father in relation to his wife and children. Mass culture has threatened the potency of the father and displaced him as the socializing agent to whom women and children now submit. The balance of forces within the family has been transformed.[32] Ironically one way of reading these views is to see them as evidence of *men's* passivity as they witness the reorientation of women's desires away from the home to the seductive environment of the cinema and stores. Women's spectatorship in both these contexts is increasingly active and inquiring. Many men – ordinary members of the public as well as intellectuals – are threatened by their exclusion from the pleasures and knowledge that consumption offers. Mass culture emerges, then, as the despised yet alluring rival of the displaced man. The insistence of the cultural critics on the passivity of the consumer can be reread as denial, as a disavowal of the profound anxiety about loss and displacement that mass culture seems to engender.

Andreas Huyssen (1986), whose indicatively entitled piece 'Mass Culture as Woman: Modernism's Other' was referred to above in relation to the way the masses have been feminized, explores in the same article the way mass culture has likewise been intricately bound up with pejorative notions of the feminine.[33] Mass culture, moreover, also takes on the attributes of the (feminized) masses, that is to say it is frequently depicted as engulfing, irrational, sentimental, and so forth. Thus it is contrasted not only with masculinity but also with cultural modernism, which is hard, rigorous and rational, and which has always been concerned to distance itself from the popular. Interestingly for my argument here, Huyssen points out that Adorno, Horkheimer and Kracauer each, at different times, explicitly sexualizes and engenders mass culture. For example Adorno and Horkheimer argue that mass culture 'cannot renounce the threat of castration' (Huyssen, 1986: 48).[34] Adorno is also of course known for his defence of modernism and high cultural aesthetics against the encroaching contamination of mass culture. Huyssen's argument about the feminization of mass culture, and mine about mass culture and consumption as the rival of the male, are obviously different yet they are not incompatible. Indeed paradoxically they confirm and complement each other methodologically. Both operate in symbolic registers – as metaphors – and centre-stage the way in which unconscious processes are at work in the formation of intellectual positions. Both insist that these must be rooted in specific historical contexts and narratives.

Walter Benjamin is another influential contributor to the debate about mass culture. His uncompleted and largely unpublished *Passagen-Werk* (The Arcades Project), reconstructed and developed with extraordinary insight and elegance by Susan Buck-Morss (1989),[35] is one of the few attempts to theorize the significance of shopping arcades in relation to modernity and commodity capitalism and, in conjunction with his other work on culture and cinema, continues to have a profound influence on contemporary debates. In the context of the argument which is being put forward here, Benjamin must be distinguished from other associates of the Frankfurt School. His criticisms of mass culture are, at least in some places, far more tempered and complex and he argues for the aesthetic and political possibilities of popular cultural forms.[36] He is not only less pessimistic about mass culture and the advent of modernity – about 'modernity's rupture of tradition' – he also welcomes the decline of 'the antiquarian effect of the father on his son'. Buck-Morss puts it thus:

In a world of objects that changed its face drastically in the course of a generation, parents could no longer counsel their children. . . . The rupture of tradition was irrevocable. Far from lamenting the situation, Benjamin saw precisely here modernity's uniquely revolutionary potential. . . . The rupture of tradition . . . frees symbolic powers from conservative restraints for the task of social transformation. . . . Benjamin insisted: 'We must wake up from the world of our parents.' (1989: 279)

Nevertheless, his Arcades Project is also at the same time full of a deeply felt ambivalence about the temptations of the metropolitan world of consumption and spectacle – the urban phantasmagoria – which both dazzles and deceives the crowd. The world of commodities is about *illusion*. Value is eclipsed by representation and display. Benjamin is simultaneously fascinated and guilty, both lustful and repelled by the luxury and decadence of city life. As Elizabeth Wilson (1992) has suggested, his views are at once utopian and dystopian. He is also manifestly ambivalent towards women, where he considers them at all.[37] In most of Benjamin's work it is the prostitute who is presented as the key female figure in the iconography of the city, and, at the same time, as *the* embodiment of commodification. In *Passagen-Werk* he argues that women use fashion to cover up the 'reality of natural decay', that fashion 'encourages the fetishistic fragmentation of the living body'. We see here the association Benjamin makes between women, commodities and consumption. Women, like commodities, are about surfaces and illusion. Yet among his notes for *Passagen-Werk*, and once more indicative of his contradictory feelings, he suggests also that fashion can be 'irreverent towards tradition . . . and emblematic of social change' (cited in Buck-Morss, 1989: 101).[38]

This major work is a unique yet contradictory and fragmented attempt to understand consumption. The ambivalence to commerce which is expressed throughout can, I think, be traced in part to Benjamin's recurring preoccupation with generational difference and his frequently documented conflicts with his own father, a financier who invested in innovative urban projects, among them a department store and ice rink. Some of what Benjamin considered his formative commercial and erotic experiences are recounted in his autobiographical essay 'A Berlin Chronicle':

> I was most lastingly affected . . . when in about 1910 . . . my father conceived the idea of taking me to . . . The Ice Palace [which was] not only the first artificial ice rink to be seen in Berlin, but also a thriving night club. . . . My attention was held . . . by the apparitions at the bar. Among these was a prostitute in a very tight-fitting white sailor's suit, who determined my erotic fantasies for years to come. . . .
>
> In those early years I got to know the 'town' only as a theatre of purchases, [where] my father's money cut a path for us between the shop counters and assistants and mirrors, and the appraising eyes of our mother, whose muff lay on the counter. In the ignominy of a 'new suit' we stood there, our hands peeping from the sleeves like dirty price tags, and it was only in the confectioners that our spirits rose with the feeling of having escaped the false worship that humiliated our mother. . . . Caverns of commodities – that was the 'town'. (Benjamin, 1986a: 39–40)

Hannah Arendt in her introduction to the collection of Benjamin's essays *Illuminations* discusses the insolubility of the Jewish question for Jewish intellectuals of Benjamin's generation 'because all traditions and all cultures as well as all ''belonging'' had become equally questionable to them' (1973: 36). This refusal of tradition casts additional light on Benjamin's hostility to what his parents represented, to commerce and thence his route to 'commodity fetishism'.[39] Demetz interprets the conflict slightly differently:

> In many Jewish families of late nineteenth-century Europe, gifted sons turned against the commercial interests of their fathers, who were largely assimilated . . . to bourgeois success, and, in building their counterworlds in spiritual protest, they incisively shaped the future of science, philosophy and literature. Articulating an insight of far-reaching implications, Karl Kraus, the belligerent Viennese satirist, suggested in his *Magical Operetta* (much enjoyed by Benjamin) that little Jewish family dramas were being played out all over, the stern fathers concerned with . . . business and the spiritual sons with . . . the less profitable matter of the pure mind. (1986: ix)[40]

Among such sons, Demetz includes Freud, Husserl, Kafka and of course Benjamin himself, for whom 'the fundamental pattern reasserts itself with particular clarity' (Demetz, 1986: ix). Benjamin's antagonism towards his parents – and his father in particular (referred to in his own autobiographical work as well as in the biographical accounts of Arendt and Demetz) – contributes to our understanding of his refusal (unlike Adorno and Horkheimer) to lament the decline of paternal authority in the family and helps explain his 'forward-lookingness', his optimism about the possibilities of the modern. A connection can also be made between his ambivalence towards commerce – his simultaneous fascination and repudiation of the 'theatres of purchases' and 'caverns of commodities' that 'create false worship' – and the anti-Semitic climate of central Europe in the 1930s described by Gregor von Rezzori in his *Memoirs of an Anti-Semite*, in which 'Commerce per se was embarrassing . . . anything connected with selling in a store was below social acceptance. This was a privilege of the Jews' (1983: 86). The humiliating anti-Semitic targeting of commerce, about which Benjamin must have felt enormously contradictory, was actualized during the period of his immersion in the writing of *Passagen-Werk* by the officially authorized Nazi boycotts of Jewish-owned department stores in Berlin, which, in April 1933, were among the first propaganda assaults of Hitler's newly elected government (Frei, 1987; Fromm, 1943).

These contextual factors help to make sense of Benjamin's equivocal and uncompleted analysis of consumption as well as his orientation towards the future – his modernism, in Berman's terms. They do not, though, explain his lack of serious attention to the ways in which consumption is *gendered*, to the ways ordinary modern women might be placed in relation to the modernity and shops he so meticulously represents. This omission, this failure to explore the significance of the feminization of such a crucial aspect of commodity capitalism and mass culture, must also be understood (like the similar omissions of other intellectuals of this and earlier periods) in the context of the broader social and psychic transformations of the period.

The shifting balance of forces between men and women in the family and the growing independence of women have already been referred to. This period was also affected by the traumatic and dehumanizing slaughter of the First World War. Challenges to the constraints and conventions of femininity reached a particularly frenzied pace during the interwar years and meshed with anxieties about the demographic crisis and the numerical disparity of the sexes resulting from the war. Concerns about 'superfluous' women – who in the popular imagination were also 'new' women: flappers, hedonists, feminists, workers, voters – can be read as evidence of a crisis of masculinity, of men's fear of being diminished, swamped and consumed (Kohn, 1992; Melman, 1988). Klaus Theweleit (1987) has analysed the cultural dread of dissolution and engulfment exhibited during this period in the writing and fantasies of German Freikorps soldiers who were later to become the vanguard of the Nazi party. He makes the point that some of these fears are articulated by men of the left as well. It would not be surprising therefore – in a context in which, additionally, German socialist feminism was still robust and the Weimar Sex Reform movement, designed to address the sexual interests of the new woman, had a membership of 150,000 (Grossmann, 1984; Thonnessen, 1973) – to find a certain ambivalence about women and a certain blindness about the feminization of mass culture and consumption in the work of the cultural critics of the period.

Conclusion

One of the innovations of feminist thought has been to alert us to the unpredictable and covert ways of the symbolic world. It has encouraged us to pose different kinds of questions of texts, authors and social processes. In this piece of work my project has been to excavate the different contexts in which influential ideas about women, modernity and consumption have developed and to refocus theoretical investigation onto gaps and inflections as well as emphases. What has emerged from this research is a history pitted by ambivalence and denial. Modernity as a narrative and experience has turned out to be far more profoundly marked by the material and imagined presence of women than the classic accounts have allowed. Yet, consumption, the sphere in which women's participation has been so culturally and economically definitive, has barely been addressed by the academy.[41] What I have tried to argue here is that this discursive marginalization must be understood partly as a consequence of the association of consumption with the destabilization of nineteenth-century femininities and the emergence of the new woman. Uneasy public fears provoked by these shifting cultural patterns and the fantasized loss of control incurred in visits to the department stores meshed in complex ways during the early part of this century with intellectual ambivalence about mass culture and disdain for commerce. This mood, the cultural formation that I have identified here, is deeply implicated in the construction of views about consumption. It has led to the repudiation of shopping and shoppers and a denial of the theoretical centrality of women to the making of modernity.[42]

Notes

1. This chapter was originally written for a book produced by members of the Department of Cultural Studies at the University of East London entitled *Modern Times: Reflections on a Century of English Modernity* (Nava and O'Shea, 1996); as the title indicates, modernity was the organizing principle. Alan O'Shea's introductory chapter, 'English Subjects of Modernity', sets out the argument for the theoretical usefulness of the concept. My thanks to all the contributors to that book for their helpful and comradely comments on earlier drafts of this piece.

2. Among the authors and texts I have drawn on for the purposes of my argument are Anderson (1984); Baudelaire (1964); Benjamin (1973, 1986a); Berman (1983, 1984); Bradbury and McFarlane (1987); Buck-Morss (1989); Frisby (1985); Lash and Friedman (1992); Nixon (1992); Sennett (1986); Simmel (1971); Williams (1989); Wilson (1991, 1992); Wolff (1985, 1990).

3. The article was first published in 1985. A slightly revised version appears in Wolff (1990). Janet Wolff (1993) has recently reiterated her support for her initial argument.

4. The reprinted version of this article (Wolff, 1990) includes a slightly longer comment on this subject than the original. See also Wolff's essay 'Feminism and Modernism' in the same book.

5. This is despite the fact that she also draws on theorists whose major concern was with the social transformations which took place later, at the end of the nineteenth and beginning of the twentieth centuries (for example, Thorstein Veblen and Georg Simmel) in order to support her argument.

6 Elizabeth Wilson's (1992: 98) phrase. Wilson is more sceptical than Wolff. For her the *flâneur* is a powerless and marginal figure, a loiterer/voyeur in the urban labyrinth.

7. Her reliance on Thorstein Veblen for the development of her comments on consumption confirms this approach. For a critique of Veblen's analysis, see McCracken (1990) and Vickery (1993a).

8. See Davidoff et al. (1976); Marriott (1996); Nava (1984); Rose (1979); Stedman Jones (1976); Walkowitz (1992); Williams (1975); Wilson (1991). Twentieth-century British versions are also more pessimistic: see, for example, the debate between Berman and Anderson in *New Left Review* in 1984; and the ideology of the garden city and slum clearance movements (Wilson, 1991).

9. European and American accounts of the city, although often ambivalent and concerned about the destruction of traditional values and modes of living, were also less fearful and more inclined to welcome – even celebrate – the rich and complex phantasmagoria of the modern metropolitan landscape. As Elizabeth Wilson (1991) has pointed out, in Paris whole families were likely to enjoy the café life on the broad new boulevards, while in the United States the city came increasingly to represent a modern architectural and social ideal. See also, for example, Theodore Dreiser's novel *Sister Carrie* (1981), first published in 1900.

10. Huyssen also quotes Gustave Le Bon: 'Crowds are everywhere characterized by feminine characteristics'(Huyssen, 1986: 52).

11. Janet Wolff is the one to have made the link to modernity and it is repeated in several of her essays. See, for example, 'The Culture of Separate Spheres: The Role of Culture in Nineteenth-Century Public and Private Life' (in 1990). Other feminist historians have also explored the separate spheres of men and women, at least as an ideal. See, for example, the extensive and important contributions of Leonore Davidoff and Catherine Hall (1987), who stress the material interdependence of the 'public' and the 'private' during the first half of the nineteenth century. See also Jenny Ryan (1992) for an example of a feminist historian whose emphasis is predominantly on the constraints of separate spheres and on the patriarchal exclusion of women from the public domain.

12. Walker (1991) showed a slide of two women in the 1890s travelling on the underground with their briefcases. Adburgham (1989) refers to the cycling craze and the new fashions that were required for it.

13. See, for example, Abelson (1989) and Leach (1984) for the United States and Adburgham (1989) and Walkowitz (1992) for England, particularly London. See Walkowitz (1992: 50–2) for a discussion of male pests and sexual harassment.

14. See also Addams (1910); Banks (1981); Nava (1984); Wilson (1978); Walkowitz (1992).

15. See Wilson's (1992) discussion of the arguments made by Wolff (1985) and Pollock (1988).

16. See also Donzelot (1979), who draws on Foucault and explores the shift in philanthropy from the gift of charity to the rendering of advice.

17. The quote from Zola's notes is taken from Ross (1992). Zola's novel was originally published in 1883.

18. Schudson (1984) has suggested that this should be understood as a democratization of aspiration and envy. For the expansion of consumer culture into the middle classes see also Abelson (1989) and Chaney (1983).

19. Among the first public toilets for 'ladies' were those provided by the department stores, obviously an added incentive.

20. It is generally estimated that 80 per cent of purchasing decisions today are made by women and that this has been the case since the beginning of the century at least (see Marchand, 1986; Pumphrey, 1987). Women were certainly identified with the internal decor of their homes and were responsible for design and domestic shopping decisions from the mid-nineteenth century onwards (Forty, 1986). Men seem never to have been very comfortable in department stores except as sellers, and even here their importance declined from the late nineteenth century onwards (Adburgham, 1979; Lancaster, 1995). Abelson (1989) claims that 90 per cent of visitors to the stores in America during this period were women.

21. There were of course regional and historical variations. Not all were as glamorous as those described here. Some were modernized while others were built from scratch. Provincial and suburban stores were oriented towards a different clientele. Yet all were designed to be attractive and make women feel welcome. The account I present here is a composite based on the research of Abelson (1989); Adburgham (1979, 1989); Bowlby (1985); Callery (1991); Covina (1978); Davis (1966); Honeycombe (1984); Lancaster (1995); Leach (1984); M. Miller (1981); Moss and Turton (1989); Williams (1982); Zola (1992).

22. The Ladies' Club at Harrods was panelled in Brecchi Sanguine, Pavannazi and Levantine marbles and onyx, according to Harrods publicity material of 1910 (Callery, 1991).

23. One of the posters in 'The Spirit of Modern Commerce' series produced by Selfridge's to mark the fifth anniversary of its opening which celebrates 'the Romance that lies in Commerce' (held in the store's archive). This poster is also interesting for its text, particularly in relation to the argument I develop later in this piece of work. Written by German industrialist Herr Rudolph Hertzog, it is a comment on the important place of the merchant in the life of the people both at home and abroad, and attempts to analyse the lack of regard with which 'princes of commerce' are viewed compared to land owners, even by their own sons. See below for further discussion of this aspect of Hertzog's comments.

24. Figure 3.2 ('Selfridge's "At Home"') was one of a series of full-page advertisements which appeared in the London daily papers in March 1909 to mark the opening of the store. The full text reads:

We are always ready with a welcome to strangers within our gates. We bid them feel at home and endeavour in every way imaginable to create and cherish that comfortable sentiment. Reception Rooms are open to them in which to meet their friends. Name Registers in the National Rooms will enable them to record their own advent and tell them of home acquaintances who may also be in London. The Library is available for correspondence and the Post Office for mailing it. The Silent Room is eloquent of quietude.

Retiring Rooms are many and perfectly appointed. If our visitor is a Gentleman the Smoke Lounge is suggestive of a meditative weed. And these accommodations belong to visitors without fee of any kind whatever and without the remotest obligation in their use to make a purchase.

The Parcel and Cloak Room takes charge of all impediments. The Bureau de Change will negotiate letters of credit. The Information Office will answer accurately any reasonable question. Seats at all theatres can be booked, and Railway and Steamship tickets taken to anywhere without going outside our doors. The Luncheon Hall and *al fresco* Tea Garden serve appetizing teas and luncheons in dainty home-like fashion at moderate charges: and from floor to floor, through the hundred or more departments, are displays of Manifold Merchandise incomparable in richness, utility and quality at London's Lowest Prices – always.

25. The stores also provided significant career and income opportunities for women. See Lancaster (1995); Leach (1984); Zola (1992).

26. This is a contentious reading of course. Cultural analysis, particularly of the left, has a well-established convention of seeing commodity culture as irredeemably bad. Richards's (1991) eloquent critique of advertising and the growth of mass consumption is an example of this. See also the discussion in 'Consumerism Reconsidered: Buying and Power' (Nava, 1992).

27. Thanks to Peter Horne for alerting me to this play.

28. Lancaster (1995) cites David Neville's MPhil, 'Women's Suffrage on Tyneside' (University of Northumbria), as a source of information about Fenwicks in Newcastle.

29. See also Nava (1992: Chapters 8 and 10). Consumption as an area of theoretical study is now finally expanding quite rapidly. Among significant contributions to the literature not cited elsewhere in this article are: Carter (1984, 1995); Morris (1988); Mort (1988); Shields (1992).

30. Wilson (1991) explores the associations between the city and seductive but threatening sexualities.

31. The Seebohm Rowntree survey reported that 50 per cent of cinema-goers were young people and children, and of the remaining adults, 75 per cent were women (Richards, 1984). Such precise information about the earlier period is not available.

32. Lasch (1979: 74) makes exactly the same point and similarly bemoans these transformations.

33. Huyssen's article was originally published in Modleski (1986b). For a complementary analysis which looks at the feminization of mass culture, see Modleski (1986a).

34. Modleski makes a similar point about Jean Baudrillard's ambivalence towards these issues. For him, she says, 'the masses function as a "a gigantic black whole", a simile ostensibly taken from physics, but perhaps owing something to (feminine) anatomy as well' (1986a: 48).

35. See also Benjamin (1968, 1973, 1986a); Brewster (1968); Buck-Morss (1983); McRobbie (1992); Wilson (1992); Miller, Chapter 2, this volume.

36. See, for example, 'The Work of Art in the Age of Mechanical Reproduction' in Benjamin (1973).

37. Susan Buck-Morss makes very little reference to this in either of her discussions of *Passagen-Werk* (1983, 1989). But see, for example, Benjamin's autobiographical 'A Berlin Chronicle' (in 1986a). See also his *Moscow Diary* (1986b), in which he constantly reiterates his ambivalence towards Asja Lacis, the woman he travelled to Moscow to see. The theme of this relationship, according to Gary Smith, is 'drawn as an erotic red thread throughout Benjamin's journal, [it] is one of obsession and denial' (1986: 141).

38. See Berman (1984) and Gaines (1990) for further discussions of Benjamin's unease.

39. See also Buck-Morss (1989); Demetz (1986), in his biographical introduction to the collection of Benjamin's essays; and Benjamin himself in his autobiographical pieces like 'A Berlin Chronicle' (in 1986a).

40. In order to place myself in relation to this narrative it is worth adding that my father, Marcel Weisselberg, and his brother and sisters, born at the beginning of the century into the Vienna that Karl Kraus describes, also engaged in these domestic intergenerational Jewish struggles about the relative value of commerce and intellectual–political life.

41. This book is of course an instance of how this has now started to change.

42. The argument and historical narrative presented in this chapter are followed up in an article about consumption and modernity in the interwar period, written subsequently but published earlier (Nava, 1995).

References

Abelson, Elaine (1989) *When Ladies Go A-Thieving: Middle-Class Shoplifters in the Victorian Department Store*. Oxford: Oxford University Press.

Adburgham, Alison (1979) *Shopping in Style: London from the Restoration to Edwardian Elegance*. London: Thames and Hudson.

Adburgham, Alison (1989) *Shops and Shopping 1800–1914: Where, and in What Manner, the Well-dressed Englishwoman Bought her Clothes*. London: Barrie and Jenkins.

Addams, Jane (1910) *The Spirit of Youth and the City Streets*. New York: Macmillan.

Adorno, Theodor and Horkheimer, Max (1973) *Dialectic of Enlightenment*. London: Allen Lane.

Anderson, Perry (1984) 'Modernity and Revolution', *New Left Review*, 144: 96–113.

Arendt, Hannah (1973) 'Introduction: Walter Benjamin 1892–1940', in Walter Benjamin, *Illuminations*. London: Fontana. pp. 7–58.

Banks, Olive (1981) *Faces of Feminism*. Oxford: Martin Robertson.

Baudelaire, Charles (1964) *The Painter of Modern Life and Other Essays*. Oxford: Phaidon Press.

Bauman, Zygmunt (1983) 'Industrialism, Consumerism and Power', *Theory, Culture & Society*, 1(3): 32–43.

Benjamin, Walter (1968) 'Paris – Capital of the Nineteenth Century', *New Left Review*, 48.

Benjamin, Walter (1973) *Illuminations*. London: Fontana.

Benjamin, Walter (1986a) *Reflections*. New York: Schocken Books.

Benjamin, Walter (1986b) *Moscow Diary*, ed. Gary Smith. Cambridge, MA: Harvard University Press.

Berman, Marshall (1983) *All That Is Solid Melts into Air: The Experience of Modernity*. London: Verso.

Berman, Marshall (1984) 'The Signs in the Street: A Response to Perry Anderson', *New Left Review*, 145: 114–23.

Bourdieu, Pierre (1986) *Distinction: A Social Critique of the Judgement of Taste*. London: Routledge and Kegan Paul.

Bowlby, Rachel (1985) *Just Looking: Consumer Culture in Dreiser, Gissing and Zola*. London: Methuen.

Bradbury, Malcolm and McFarlane, James (eds) (1987) *Modernism 1890–1930*. Harmondsworth: Penguin.

Brandon, Ruth (1990) *The New Woman and the Old Men: Love, Sex and the Woman Question*. London: Flamingo.

Breward, Christopher (1994) 'Femininity and Consumption: The Problem of the Late Nineteenth Century Fashion Journal', *Journal of Design History*, 7(2).

Brewster, Ben (1968) 'Walter Benjamin and the Arcades Project', *New Left Review*, 48.

Buci-Glucksmann, Christine (1987) 'Catastrophic Utopia: The Feminine as Allegory of the Modern', in C. Gallagher and T. Laqueur (eds), *The Making of the Modern Body*. Berkeley and Los Angeles: University of California Press. pp. 220–40.

Buck-Morss, Susan (1983) 'Benjamin's *Passagen-Werk*: Redeeming Mass Culture for the Revolution', *New German Critique*, 29: 211–40.

Buck-Morss, Susan (1989) *The Dialectics of Seeing: Walter Benjamin and the Arcades Project*. Cambridge, MA: MIT Press.

Callery, Sean (1991) *Harrods Knightsbridge: The Story of Society's Favourite Store*. London: Ebury Press.

Campbell, Colin (1987) *The Romantic Ethic and the Spirit of Modern Consumerism*. Oxford: Basil Blackwell.

Carter, Erica (1984) 'Alice in Consumer Wonderland', in A. McRobbie and M. Nava (eds), *Gender and Generation*. London: Macmillan.

Carter, Erica (1995) *How German is She? National Reconstruction and the Consuming Woman in the FRG and West Berlin 1945–1960*. Ann Arbor, MI: University of Michigan Press.

Chaney, David (1983) 'The Department Store as Cultural Form', *Theory, Culture & Society*, 1(3).

Covina, Maurice (1978) *Fine Silks and Oak Counters: Debenhams 1778–1978*. London: Hutchinson Benham.

Davidoff, Leonore (1973) *The Best Circles: 'Society', Etiquette and the Season*. London: Croom Helm.

Davidoff, Leonore and Hall, Catherine (1987) *Family Fortunes: Men and Women of the English Middle Class 1780–1850*. London: Hutchinson.

Davidoff, Leonore, L'Esperance, Jean and Newby, Howard (1976) 'Landscape with Figures: Home and Community in English Society', in J. Mitchell and A. Oakley (eds), *The Rights and Wrongs of Women*. Harmondsworth: Penguin. pp. 139–75.

Davis, Dorothy (1966) *A History of Shopping*. London: Routledge and Kegan Paul.

Demetz, Peter (1986) 'Introduction' to Walter Benjamin, *Reflections*. New York: Schocken Books.

Donzelot, Jacques (1979) *The Policing of Families*. London: Hutchinson.

Dreiser, Theodore (1981) *Sister Carrie*. Harmondsworth: Penguin.

Eckert, Charles (1990) 'The Carole Lombard in Macy's Window', in J. Gaines and C. Herzog (eds), *Fabrications: Costume and the Female Body*. London: Routledge. pp. 100–21.

Ewen, Stuart (1976) *Captains of Consciousness: Advertising and the Social Roots of Consumer Society*. New York: McGraw-Hill.

Ewen, Stuart (1988) *All Consuming Images*. New York: Basic Books.

Ewen, Stuart and Ewen, Elizabeth (1982) *Channels of Desire: Mass Images and the Shaping of American Consciousness*. New York: McGraw-Hill.

Featherstone, Mike (1983) 'Consumer Culture', *Theory, Culture & Society*, 1(3): 4–9.

Forty, Adrian (1986) *Objects of Desire*. London: Thames and Hudson.

Foucault, Michel (1980) *Power/Knowledge*. Brighton: Harvester.

Frei, Norbert (1987) *National Socialist Rule in Germany: The Führer State 1933–1945*. Oxford: Basil Blackwell.

Frisby, David (1985) *Fragments of Modernity: Georg Simmel, Siegfried Kracauer and Walter Benjamin*. London: Heinemann.

Fromm, Bella (1943) *Blood and Banquets: A Berlin Social Diary*. London: Geoffrey Bles.

Gaines, Jane (1990) 'Fabricating the Female Body', in J. Gaines and C. Herzog (eds) *Fabrications: Costume and the Female Body*. London: Routledge. pp. 1–27.

Gramsci, Antonio (1973) 'Americanism and Fordism', in his *Prison Notebooks*. London: Lawrence and Wishart.

Granville Barker, Harley (1977) *The Madras House*. London: Eyre Methuen.

Greenhalgh, Paul (1988) *Ephemeral Vistas: The Éxpositions Universelles, Great Exhibitions and World's Fairs, 1951–1939*. Manchester: Manchester University Press.

Grossmann, Atina (1984) 'The New Woman and the Rationalisation of Sexuality in Weimar Germany', in Ann Barr Snitow, Christine Stonsell and Sharon Thompson (eds), *Desire: The Politics of Sexuality*. London: Virago, pp. 190–210.

Hake, Sabine (1987) 'Girls in Crisis', *New German Critique*, 40: 147–66.

Hansen, Miriam (1983) 'Early Silent Cinema: Whose Public Sphere?', *New German Critique*, 29: 147–84.

Held, David (1980) *Introduction to Critical Theory*. London: Hutchinson.

Hollis, Patricia (1979) *Women in Public: The Women's Movement 1850–1900*. London: George Allen and Unwin.

Honeycombe, Gordon (1984) *Selfridges*. London: Park Lane Press.

Horkheimer, Max (1972a) 'Authority and the Family', in his *Critical Theory: Selected Essays*. New York: Heider and Heider, pp. 47–128.

Horkheimer, Max (1972b) 'Art and Mass Culture', in his *Critical Theory: Selected Essays*. New York: Heider and Heider.

Horowitz, Daniel (1985) *The Morality of Spending: Attitudes towards Consumer Society in America, 1875–1940*. Baltimore: Johns Hopkins University Press.

Huyssen, Andreas (1986) 'Mass Culture as Woman: Modernism's Other', in his *After the Great Divide: Modernism, Mass Culture and Postmodernism*. Basingstoke: Macmillan. pp. 44–64.

Jay, Martin (1984) *Adorno*. London: Fontana.

Jay, Martin (1992) 'Scopic Regimes of Modernity', in Scott Lash and Jonathan Friedman (eds), *Modernity and Identity*. Oxford: Basil Blackwell. pp. 178–92.

Kohn, Marek (1992) *Dope Girls: The Birth of the British Drug Underground*. London: Lawrence and Wishart.

Kracauer, Siegfried (1987) 'The Cult of Distraction: On Berlin's Picture Palaces', *New German Critique*, 40: 91–6.

Kuhn, Annette (1988) *Cinema, Censorship and Sexuality 1909–1925*. London: Routledge.

Lancaster, William (1995) *The Department Store: A Social History*. London: Pinter.

Lasch, Christopher (1979) *The Culture of Narcissism*. New York: Norton.

Lash, Scott and Friedman, Jonathan (eds) (1992) *Modernity and Identity*. Oxford: Basil Blackwell.

Leach, William (1984) 'Transformations in a Culture of Consumption: Women and Department Stores, 1890–1925', *Journal of American History*, 7(2): 319–42.

McCracken, Grant (1990) *Culture and Consumption*. Indianapolis and Bloomington: Indiana University Press.

McKendrick, Neil, Brewer, John and Plumb, J. H. (1982) *The Birth of a Consumer Society: The Commercialization of Eighteenth-Century England*. London: Europa.

McRobbie, Angela (1992) 'The *Passagen-Werk* and the Place of Walter Benjamin in Cultural Studies', *Cultural Studies*, 6(2): 47–57.

Marchand, Roland (1986) *Advertising the American Dream: Making Way for Modernity 1920–1940*. Berkeley and Los Angeles: University of California Press.

Marriott, John (1996) 'Sensation of the Abyss: The Urban Poor and Modernity', in Mica Nava and Alan O'Shea (eds), *Modern Times: Reflections on a Century of English Modernity*. London: Routledge. pp. 77–93.

Mast, Gerald (1982) *The Movies in our Midst: Documents in the Cultural History of Film in America*. Chicago: University of Chicago Press.

Melman, Billie (1988) *Women and the Popular Imagination in the Twenties*. London: Macmillan.

Miller, Michael B. (1981) *The Bon Marché: Bourgeois Culture and the Department Store, 1869–1920*. London: Allen and Unwin.

Minsky, Rosalind (1994) 'Women as Shoppers'. Unpublished paper.

Modleski, Tania (1986a) 'Femininity as Mas(s)querade: A Feminist Approach to Mass Culture', in C. McCabe (ed.), *High Theory/Low Culture*. Manchester: Manchester University Press (reprinted in Tania Modleski, *Feminism Without Women*. London: Routledge, 1991).

Modleski, Tania (ed) (1986b) *Studies in Entertainment: Critical Approaches to Mass Culture*. Indianapolis and Bloomington: Indiana University Press.

Morris, Meaghan (1988) 'Things to do with Shopping Centres', in Susan Sheridan (ed.), *Grafts: Feminist Cultural Criticism*. London: Verso. pp. 193–225.

Mort, Frank (1988) 'Boys Own? Masculinity, Style and Popular Culture', in R. Chapman and J. Rutherford (eds), *Male Order: Unwrapping Masculinity*. London: Lawrence and Wishart.

Moss, Michael and Turton, Alison (1989) *A Legend of Retailing: House of Fraser*. London: Weidenfeld and Nicolson.

Nava, Mica (1984) 'The Urban, the Domestic and Education for Girls', in G. Grace (ed.), *Education and the City*. London: Routledge and Kegan Paul (reprinted in Nava 1992). pp. 159–91.

Nava, Mica (1992) *Changing Cultures: Feminism, Youth and Consumerism*. London: Sage.

Nava, Mica (1995) 'Modernity Tamed? Women Shoppers and the Rationalisation of Consumption in the Interwar Period', *Australian Journal of Communication*, 22(2): 1–19.

Nava, Mica and O'Shea, Alan (eds) (1996) *Modern Times: Reflections on a Century of English Modernity*. London: Routledge.

Nixon, Sean (1992) 'Have You Got the Look? Masculinities and Shopping Spectacle', in Rob Shields (ed.), *Lifestyle Shopping: The Subject of Consumption*. London: Routledge.

O'Shea, Alan (1996) 'English Subjects of Modernity', in Mica Nava and Alan O'Shea (eds), *Modern Times: Reflections on a Century of English Modernity*. London: Routledge. pp. 7–21.

Petro, Patrice (1987) 'Modernity and Mass Culture in Weimar', *New German Critique*, 40: 115–46.

Pollock, Griselda (1988) *Vision and Difference*. London: Routledge.

Poster, Mark (1978) *Critical Theory of the Family*. London: Pluto Press.

Pumphrey, Martin (1987) 'The Flapper, the Housewife and the Making of Modernity', *Cultural Studies* 1(2).

Richards, Jeffrey (1984) *The Age of the Dream Palace: Cinema and Society in Britain 1930–1939*. London: Routledge.

Richards, Thomas (1991) *The Commodity Culture of Victorian England: Advertising and Spectacle 1851–1914*. London: Verso.

Robins, Elizabeth (1980) *The Convert*. London: Women's Press.

Rose, Nikolas (1979) 'The Psychological Complex: Mental Measurement and Social Administration', *Ideology and Consciousness*, 5: 5–68.

Ross, Kirstin (1992) 'Introduction' to Émile Zola, *The Ladies' Paradise*. Berkeley and Los Angeles: University of California Press.

Ryan, Jenny (1992) 'Women, Modernity and the City', Working Papers in Popular Cultural Studies no. 1, Manchester Institute for Popular Culture.

Sackville West, Vita (1983) *The Edwardians*. London: Virago.

Schudson, Michael (1984) *Advertising: The Uneasy Persuasion*. New York: Basic Books.

Schwarz, Bill (1991) 'Rationalism, Irrationalism and Taylorism', *Science and Culture* 8: 144–52.

Sennett, Richard (1986) *The Fall of Public Man: On the Social Psychology of Capitalism*. London: Faber and Faber.

Shields, Rob (ed.) (1992) *Lifestyle Shopping: The Subject of Consumption*. London: Routledge.

Showalter, Elaine (1992) *Sexual Anarchy: Gender and Culture at the Fin de Siècle*. London: Virago.

Simmel, Georg (1971) 'The Metropolis and Mental Life', in his *On Individuality and Social Forms*. Chicago: University of Chicago Press. pp. 409–24.

Smith, Gary (1986) 'Afterword' to Walter Benjamin, *Moscow Diary*. Cambridge, MA: Harvard University Press.

Stedman Jones, Gareth (1976) *Outcast London*. Harmondsworth: Penguin.

Stein, Sally (1985) 'The Graphic Ordering of Desire: Modernisation of a Middle-Class Women's Magazine 1914–1939', *Heresies*, 18.

Strachey, Ray (1978) *The Cause*. London: Virago.

Theweleit, Klaus (1987) *Male Fantasies*. Cambridge: Polity Press.

Thonnessen, Werner (1973) *The Emancipation of Women: Germany 1863–1933*. London: Pluto Press.

Tickner, Lisa (1987) *The Spectacle of Women: Imagery of the Suffrage Campaign 1907–1914*. London: Chatto and Windus.

Trimberger, Ellen (1984) 'Feminism, Men and Modern Love: Greenwich Village 1900–1935', in Ann Barr Snitow, Christine Stonsell and Sharon Thompson (eds), *Desire: The Politics of Sexuality*. London: Virago. pp. 169–89.

Valverde, Mariana (1989) 'The Love of Finery: Fashion and the Fallen Woman in 19th Century Social Discourse', *Victorian Studies*, 32: 169–88.

van Vucht Tijssen, Lieteke (1991) 'Women and Objective Culture: Georg Simmel and Marianne Weber', *Theory, Culture & Society*, 8(3): 203–18.

Veblen, Thorstein (1979) *Theory of the Leisure Class*. Harmondsworth: Penguin.

Vickery, Amanda (1993a) 'Women and the World of Goods: A Lancashire Consumer and her Possessions, 1751–81', in John Brewer and Ray Porter (eds), *Consumption and the World of Goods*. London: Routledge. pp. 274–301.

Vickery, Amanda (1993b) 'Shaking the Separate Spheres', *Times Literary Supplement*, 12 March.

von Rezzori, Gregor (1983) *Memoirs of an Anti-Semite: A Novel in Five Stories*. London: Pan Books.

Walker, Lynne (1991) 'Women and Victorian Public Space'. Paper given at 'The Cracks in the Pavement' Conference, Design Museum, London.

Walkowitz, Judith (1980) *Prostitution and Victorian Society*. Cambridge: Cambridge University Press.

Walkowitz, Judith (1992) *City of Dreadful Delight*. London: Virago.

Ward, Ken (1991) *Mass Communication and the Modern World*. London: Macmillan.

Weeks, Jeffrey (1981) *Sex, Politics and Society*. London: Longman.

Williams, Raymond (1975) *Country and City*. Harmondsworth: Penguin.

Williams, Raymond (1989) *The Politics of Modernism*. London: Verso.

Williams, Rosalind (1982) *Dream Worlds: Mass Consumption in Late Nineteenth-Century France*. Berkeley and Los Angeles: University of California Press.

Wilson, Elizabeth (1978) *Women and the Welfare State*. London: Tavistock.

Wilson, Elizabeth (1991) *Sphinx in the City*. London: Virago.

Wilson, Elizabeth (1992) 'The Invisible Flâneur', *New Left Review*, 191: 90–110.

Wolff, Janet (1985) 'The Invisible Flâneuse: Women in the Literature of Modernity', *Theory, Culture & Society*, 2(3): 37–46.

Wolff, Janet (1990) *Feminine Sentences: Essays on Women and Culture*. Cambridge: Polity Press.

Wolff, Janet (1993) 'Memoirs and Micrologies: Walter Benjamin, Feminism and Cultural Analysis', *New Formations*, 20: 111–23.

Wollen, Peter (1993) 'Modern Times: Cinema/Americanism/The Robot', in his *Raiding the Icebox: Reflections on Twentieth Century Culture*. London: Verso. pp. 35–51.

Zola, Émile (1992) *The Ladies' Paradise*. Berkeley and Los Angeles: University of California Press.

Zukin, Sharon (1988) 'The Postmodern Debate over Urban Form', *Theory, Culture & Society*, 5(2–3): 431–46.

4

SUPERMARKET FUTURES

Rachel Bowlby

'Big Bear crashes into New Jersey'

On 8 December 1932, the vacant Durant automobile plant in Elizabeth, New Jersey, was the site of a much-remarked event, the result of a recent alliance between two entrepreneurs and a Hoboken wholesaler. Five years later, the occasion is enthusiastically recalled as a media event, as newspaper stories

> flashed around the country . . . described the barny structure with its crude interiors, fixtures made of rough pine lumber and its huge displays of merchandise as the center of attraction, with thousands of people who were swarming around them with baskets on their arms, content to wait on themselves.
>
> From the fantastic stories that were spread around the country, the prevailing opinion was that the Big Bear was some kind of a circus stunt of a temporary nature, organized to get rid of surplus merchandise. (Zimmerman, 1937: v–vi)

But no! M.M. Zimmerman, the writer of the account, was a man who prided himself on spotting the futures of shopping history. Some years earlier, he had covered the development of chain stores in the advertising journal *Printers' Ink*, and after the war he would make himself into a missionary for American self-service selling in Europe and elsewhere in the world. For Zimmerman, this 'swarming' to the 'barny' place from miles away was no one-off depression production of a run-down farmyard or circus; it was nothing less than the inauguration of the next glorious phase in the continuing history of retail progress. The 'super market' was here to stay, here to spread.

Zimmerman focuses in on just one of many comparable beginnings at this time. Outfits similar to the Big Bear were appearing in many states and regions, from the first King Cullen Market on Long Island, opened in 1930, to stores in the Los Angeles area as early as 1927. By 1937, in typically triumphalist prose, Zimmerman can write:

> Contrary to the prognostications of Big Bear's early demise, it not only survived but many other Big and Little Bears have appeared in many of the large Metropolitan cities throughout the country, under such fantastic names as Giant Tiger, Big Chief, King Kosh, the Whale and what not. Today there are more than two thousand of these Big and Little Bears operating in thirty-two states. (1937: vi)

The supermarkets seem to proliferate as readily as their masses of swarming customers, but they are a special kind of animal: jolly kiddy creatures, big and fun and cartoon-like. The 'fantastic names', like the 'fantastic stories', suggest some kind of children's wonderland, with gentle giants performing in a friendly arena.

Even though Zimmerman leads up to the continuation and expansion of the new kind of circus store, he does want to stress its makeshift qualities. He describes the 'crude' interior and the 'rough' pine matierials; 'the entire layout of fixtures was of cheap construction, giving a temporary bazaar-like appearance' (Zimmerman, 1937: 8). The point is partly a pioneer spirit – back to the simple nature of rugged commercial pre-civilization. And in the context of post-Crash retailing, what it implies in particular is a reduction in unnecessary marketing costs. For Zimmerman, 'the ultimate goal' of retailing developments is the progressive elimination of steps and costs in an ever smoother economic journey, 'the flow of goods towards the consumer's home' (1937: v).

There were two specific innovations which directly eliminated distribution costs. First, the customers travelled to the goods instead of the goods going all the way to them. The store was miles away from where the customers lived. The Model T Ford had made car-owning widespread; they could drive there themselves, parking in a a special lot across the road. But the most striking way in which supermarkets turned distribution over to the customer was inside the store itself, through the 'hundreds of market baskets' (Zimmerman, 1937: 8) piled up near the entrance. This produced the amazing spectacle of people 'content to wait on themselves':

> Its appeal to the consuming public is, Help Yourself, Serve Yourself, Pay Cash, Carry Your Goods Away and Save the Difference. (Zimmerman, 1937: 6)

The shouting capitals seem to hover between invitation and forceful imperative: an offer you can't refuse. But soon, this would vanish into the unremarkable obviousness of supermarket self-service.

Bear facts

'Bear Facts' was the title of a broadsheet produced by the Big Bear operators to counter the opposition from representatives of more traditional forms of food retailing, which had issued in a ban on their advertising in local newspapers. The phrase may serve as a cue for the following selection of supermarket data. For in the world of supermarkets, facts are always more bear facts than bare facts.

First, this is because representations of supermarkets, whether negative or positive, critical or promotional, have always been packed and packaged with vivid images. Far from the supposed neutrality or bareness of shopping centres or malls, they have been placed in animal, magic or technological worlds that may be benign or hostile – jungle, circus, wonderland, power grid. The cute associations of the 1930s images shade into the networks of entrapment and manipulation that characterize the supermarket seen through the eyes of its critics in the post-war decades. In the most extreme version of this, the supermarket can itself come to stand for the all-encompassing powers and controls of modern society. A French novel of the early 1970s, J.M.G. Le Clézio's *Les Géants* (The Giants) (1973), which takes the giant supermarket as a microcosm of contemporary culture, metamorphoses those friendly Big Bears and other such creatures into the insuperable controls of systematic power, 'big' business. The novel's primary title is the universal electricity danger sign, ⚡.

Second, supermarkets have been one of the principal outlets for brand-name, mass-produced goods identified by packaging and promoted by advertising. Both of these, among other functions, intervene to dress up the bare article for sale in a distinctive mode, verbally or visually or both, so that the bare and the bear are part and parcel, wrapper and contents, of the same product. This is true even, or especially, when the package, or the advertisement, proclaims its imparting of the facts, and only the facts. The plainness of information carries its own persuasions. In a similar way, the supermarket, from the outset, presented itself as the bare, functional store, basic things at basic prices.

Supermarket histories

Zimmerman's celebratory story, an extract from an implied perpetual improvement in methods of selling, is not an uncommon type within the institutions of marketing and retailing. The relation between the benefits to manufacturers and entrepreneurs and the benefits to customers is never at issue; it is simply assumed that the two automatically coincide. So Zimmerman posits a seamless evolution from department stores, to mail order, to chain stores, to the latest retail development pinpointed in the events of the early 1930s.

Critiques of supermarket shopping start from the opposite assumption, that this relation does not hold, or rather that it holds inversely: the more the capitalists benefit, the less the customers do. Progress in the positive account is mirrored by a story of inexorable and increasing exploitation, as consuming institutions take over the minds and the purses of their vulnerable victims, including the employees. These two stories place themselves at opposite points in the supermarket: one at the cold checkout counter where the customer pays, and the underpaid worker suffers, the other in the bright lights of an ever-welcoming store interior.

If we tried to drop both versions, and simply to look at 'the facts' of the history of the supermarket, where might we begin? What would be its archives? Nothing, it might seem, would be more free of distracting values and stories than bare sequences of names and figures. So we could turn first to the millions of shopping lists compiled by millions of customers over the decades, bearing but not baring some unidentifiable relation to what they actually bought, and some other unidentifiable relation to the purchases of all the customers who never made lists in the first place. Then there might be the till receipts, preserved by circumspect shoppers, but until the invention of the barcode providing no information apart from a series of prices and a grand, or meagre, total. And except for a few chance exceptions, all these careful plans and quantifiable results would have gone the way of the packages and leftovers and food gone rotten, off into the unlocatable, decomposing garbage tips of Western consumer culture.

To remedy such lack of data on the consumer side, we could turn instead to the inventory and sales records from within the stores. There might be more or less complete and accurate records of costs and profits. Records of the quantities and rate of sale for individual products would be less exact, given the thousands of different lines that are stocked – until, that is, the advent of the barcode in the 1980s, which has meant that inventory and turnover records are rapidly attaining states of infallibility and comprehensiveness undreamt of a few decades ago.

But what would perfect barcode knowledge tell us, either about the stores or about the customers? One kind of supermarket research has always sought to maximize information about the ins and outs of the products and the people and the money: what goes in and who takes it out, or who comes in and what they take out. The techniques of market research classify customers according to an infinitely expandable set of variables. Just as each product is a unique but computer-classifiable individual, so every customer is a unique and computer-classifiable target, marked up ever more precisely according to lifestyle, understood as likely, calculable dispositions to buy. Already, in one forward-looking account of 1935, 'The customer is considered a bundle of sales possibilities' (Dipman, 1935: 7).

Apart from the possible facts and figures of who and what, imagine all the possible unstatistical histories in and around the stores – the routines and dawdles and encounters and desires and decisions, all of which pass all the time through the checkout with barely a trace behind them. There might be the millions of conversations on the way there and back, disappeared out of the window of millions of suburban automobiles; and the arguments at home, at work, in the papers, on TV, about the qualities or disadvantages of this or that new store, and this or that kind of shopping. There might be the accounts in novels and films and letters and phone calls, the more and less durable media of supermarket stories, imagining the store as freedom or oppression or just as a place of everyday boredoms and pleasures and annoyances.

For writers are not the only ones drawn to the making of plausible shopping histories. This is a part of life where everyone has theories and histories, both personal and general: about the merits and drawbacks of recent and local, distant and ancient developments; about the implications of different marketing strategies; about the quirks and perversities of shopping behaviour, their own and other people's.

In such mixed contexts, the following pieces are not, of course, the whole story, all the thousands of lines – an impossible fantasy – but a series of short extractions from some possible supermarket histories. These histories, at every turn, are inseparable from the futures that they imagine. As such, they are meant to offer food for thought at a time when supermarkets have come to occupy a position of peculiar centrality in our culture.

The supermarket and the department store

In the nineteenth century was the department store; in the twentieth century was the supermarket. A schematic comparison of the dominant traits of each animal – as much in their image as in their never-bare facts of life – may begin, provisionally, to point out some of the characteristics of the supermarket.

Both are large-scale retailing institutions, selling a vast range of goods under one roof and making use of modern marketing principles of cost-effectiveness, high turnover rates and low profit margins. Both encourage the customer to look and sometimes to handle, with no obligation to buy. Both are taken, in their times, as emblematic of contemporary developments not only in marketing, but in social life more generally: cities and leisure in one case, suburbs and automobiles in the other.

Both come to be represented in terms of magic and enchantment, seen – as in so many of these double-faced images – as either pleasurable or insidious, the work of friendly or evil wizards. Department stores, and supermarkets in their later developments, dazzle with their lighting and displays of goods. Both are thought to produce in their female customers states of mind that are far removed from the normal: the collective ecstasy of the nineteenth-century crowd of women in front of the array of fabrics, the hypnotic trance of the 1950s housewife numbed by the muzak and the psychologically selected colours of the packets of washing powder (see Packard, 1960: Chap. 10; Zola, 1992).

But the differences between the two stores are equally crucial in their respective mythologies. First, what they sell. The department store offered everything and anything, though with a concentration on clothes and furnishings. The supermarket is associated with something the department store did not always sell: food. Whereas the nineteenth-century department stores were represented as bringing the luxury of fashion to the middle classes, the supermarket brought cheap food to 'the masses'. In one case, luxury items for a class aspiring to an image of affluence (and a sex aspiring to an image of beauty); in the other, necessities for all.

The department store offers an image of service: anyone can enter and be treated like a queen. Assistants will come to your aid; you may partake of the free refreshments, the reading room, and all the other facilities laid on to encourage you to spend the whole day there enjoying the new leisure activity called shopping. The supermarket's image is functional. Costs are minimized because you are serving yourself, and because there is (at first, as in Zimmerman's account) a vaunted lack of deliberate display: here it is, nothing fancy, no extras. Shopping is a task to be got through with minimum time and minimum expenditure: cost-effectiveness is on the side of the customer as much as on that of the entrepreneur.

The department store is European; the supermarket is American. The association in the first case is false, in the sense that department stores arose in the United States at the same time as in Paris or London or Berlin. In the second case, it's more or less true. But the contrast functions to reinforce other department store/supermarket distinctions. The department store is considered to be feminine, frivolous, French and fashionable; in its Parisian form, it is one of the emblems of nineteenth-century modernity for Walter Benjamin's retrospect in the first part of the twentieth. The supermarket, initally 'crude' (Zimmerman) and basic, often vulgar and hardly tasteful, figures above all as an American invention which is then exported to Europe. So, as with other features of twentieth-century consumer culture – mass-marketing and advertising techniques, brand-name products – which are themselves inseparable from the development of supermarket selling, the supermarket is seen unequivocally as American.

The department store is the 'cathedral of modern commerce' (Zola); and it appears as a 'palace' for the middle classes, symbol of 'the democratization of luxury' (Georges d'Avenel). As a palace, it affects an image of opulent leisure accessible to anyone who cares to enter and participate vicariously in an image of the aesthetically aristocratic life. As a cathedral, it takes over from religion; it has its consecrated building, and its own rituals and festive seasons (designated times for sales and events in relation to particular themes and product groups).

The supermarket has no such grand pretensions (though the uproar in England about supermarkets opening on Sundays may be an acknowledgement of the way that the weekly shopping trip is indeed in some sense symbolically akin to the traditional family ritual). In the Big Bear circus, the emphasis is less on the show as display than the show as performance or stunt, later to become a markedly dirty trick. In the 1960s, at the height of consumerist protests against exploitation by the big food corporations, it took on dramatically negative appearances, as a 'jungle' or 'trap', each giving titles to bestselling critiques of the period (Cross, 1970; Leinwand, 1970). Where the department store invites you in, the supermarket catches you and won't let you out. The jungle and trap images imply primitive aggression – big bears eating little ones – but also a confusing forest or maze from which you cannot escape.

The supermarket may be no more than a 'warehouse', signifying the minimization of distribution costs; simply a way-station between the factory and the home. At a later stage than the jolly frolics of Big Bear and his friends, the supermarket moves on from its makeshift beginnings to take on an image of streamlined efficiency: convenience, hygiene, reliability. But here, the contrast is not so much with the department store as with earlier phases of food merchandizing.

Self-service and the modern food store

In the history of big stores, the supermarket's natural analogue and predecessor is the department store. In the history of food retailing, it is principally the local grocery store. From the late nineteenth century, chain stores of various types had come to supplement and compete with grocery stores, general stores, and the stores selling fresh or specialist products – meat, produce, tea and coffee. Some of these expanded directly into the larger, self-service stores that came to be called supermarkets. One American example of this is A & P (the Great Atlantic & Pacific Tea Company); another is the midwestern Kroger's, which expanded in the 1890s from Barney Kroger's Cincinnati tea and coffee store, via a growing chain in the early part of this century. Whatever their particular product group, the chains were developing the economies of scale – bulk-buying, vertical integration, low profit margins – that would be deployed by their larger modern cousins. Chains developed in Europe as well, and there, too, they provided one existing basis for the development of the new kind of store, with the cooperative societies playing a particularly prominent role.

The invention of self-service is attributed to Clarence Saunders, who opened his first Piggly Wiggly store in Memphis, Tennessee, in 1916. The design, including high rows of shelves arranged in aisles, turnstiles for entrance and exit, and a checkout counter, was patented the following year. In effect, the Piggly Wiggly was a prototype supermarket, anticipating what would later become the normal mode of direct customer access to goods.

During the 1930s, Carl W. Dipman produced a series of descriptions and projections of developments in food retailing, published under the auspices of the American trade journal *The Progressive Grocer*. Without the flash and drama or the sheer size of Big Bear and his numerous peers, these conceptions of the futures of food stores look to other features which will differentiate them from their precursors. The element in common is the emphasis on self-service. But self-service is associated not only with the saving of running costs, but also with the unprecedented idea of the food store as potentially an attractive and comfortable place for the consumer to enjoy.

The image of the warehouse here becomes negative, attributed not to the new stores, but to the old, with their lack of understanding of 'modern' selling principles. These principles are represented, strikingly, as aesthetic. In 1931, Dipman writes:

> The grocery store today must be both pleasing to the customer – a thing of beauty – yet so constructed that work and labor are reduced to a minimum. . . . The application of sight and touch, coupled with efficiency of operation, are the most important factors in the new retail salesmanship. (1931: iv)

'The application of sight and touch' make shopping a matter of carefully prepared perceptions and pleasures. The consumer is a looker and a feeler, her likely natural responses beginning here to be charted in ways that will subdivide to an infinitely expandable range (or 'bundle') of responsive possibilities – different senses, particular colours or textures or shapes.

Efficiency and 'pleasing' qualities are separated in one way, but come together in another, since the modern 'thing of beauty' is produced by the application of principles taken to be just as scientific as those deployed to minimize the costs of 'work and labor'. The reduction of 'work and labor' is as much for customers as for staff: shopping is to be an *experience*, not just a job to be done. But there is also the implication that employees' activities, disruptive of store displays, should be hidden from the aesthetic view. Self-service may further involve the partial removal of this element: 'Rearranging a floor plan so the benefits of self-service arrangement can be acquired is often the means of reducing the selling expense, sometimes by the elimination of an employee or two' (Dipman and O'Brien, 1940: 8).

Sales clerks, counters, shelves, in fact anything else not for sale is an obstruction to the direct encounter of customer and product:

> The properly arranged store . . . has no unnecessary barriers. It lets women and merchandise meet.
> As far as possible every square inch of the eyes' range of vision, from the top of the shelving down to the floor, wherever the customer stands, wherever she looks, should display merchandise. (Dipman, 1935: 11)

The passage encapsulates the combination of control and licence that the self-service store was to promote. On the one hand, the woman's vision (it's always a woman at this time), mathematically measurable, is completely taken over: there is no getting away from the goods which come directly to confront her. On the other hand, there are 'no unnecessary barriers' to the casual encounters of customer and merchandise. For the time she is in the store, the shopper is free to move back and forth, to put into her trolley whatever she wants: the looking and touching encouraged by the open displays suggest and permit a taking that is not (yet) a commitment to purchase. In this interim, provisional space, between the entrance and the checkout, she really can have anything. This is the dreamlike face of self-service, when all is possible, possessable, until the moment of reckoning.

In this regard, the rationale of the self-service store is much like that of the department store, equally devoted to the careful construction of a fantasy experience for women. The difference – ironically, in light of the massive future of self-service – was in the scale, since Dipman's 1930s food store is intimately small. After the war, the big food corporations metamorphose into 'the giants', characters who no longer have much to do with the childish play of Big Bear and his pals. The names of supermarkets opened in the 1950s often loudly proclaim their GIANT size, recapitulated in the mega-miniature of the *giant* or *jumbo* packs of what they sell inside. But during the period of anti-supermarket consumer activism beginning in the mid-1960s, as in Le Clézio's novel, 'the giants' become ominously inhuman, towering corporately over defenceless swarms of crawling, dazed consumers.

Like packaging, to which it is intimately related, display is thought of as taking over the salesman's job, replacing an aural appeal – his sales talk – with a visual one. In 1935,

> The modern food store is a scientific salesroom. . . . In this evolution there has come into use a new type of salesmanship. For the want of a better term let us call it *silent salesmanship*. While personal salesmanship still has and always will have, a valuable place in food retailing, yet it must be supplemented with the new *silent salesmanship* – sometimes called display. (Dipman, 1935: 7)

The assumption here is that display is something added to the goods, a selling force they would lack without it. It will therefore move the goods faster, increasing turnover and ultimately reducing costs, in keeping with the aims of the 'scientific salesroom'.

But just as often, the opposite assumption is made: that supermarkets should appear as spaces which do without display, considered as a luxury that adds to prices and thus deters a buyer who is shopping primarily to save money and obtain essential commodities, not to be charmed by beauty. Throughout supermarket history, the issue of display has provided a point of argument around which different sides can lay claim to superiority according to disputed criteria of customer preference. Supermarkets regularly present themselves as minimizing costs by doing without the luxuries of old-fashioned service or the lavish displays of stores selling luxury goods.

After the war, when it pioneered self-service selling in Britain, the Tesco chain used the slogan 'Pile it high and sell it cheap'. The point of the slogan was not to suggest that piles of it had any intrinsic appeal, even though this is precisely what American proponents of 'mass displays' – such as huge pyramidal heaps at the end of the aisle – were advocating at the time. In the early 1990s, the Tesco slogan was revived by the cut-price chain Kwik Save, which expanded rapidly during the recession, occupying town-centre sites and thus going against the trend towards large, out-of-town 'superstores'. The adoption of the old slogan on posters combines playful nostalgia – the good old days when supermarkets were supermarkets – with pointed mockery of the gentrified Tesco, abandoning its former cheapo glory as champion of price-cutting for the consumer, and now indistinguishable from any of the other big chains.

The homely store

Home is the ultimate destination, the final resting place, of the goods which have made the journey from their place of production with more or less efficiency, more or less elimination of waste. Where the supermarket is represented as merely functional, simply the point of sale, it has none of the calm, peaceful and extra-commercial associations of home.

Yet some suggestions for the modern self-service store imagine it as a kind of second home. Carl Dipman's advocacy of display as an appeal to feminine 'whims and fancies', and to women's natural sense of beauty, is accompanied by a suggestion that domestic comforts, too, should form part of the store's scientifically coordinated appeal. In 1931 the modern store is to be recognizably domestic in scale; or, rather, it is to produce domestic cosiness as another point of aesthetic appeal, set apart from the merchandise itself:

> Little imitation window effects with mirror backings are another particularly successful wall treatment. These help greatly to give the store the appearance of a cheery cottage kitchen – and that is an atmosphere that makes a big appeal to the beauty-loving nature of women – it is the sort of atmosphere they like to be in, to linger in. . . . A third method of adding attractiveness above the wall shelving is by several pleasing pictures. Country scenes of meadows or books, or pictures of children at play, are always appropriate. So are pictures such as farming scenes that relate directly to the grocery business. (Dipman, 1931: 143–6)

The 'cheery cottage kitchen' is a long way from the modern store; the 'pleasing pictures', likewise, are reassuringly pastoral, lest there be any doubt that the 'grocery business' has its roots anywhere else than on the traditional farm. And the food store – like the department store – appears as a place 'to linger in'.

Such lingering comes to a complete halt in Dipman's most whimsically delightful proposal:

> *Women Appreciate a Rest Corner*
> Many stores can afford a small space to be used as a customers' rest corner. It should be a friendly spot – a grouping of table, comfortable, colorful chairs, and if possible a telephone, fern stand, lamp, pads and pencils, a magazine or two. This is a good spot, too, for a radio or a canary, if the store has them. The rest corner should be located where customers can observe store activity, for people like to watch others at work or play. (Dipman, 1931: 148–9)

Here, in some golden age of the pre-supermarket imaginary, we find tucked away a little idyll of feminine comforts, lovingly detailed down to a surrealistically perfect juxtaposition of the canary and the telephone. This secluded spot provides an outlet for an innocent natural voyeurism – 'people like to watch others' – which even allows the customer to look at something other than the merchandise.

This is a vision in another world from the store surveillance programmes that would make in-store people-watching into the antithesis of a harmless customer sideline. Discussions a decade or two later about whether to provide supermarkets with restrooms (let alone rest corners) worry about their advantages for shoplifters, who will be able to stow their goods away in the much too private space. In the 1960s, restrooms are once again considered 'relatively new' as an idea; and despite the pilfering problem which is mentioned as an objection, some of the features of the 1930s 'rest corner' return with the accoutrements of the modern high-tech home:

> The lounges furnished in some of the supermarkets consist of an air-conditioned room; magazines, newspapers, and in some cases television sets, are provided. (Brand, 1965: 7)

(Alas, poor canary!)

The home a store

In her book *Household Engineering* (1920), Christine Frederick recommends the keeping of storage records for canned goods. These should show sizes, prices and the quantity in stock: 'then, as a can of peas or peaches is used, it should be crossed off the list, so that at a glance the number of cans on hand of any particular product can be seen without poking around the storage and actually counting the cans' (Frederick, 1920: 304; quoted in Strasser, 1982: 249). The purpose of this procedure is to make the shopping list; the housewife is the manager of her own store, exercising a regular inventory control, with records kept in an 'office corner' set aside for administrative purposes.

At this point, the crossover between home and store operates in terms of common principles of scientific management or 'engineering'. Other writers emphasize the way that the new self-service system transfers to customers functions that were previously performed by stores. Buyers do their own warehousing and their own distribution, in reverse order, travelling long distances to the store in their own delivery vehicles which then take back large quantities of goods to be stored at home until needed.

Later images of the home in advertising and elsewhere would suggest not so much its functional resemblance to the store, as its tendency to serve as a supplementary space for the display of merchandise. The door of the refrigerator opens enticingly on an array of technicolour produce; larder shelves display a dazzling array of canned foods; freezer compartments offer you a selection of instant meals. As in the supermarket, you have only to take what you want from the home store. The customer still has a wide choice, and this time it is free as well:

> The consumer has taken over the problem the retailer used to have, of making goods available frequently rather than infrequently. All he has to do now is to go and open his refrigerator door, and there his product is; but he had to put it there in the first place. (Cox, 1957: 54–5)

Shopping

There is a difference between 'going shopping' and 'doing the shopping'. Going shopping is a vague activity, an *extravagance* – literally, 'wandering out'. It is open-ended, with no precise plans or destinations: you can spend all day or not, you may just look and not buy. Going shopping is pleasurable, and possibly transgressive and excessive: you may spend too much time or too much money.

Doing the shopping, on the other hand, suggests an obligation or a regular routine. 'The' shopping implies something both planned and limited: the definite article, with no extras or deviations. Going shopping points to fashion, clothes and leisure; doing the shopping is food shopping, for the most part regarded as a chore. Food is necessary, fashion is fun and spontaneous. The weekly trip to the supermarket is an ordeal or at best a predictable and boring job that has to be done.

Sometimes the functionality of doing the shopping was the focus of supermarkets' self-declared appeal, as for this commentator at a policy seminar in Pittsburgh in 1957:

> It has been necessary to meet changed buying habits, since shopping is no longer a major diversion, but rather a task or chore to be performed as expeditiously as possible. The desire to shop quickly, conveniently, and informally, and to do it by automobile, has had to be met not only by decentralized locations, new store architecture, and the provision of adequate off-street parking facilities but also by measures to expedite purchases after the customer has entered the store, including open display, functional fixturing, brand promotion, and varying degrees of self-service or simplified selling. (McNair, 1957: 6)

In the imagined shift here from 'diversion' to 'chore', from going shopping to doing the shopping, the supermarket is there to fulfil an existing social need, in the form of the 'changed buying habits', to which the stores themselves are passive, only waiting to serve it.

But more often, planners attempted to shift the association of food shopping from work to leisure: if customers can be persuaded to linger and dally and enjoy, they will spend more than if they see themselves in the same role as the operators themselves, interested only in minimizing their expenditure of time, effort and money. Hence the promotion of self-service as a positive pleasure by contrast to the delays and dullness of over-the-counter serving, or, later, the regimented monotony into which the image of self-service had itself declined.

Discussions in the 1960s of how to increase sales focused on the potential for such a shift away from the dull routine of doing the shopping:

> Each customer service must, as one of its main objectives, make the weekly shopping tour less of a 'bore and chore' and more a pleasant interlude for the customer. (Brand, 1965: 6)

The question is always put in terms that imply an either/or decision: at any one time, what you are doing is work or pleasure, one or the other, never some combination or nebulous mixture of the two, and never something that might fall outside the understanding of either term. For supermarket designers, parallel separations distinguish attractive displays and comfortable 'services' – the little luxuries, descendants of the rest corner, that will make the visit enjoyable – from provisions that will reinforce a sense of the supermarket as a place where the customer gets a necessary job done as fast and painlessly as possible.

The list

In making a list, the customer plans and circumscribes: her shopping trip will be efficient and limited. The list may be planned out to follow the order of the passage round the supermarket aisles, preparing in advance for an expedition that will be smooth, familiar and without interference. For the supermarket, the housewife 'armed' with a finite list may well be bad business; so a counter-strategy of displays and offers attempts to throw her off her planned course, to get her to do what the unprepared customer, by implication, will always be likely to do: buy something unintended, an 'impulse purchase'. This is achieved by changing what appears along the route, so that the list no longer serves as a plan of the path round the store. Parts of the established arrangement are moved around, and special displays and special offers thrust themselves forward along the route with additional suggestions – in the ideal supermarket world where commodities take the initiative, they 'fall' into the unsuspecting trolley as it passes (in the 1950s, they were even known to 'jump').

In its functional image, self-service gives the customer control over exactly what she buys: with nothing, and no one, between her and the goods, she can carry through her plan from home to store and back again. But the expansion of supermarkets is accompanied not by an increase but by a decline in the use of shopping lists, one of the behavioural variables regularly tabulated by investigators. The customer's rationale for listlessness is that she will pass every item on sale as she goes up and down the aisle: nothing will therefore be missed. The initiative thereby moves from the customer to the goods. Without a list, every product, without distinction, offers itself to her along the route, as a possible satisfaction of possible needs.

> People depend less on written shopping lists than formerly. Today they think of the super market itself as a giant shopping list. (Alexander, 1958: 29)

Convenience

Supermarkets themselves and supermarket products offer this characteristically twentieth-century value as part of their promotion. More recently, the 'convenience store' has become a local extra, charging higher prices to compensate for the service it provides through its location near the home and its long opening hours (even more significant in Britain where, apart from the factor of distance, the supermarkets are not yet open twenty-four hours a day – except for the first experiments implemented in a few out-of-town supermarkets in early 1997). But the idea gains purchase alongside the pre-war development of the proto-supermarket: self-service and everything under one roof, meaning no need to stand in line at innumerable counters in a succession of different food stores. Convenience ties in with the supermarkets' functional emphasis: this is what you need, not a luxury or extra; this is what serves your (already established) purposes.

Convenience also implies the saving of the housewife's time, conceived of, like money, as finite and divisible into separate, countable units. The convenience food appeals to a housewife assumed to be short of time: her meal will be ready-to-hand, and ready-made. It is as if, ideally, there were no distance in space or time between store and home and consumption, and no labour to be done at any of these junctures; conversely, it is as if any time or effort devoted to seeking or preparing food were to be understood as too much, as waste or chore to be eliminated as far as possible.

Convenience removes the panic of time imagined as rush and hurry, something which is always and only getting lost and which is always speeding up; so even for Jennifer Cross (1970: 29), a critic not an exponent of supermarketing practices, it is simply 'the increased tempo of modern life' that has 'created a market for convenience products' – not the convenience products that have helped to create the sense of modern life as a rush. The natural culmination of this is the 'instant' food, which abolishes time altogether.

Lines

The shopping list marks out one customer's selection from the infinite number of possible purchases available in the supermarket. In the United States, the average number of lines stocked by any one store increased from three to eight thousand in the years between the end of the war and the late 1960s, and continued to rise at an ever-accelerating rate in the years afterwards. Only a fraction of these could make their way into the passing customer's consciousness, let alone into her shopping cart. But before this inter-product war for the carts and minds of the customer can even begin, the new line has to struggle its way into visibility by winning an initial victory in 'the battle for shelf space'.

Nothing limits the proliferation of products. To gain a place on the shelves, they must be able to represent themselves as different from all the rest (a difference which may be limited to the fact of newness). The categories that differentiate are themselves capable of infinite modification and supplementation, coming and going with the fluctuations and wars of the cultural values they also contribute to shaping: 'modern' now sounds dated, 'eco-friendly' figures, 'low' – cholesterol, fat, tar, and so on – rates ever higher, 'new' is perennial.

An American study of product innovation in the mid-1960s tried to distinguish the really new from the not really new, according to three categories of newness: 'innovative' (genuinely new), 'distinctly new' (sort of – the manufacturers had to do some preparatory research and test marketing) and 'me-too' (new only in the shape, the size, the flavour, the fact that this company is making it, and so on).

According to this particular set of standards, the following products were found to be truly 'innovative':

> dehydrated (flaked) potatoes, all-purpose instant flour, frozen juice and synthetic juice concentrates, liquid diet foods, instant nonfat dry milk, recooked rice, semi-moist dog food, powdered non-dairy creamers, three types of cold breakfast cereal (pre-sweetened, nutritional, and with dried fruit), soft margarine, freeze-dried soluble coffee, boil-in-the-bag vegetables, and frozen dinners. Since then, two

others could be added: dry cocktail mixes and space food sticks. (Cross, 1970: 30; citing Buzzell and Nourse, 1967)

Thirty years on, this distinctive shopping list reads more like a pop-art caricature of 1960s fantasy – instant, high-tech, space age. For the health- and environment-conscious 1990s, the gap is far enough to gloss the debris with retrospective nostalgia and incredulity: could it ever have been like that? At the same time, most of the products cited here can still be found on the shelves, relegated or resigned to the status of 'standard' now, their 'new' days a long-forgotten technicolour past.

But as they grow older and linger on the shelves, watching new generations take their place and fondly remembering their moment of pride on an end-of-aisle display, the products of the 1960s must console themselves with the reflection that they were lucky to be born at all, that the attainment of any form of shelf life is after all a matter of some pride. Only a few potential products at this time even made it past the 'birth control' (so they named it) prudently exercised by manufacturers unable to nurture too many new ones; and after conception, they had to get through numerous trials and screenings during the process of development and test marketing. Indeed, only one in twenty product embryos was carried through to the moment of being launched upon the world – out of the shelter of the laboratories into the struggle for existence in the 'battle for shelf space' (Cross, 1970: 29).

The flow

Supermarket designers attempt to regulate two 'flows' through the store: one of customers and the other of goods. Speed on one side, slow-downs on the other: the faster the goods flow through, the more the profits; the slower the customer flow, the more time for goods to find their way into the cart. But the customer must none the less be kept moving (no seating or other stop-offs), and the minor distractions thrown in her way should not go so far as to detract from a general impression of orderly routes, familiar arrangements and open access (wide enough aisles to avoid the clashing of carts).

Post-war architects and planners occupy themselves with speculations as to the optimum layout of the store, conceived of as a city street plan (see, for example, Ketchum, 1948). For food markets, customer traffic flow never defies gravity: the street remains on the ground, without the vertical selling suggested for other types of store by the addition of extra floors above or below. The dominant layout is the grid without cross-streets: parallel aisles surrounded on three sides by a wider perimeter, on the fourth by the row of checkouts, like turnpike toll-booths.

Surveys tirelessly follow the directions and deviations of trolley movements, attempting to arrive at a map and timetable of the typical passage through the store. So we find, say, in the 1950s that the average customer will go round the perimeter first, spending in all some 25 to 27 minutes in the store. Backwards and forwards, up and down the aisles, her every gesture, pause and acceleration is minutely noted and assessed, before being factored in to the construction of a hypothetical pattern of customer flow.

The flow of merchandise is equally hard to tabulate, the impression of regularities being obtainable only from the bare statistics of inventory and checkout. For the individual product, like the individual customer, life is rather more confused than the impression given by the averages. Rapidly and untimely ripped from the security of the cardboard box where it nestles with its peers, the product is stashed inhumanely out on the open shelves, hidden at first behind some of the others in a darkness not much different from that of the carton. Unless intruded upon by groping hands searching out a later sell-by date, it remains in this nebulous half-life until the moment arrives when it reaches the front, suddenly exposed to all the glares and stares of lights and eyes which ultimately – in seconds, hours or humiliating months – lead to its rescue by gentle fingers carefully transferring it to an attendant cart.

In the meantime, there is nothing to do but wait, flaunting or sitting quietly according to your well-researched nature, and hoping at least to avoid the embarrassment of falling into the wrong hands, the ones that pick you up and look you over, only to cast you brutally back on the shelf. Once in the trolley, there is the encounter with all sorts of unfamiliar new neighbours. Before this, the only entities the product knew apart from its own kind were those who could be seen across the aisle, regarded with envy or attraction according to mood and the relative rates of disappearance between its sort and theirs. But now, in the cart, to touch as well as to see, is a whole new world of textures, shapes and sizes never before imagined. All at once, the thing comes to a halt, and for a while there is no movement at all, though by peering through the bars you can pick up the outlines of other carts similarly stalled, and even recognize one or two of your former companions of box and shelf. Then suddenly hands are lifting you out and up and the ground is moving and something flashes on and over you in a moment of blackout. Then a dark interior space, and once more you are moving on wheels again, this time at a faster, more even pace than before. Eventually, after more upheavals, there is a snap, utter darkness, then a roar beneath and a sense of being moved, perhaps to a final destination.

The supermarket of the future

In 1962, the British trade journal *The Grocer* published a centenary number which included a fanciful feature on 'The Grocery Shop of the Future?' The accompanying illustration, a black-and-white drawing, shows mother, daughter and dog taking off to the supermarket in their circular helicopter from a ranch-style suburban dwelling outside which father and son stand waving goodbye in the distance. In the article, Howard Fox (1962: 180) runs through possible prospects for stores that in the 1970s will move from rectangular to circular designs, perhaps with 'a series of little personal shops' round the perimeter. The customer stands on moving aisles, getting off whenever she wishes. In the dim distance that can be glimpsed beyond the 1970s, the shoppers have come to a complete standstill as the goods circulate to offer themselves for her inspection: 'Eventually, the entire perimeter of a store may be arranged in lounges, with the shopping area a huge revolving island. The housewife would sit, talk with her friends and pick items as they pass by' (Fox, 1962: 181).

This passage is quoted from an American source on which the whole article is based; characteristically, the future of supermarket shopping is imagined in an American mode. And in numerous respects, the piece returns us to earlier histories, of supermarkets themselves, of their antecedents, and of the first projections of their futures. With those little shops round the edge, the old High Street or Main Street is back, now inside the single store. Shopping, we learn, is to be 'a pleasure rather than a chore' (Fox, 1962: 180). The chatty lounges might almost include the odd canary.

From the perspective of 1990s Britain, these 1960s fantasies, in their own time echoing futures past, become strange in another way, comfortably and uncomfortably familiar in their partial anticipation of our own present. There is the out-of-town site reached by private transport; the deli and fresh fish and bakery counters round the edge to signify service alongside self-service, the best of all worlds under one roof; the place to sit and talk. Supermarkets may not have changed their classical four-sided structure, to transform themselves into circles with moving aisles, but, in certain ways, they have almost gone further than Fox's projections. It is as though they were turning the wheels of retailing revolutions full circle, coming to be all shops to all people, to recapitulate all the phases of retailing history under their single roof.

Evoking the fonder memories of the high street and the market they have supplanted, supermarkets parade their counters with personal service, the bakery, the fish shop, the butcher and even the post office. In the wake of their general upmarketing, as they come to sell more and more expensive, recherché lines, they loudly proclaim their fidelity to their cheap origins, still piling it high and selling it low with 'basic' ranges of minimally priced own-brand goods. At the same time, like the grand department stores, they now sell fashion as well as cheapness. Where the department stores collected the exotic products of the colonies, supermarkets sell 'ethnic' cuisine as fashion. And where they were once associated solely or primarily with the selling of food, supermarkets as superstores have extended their range of non-food lines so far that they have come to resemble the department stores in contents as well as in forms. The introduction of cafés, inviting the slower time of an outing, puts an end to the identification of food shopping as a definite task to be completed as quickly as possible. Now you can be doing the shopping and going shopping, getting the basics and enjoying yourself, all in one place and one time.

Or indeed, it might seem, at all times and everywhere. For supermarkets in Britain have risen in the 1990s to a position of unprecedented prominence in that blur between media representations and actual behaviour which makes up the fabric of our daily lives. They seem to be occupying every possible space and time, from daytime and prime-time TV advertising to Sunday morning family shopping in the wake of the relaxation of the laws on opening hours in 1994. In their metamorphosis into out-of-town super-stores, they have become the focus for a new environmental argument about the decline of urban centres and the growth of a car-dependent culture. The 1960s image of the supermarket shopper as a female zombie has given way to a much less identifiable figure, anyman, anywoman and especially anybaby – for we all have our special trolleys now, thoughtfully provided to meet our aisle-cruising needs from Pampers to eternity.

The future of supermarkets in the twenty-first century is in one sense anybody's guess, anybody's choice. Yet it sometimes appears that the future itself is envisaged in the image of a great supermarket in which citizen-consumers move about making their more or less informed, more or less random individual choices. Whether that image draws on a hope or a fear depends on the persuasions of the speaker; but it is perhaps not an irrelevant fact that in Britain stores are almost invariably designed so that customers start with the fresh produce on the left and come out, after the drinks, on the right.

Acknowledgement

The research for this piece was supported by a fellowship in 1993 at the Rutgers Center for Historical Analysis, during the two-year project on 'Consumer Cultures in Historical Perspective'. I would like to thank the organizer, Victoria de Grazia, and others at Rutgers for their many contributions.

References

Alexander, Milton (1958) *Display Ideas for Super Markets*. The Progressive Grocer. New York: Butterick Publishing Co.

Brand, Edward A. (1965) *Modern Supermarket Operation*. New York: Fairchild Publications Inc.

Buzzell, Robert D. and Nourse, Robert E.M. (1967) *Product Innovation in Food Processing*. Boston: Harvard Business School.

Cox, Reavis (1957) [n.t.], in Albert B. Smith (ed.), *Competitive Distribution in a Free High-Level Economy and its Implications for the University*. Pittsburgh: University of Pittsburgh Press.

Cross, Jennifer (1970) *The Supermarket Trap: The Consumer and the Food Industry*. Bloomington: Indiana University Press.

Dipman, Carl W. (1931) *The Modern Grocery Store*. The Progressive Grocer. New York: Butterick Publishing Co.

Dipman, Carl W. (ed.) (1935) *Modern Food Stores*. The Progressive Grocer. New York: Butterick Publishing Co.

Dipman, Carl W. and O'Brien, John E. (1940) *Self-Service and Semi-Self-Service Food Stores*. The Progressive Grocer. New York: Butterick Publishing Co.

Fox, Howard (1962) 'The Grocery Shop of the Future?', *The Grocer*, Centenary Number.

Frederick, Christine (1920) *Household Engineering: Scientific Management in the Home.* Chicago: American School of Home Economics.

Ketchum, Morris Jr. (1948) *Shops and Stores.* Progressive Architecture Library. New York: Reinhold Publishing Corporation.

Leinwand, Gerald (ed.) (1970) *The Consumer.* New York: Simon and Schuster, Inc.

McNair, Malcolm P. (1957) 'Significant Trends and Developments in the Postwar Period', in Albert B. Smith (ed.), *Competitive Distribution in a Free High-Level Economy and its Implications for the University.* Pittsburgh: University of Pittsburgh Press.

Packard, Vance (1960 [1957]) *The Hidden Persuaders.* Harmondsworth: Penguin.

Strasser, Susan (1982) *Never Done: A History of American Housework.* New York: Pantheon.

Zimmerman, M.M. (1937) *Super Market: Spectacular Exponent of Mass Distribution.* New York: Super Market Publishing Company.

Zola, Émile (1992 [1883]) *The Ladies' Paradise.* Berkeley and Los Angeles: University of California Press.

5

THE MAKING OF A SWEDISH DEPARTMENT STORE CULTURE

Cecilia Fredriksson

Prelude: a lunch break at EPA

Kerstin looked at the green neon sign in the distance. She quickened her step so that she would have time to pop into EPA before her lunch break came to an end. She might meet Eva or Siv in there, so that they could have a quick cup of coffee in the bar. In the foyer she was immediately overwhelmed by the characteristic department store smell: soap, after-shave, and sweet lily-of-the-valley perfume. A little further into the store she noticed the smell of newly manufactured plastic, recently unpacked leather goods, cold steel, and impregnated nylon shirts. Hovering over it all was a vague hint of freshly made coffee and the green marzipan buns awaiting her. The smell of EPA was green and enticing, roughly like a green plastic hair-roller.

Kerstin stopped at the make-up counter and let her gaze sweep over the newly wiped glass top. It felt almost as if her gaze bounced back from the hard, shiny surface, while at the same time the articles under it drew her towards them in an almost irresistible way. Yet not everything was under glass. Just beside the make-up counter was the counter selling jewellery and trinkets. If you let your fingers play among the tangled necklaces it made a very distinctive jingling sound – not the brittle sound of glass but a duller rustle. You could pick up a necklace and hold it in your outstretched hand, or let several of them hang there in a row, clattering against each other. Kerstin looked at them, her eyes full of wonder, but quickly hung them back in their place. She wasn't going to buy anything. She couldn't afford anything anyway.

The store had become crowded. People seemed to be pouring in from all sides, and she felt warm in her coat and scarf. She loosened her scarf and let it slide down into one of her coat pockets, and once again she let a green necklace dangle against the palm of her hand. As it hit her hand, she could feel her heart beating faster and faster, keeping time with the necklace, and she suddenly became aware of herself in a new, rather frightening way. She sensed that someone was watching her. Her back felt as if it was burning, as if someone was looking right through her. It was as if someone at the counter behind her could see that beating heart. She did not dare turn round. The necklace had stopped dangling. For a moment Kerstin stood stock-still, holding her breath, and then she fished the scarf out of her pocket. Without moving more than her arms and hands, she then lowered her left hand with the necklace in it. Under the cover of her own body and her coat, she let the scarf gently enclose the necklace, and then she carefully put the scarf back in her right-hand pocket.[1]

In the classroom of consumption

This chapter is about learning the art of mass consumption. As an arena[2] for this, I have chosen EPA, a chain of department stores that existed in Sweden between 1930 and 1977. EPA was a very modern cheap store, opening a whole new world of goods to Swedes who had previously had nowhere to go except small shops and specialist stores. EPA was also the first department store that allowed children and young people to enter the stage of the modern commodity market. EPA became a new public space and a meeting place for several generations of young people in Sweden. At EPA they could learn how to consume in a new way, and also try out forbidden things; shoplifting was one such activity. Above all, however, EPA communicated modernity and provided a place to which one could channel one's longing. What did people long for? What dreams could EPA arouse, and what space in people's lives was suddenly filled with planned and unplanned visits to EPA? 'It was fun and exciting to go there and fantasize about the things you saw, and what you would do if you could have them,' says a woman who often visited EPA during her childhood in the 1930s and 1940s. Consumption is also related to daydreams (Campbell, 1987) which are materialized in objects in a pleasurable way, and EPA appears to have been able to satisfy this need.

In contrast to primitive bargaining, the department store stands as a monument to 'civilized consumption' (Williams, 1982: 67). In the new department store it was impossible to haggle about prices; every article was marked with a fixed price, and no one would have thought of arguing about it. Yet although the department store had a civilizing function, it also brought a new kind of licentiousness. The nineteenth-century stage-managers of the department stores knew how to associate consumption with seductive interior design, sensuality, technical novelties and a promise that you were not forced to buy anything. It was supposed to be a pleasure to go shopping. Not only did the customers not need to haggle and get involved in the commercial side of shopping, they were under no obligation to buy anything at all. A completely new way of idly strolling around among the new items on the commodity market was established. The department store could also offer a slightly more relaxed atmosphere than the bustle and immensity of the growing city, making it possible to escape from it for a while (see Falk, Chapter 8, this volume).

The department store today can still be seen as a commercial oasis in a city, a place where one can wind down during one's lunch break, browse through the records or pantyhose, wander round and bump into acquaintances. Some people may find the department store more relaxing than an aimless walk along the streets, where one is forced to meet the eyes of passers-by. The department store always offers something to look at; there is always something within reach to touch, to contemplate buying, and perhaps to put back in its place. No one in a department store asks what your business is, no troublesome conversations need be started; the doors open and close automatically, and no greetings are necessary. The department store as recreation, relaxation and as a place for outings is a consumption arena with its roots in the new view that arose in the nineteenth and early twentieth centuries of human existence as one of yearning and change. The continuity can reveal fascinating patterns for combining consumption with seduction. It is important to remember, however, that EPA was a completely different type of department store from the consumption palace of the nineteenth century: EPA was functional, modern, and above all it was a department store for everyone.

The following account is based on a large number of recent interviews with former EPA staff and customers. The account employs government inquiries, daily newspapers, and the company's staff newsletter, *EPA-nytt*, which appeared four times a year during the period 1930–77 covered by this study.

The history of a department store

> I have read in all sorts of newspapers about a big department store in a nearby town, a department store which is supposed to sell everything so tremendously cheap that it is likely to strike the whole world with amazement. I was simply forced to go there myself and see what it looked like.

This appeared on 17 December 1931 in the Swedish daily newspaper *Arbetet*. The writer, who called himself 'The Mysterious X', went on to describe his first visit to the store. He could not deny that everything was cheap. He estimated that about 9,000 of the articles were cheaper than in other stores, but this must have been an exaggeration since the total range of items available was less than half that number.

This new form of consumption was established in Sweden in the early 1930s, opening its doors to a delighted and overwhelmed public. The company was called Enhetsprisaktiebolaget EPA (The Standard-Price Corporation). Standardization and mass production were the secrets behind this new type of early mass consumption, and the target group were people 'who value being able to obtain a good article at a low price and thereby have a chance to acquire many more of the things they desire'.[3] The goods were not intended for an exclusive clientele; the product range concentrated on everyday articles, and the original idea was the standard-price system with just a few price classes, the highest class being just 1 krona.

The first EPA store was opened in a small town in central Sweden in 1930. At the end of the 1930s there were eighteen EPA stores in sixteen Swedish towns. By 1945 the number had risen to twenty-five. Development proceeded rapidly in the 1950s and 1960s, and in the mid-1960s there were almost a hundred EPA stores throughout the country. The idea of standard prices was abandoned in the 1940s, and the name was changed, omitting the word Enhetsprisaktiebolaget to leave only the abbreviation EPA. After the

Figure 5.1   *Opening day in Kristianstad at the end of the 1930s*

golden age of the 1960s, EPA began to decline, and the stores closed down for good in 1977.

The dark years

EPA had great difficulties when taking its first shaky steps into the commercial scene in the 1930s. It met solid resistance from the established trade, which mounted concerted campaigns to block deliveries to EPA. In political terms, too, EPA was a hot potato, and the standard-price system was the subject of an inquiry by the Ministry of Commerce in 1935. Some people wanted to legislate against EPA and similar standard-price companies because it was feared that their stores would drive other retail shops out of business through their low prices for everyday commodities.

Yet there were other elements which contributed to the general threat. It was thought that the standard-price idea was based on 'a kind of psychosis': 'people are influenced by suggestion into buying from these companies, not primarily because they need a particular item on a particular occasion, but because it is cheap'.[4] There was heated discussion of the risk that tastes would deteriorate, even 'be corrupted', and people were afraid of 'a generally lax attitude to what is solid and genuine'.[5] It is highly informative to follow the argumentation used on this issue. Few things have such a high moral charge as consumption, and the charge of course comes from arguments about controversial or threatened contemporary matters. The opponents of EPA, for instance, spoke about the importance of preserving the Swedish cultural heritage, both spiritual and material.

EPA was launched as a decidedly modern phenomenon; the very idea of department stores was not generally established in Sweden, and the system of large groups of items with a standard price was also new. The idea came from America – everyone agreed about that – but the foreign influences were interpreted in slightly different ways. In the Ministry of Commerce inquiry of 1935 it was observed that the *attitude* of the buying public was what made such an early development of this form of distribution possible in America. This claim was based on the generally accepted assumption that the American consumer has 'a pronounced inclination for uniformity and standardization as regards clothes, food, and living habits as a whole' (SOU, 1935: 14). F.W. Woolworth was regarded as the founder of this form of business; in 1879 he had opened the first store where all the goods cost 5 cents, in Utica, New York. The agitators against the EPA system expressed their fears that Americanization[6] would have a detrimental effect on genuine Swedish culture, destroying the high standard of commodities that Sweden had achieved, unless Swedes stood guard to protect the qualities of their cultural heritage. The following is a description of a visit to Stockholm in 1931 by the heir to the Woolworth Company:

> Stockholm had a remarkable visit at the start of June. It was Mr Norman B. Woolworth who honoured the capital with his presence. Mr Woolworth is the world's biggest standard-price director, and he came in his own Ocean yacht, which cast anchor at Strömmen.
>
> Mr Woolworth was interviewed about the standard-price idea. The great man was frank in his statements – so much must be said in all fairness about him.
>
> 'The standard-price idea,' he said to begin with, 'is a greater invention than most other modern systems.'
>
> The surprise revealed by the interviewer over this at once unexpected and categorical statement was naturally observed by Mr Woolworth, and the American gentleman continued:
>
> 'Yes, I notice that you are amazed that I say so myself, but the fact remains. It is psychosis that the modern businessman must deal in. More so than in goods at higher or lower prices. And that's what I've gone in for.'[7]

Selling a large number of goods (which have no mutual relation to each other) at a standard price offended a deep-seated notion about the special value of an individual article and the unique qualities that the price tag guaranteed. Mass sales and quality became two diametrically opposed concepts. Right from the start, suspicions were cast on EPA for compromising on quality. Cans of conserved food were opened and their content was measured, counted and weighed for comparison with similar cans sold in other shops. The Swedish Mint checked the silver content in the cutlery sold at EPA, and someone on the government committee of inquiry had counted the number of pages in the notebooks that could be bought at the store.

After the opening of a store in a central Swedish town in 1932, some of the local retailers claimed that EPA had displayed a kind of soap in its window, priced at only 25 öre a bar, but this had melted after a short time on display (SOU, 1935: 96). EPA explained in its defence that 'this episode was quite accidental, being due to the inappropriate display of a batch of soap in excessively bright sunlight'. The incident nevertheless led to an inquiry into EPA's soap sales and a comparative analysis by the National Testing and Research Institute of different types of soap bought at EPA and other shops. The study showed that EPA's soaps were not of inferior quality; the difference seemed to consist rather in 'the degree and nature of the perfuming', which was more a question of individual taste than of quality. It was also observed that EPA's soap, at 25 öre a bar, was much cheaper than

Figure 5.2   *The new world of goods*

soap in other shops. In addition, the study noted that 'the consequence of a higher water content is that the soap is used up faster'.

Similar analyses were performed of many goods sold at EPA: did the candles burn for a shorter time than other candles? Was the toilet paper worse? Were the soles of the clogs machine-made, and was the leather on the uppers of the slippers made from the thinner hide of the animals' bellies instead of the sturdier hide from the back? The Ministry of Commerce examined everything from gym shoes to canned herrings, but could not find that the goods sold at the standard-price stores were inferior to those sold elsewhere.

EPA – between tradition and modernity

People naturally wondered how EPA could sell the goods so cheap. In the first issue of EPA's staff magazine in January 1932, the company tried to answer this by explaining the modern idea behind EPA:

> You might as well ask what has made the American standard-price stores, organized in the 'chain-store' system, despite their modest start over fifty years ago, develop into gigantic companies, some of which have thousands of branches and turn over several hundred million dollars every year. Why has this form of shop been so successful in America, and from there spread further to England, France, Germany, the Netherlands, Switzerland, Sweden, and other countries? The answer to these questions is simply: They are working in the way of modern business, while the rest of the retail trade is still practising antiquated methods.[8]

The secret of EPA's success was thus rooted in the inevitable progress of modernity. If one wanted to be part of the spirit of the new age, then EPA was a splendid arena for this. The battle between old and new, traditional and modern, was obvious in the debate about EPA and its right to exist. But it was a modernity that in many ways lagged behind what was considered progressive and innovative. EPA never really managed to become accepted by anyone outside the working class and the lower middle class. EPA was thus in an interesting intermediate position between traditional and modern, giving the working class an opportunity to advance. Yet the success achieved in this way was still a second-class success. A worker who became an engineer by correspondence course or evening classes was known as an 'EPA engineer'; the mass-produced housing estates of the 1950s and 1960s were called 'EPA Valley'; an excessively glamorous girl in nylon stockings and blue eye-shadow was colloquially known as an 'EPA Doris' (and if she talked too much as well, it could be said that 'her mouth opened and shut like an EPA door in the Christmas rush'). It was not easy to attain modernity in this way, and EPA was an excellent means of distinction in welfare-state Sweden. Although EPA was closed down almost twenty years ago, it still lives on in the Swedish language as a synonym of poor quality.

Despite all the attempts to prohibit the standard-price system, EPA was a great success. During a period of almost fifty years, from 1930 to 1977, EPA was an ambiguous concept in the consciousness of every Swede. Each Swedish town had its own EPA, and for rural children on class outings or adults on excursions to the big towns, a visit to EPA was a natural part of the programme. EPA functioned as a meeting place, an innovator, a classroom, and for the everyday consumer the EPA store became an inescapable source of dreams of a more modern life. EPA also gave most Swedes a chance to acquire things that were previously available only to the few. At times, however, it was important to hide the EPA plastic bag inside one's own shopping bag to avoid being identified as an EPA customer.

The impact of EPA is a rewarding reflection of the Swedish consumer society during an important and eventful period. In my research into EPA I have also encountered another interesting phenomenon: the disappearance of EPA has given rise to nostalgia for the days of the welfare state. Suddenly everyone has personal recollections of EPA. Time has turned EPA into a collective, harmless cultural treasure that is considered well worth preserving.

'Did you pinch it from EPA, or what?'

The new everyday commodity market

During the depression in the 1930s, EPA was often called 'the warm shelter for the unemployed'. The EPA bars with their red and silver décor offered cheap coffee, and the department store was a warm and open place for everybody. EPA was not the first department store in Sweden,[9] but it was the first chain of stores that everyone was able to visit – it was affordable and socially permissible to shop there. Strolling freely around in the new landscape of the open-plan store was an experience that many people had never tried before. No one hovered around to ask officiously 'Can I help you?' or 'Were you looking for anything in particular?' The new self-service system avoided this form of control, giving a new sense of space and freedom inside the store. It was easy to disappear in the crowd, and it was easy to slip something into your bag, or your pocket.

Many informants say that shoplifting was a great problem at EPA right from the start, while some say that it was a problem that grew, and others say that it was never worse than in the 1970s. It is hard to determine the extent of shoplifting since no statistics are available before the middle of the 1960s. The statistics are one-sided anyway, in that they show only the cases that were actually reported; EPA personnel often chose not to report young children and old people. It is remarkable, however, that the total wastage seems to have been stable at around 1–3 per cent during the period (Ekberg, 1990). This percentage can be roughly divided into three equal parts: 1 per cent shoplifting, 1 per cent staff theft, 1 per cent stolen during delivery. It is not my aim, however, to investigate the extent of shoplifting a ʒPA. What I am interested in is the role played by theft and shoplifting in the newly created department store culture, and the way EPA treated, narrated and described this dark side of its history. When did shoplifting come into focus as a phenomenon, and who were the shoplifters?

Time was an important factor in the new department stores. There were no limits to how long you could spend on the premises. The interior was vast and diverse enough to swallow all the visitors. Glass, stainless steel and mirrors attracted, reflected, and multiplied the range of goods. The mirrors could be deceptive: people sometimes waved to themselves in them. EPA affected the senses just as described in Zola's *The Ladies' Paradise* (1992), but the things at EPA were perhaps closer to reality for the people who visited the early EPA stores. All the small things that were needed for everyday life were suddenly assembled under one roof: wallets, combs, brushes, underwear, socks, shoe-polish, gloves, ties, pocket mirrors, station-ery, tools, onion sets, canned fruit, sweets, toys, records, cosmetics, and much more besides. Before the 1960s there was no separate food depart-ment; the store sold only canned goods and sweets. Clothes were not sold on any great scale until the last few decades. EPA specialized instead in everyday articles that were affordable and necessary. Lamps, crockery, cutlery, household utensils and ornaments were also important items. The goods at EPA were to be taken home from the public light of the store to the privacy of the home; for this reason they were at first modestly displayed. The temptation consisted of the *quantity* of cheap goods. The super-abundance was made manageable by the division of the range into different groups of articles and by the kaleidoscopic structure of the store. Glass counters and cases kept the goods safe from the touch of inquisitive hands. The glass marked the difference between seeing and touching.

Controlling the senses

The window display was an excellent civilizing instrument. The primacy of sight has often been discussed (Synnott, 1993), and it is probably true that the distinction of sight from the other senses was most important for the distanced orientation of the urban body. Those who did not let their interest in the goods stop at visual appreciation but went one step further and *took* them were classified under the term 'kleptomania', one of the urban sicknesses that afflicted people who were not in full control of their senses. The first diagnosis of this complaint is variously dated, but the condition was described in 1840 by a French doctor named C.C.H. Marc as 'a distinctly irresistible urge to steal' (Miller, 1981: 198). *Monomania* was a covering term used at this time for various fixations and obsessive compulsions which made people unable to control their impulses. The irresistible urge to steal was explained on the basis of monomania, but for safety's sake it was also given a separate designation of its own. People afflicted by monomania, according to Marc, should be classified as being mentally ill, which meant that they could not be punished. Interest gradually grew in kleptomania as an illness, and the number of cases rose. The first department stores were established, and suddenly the phenomenon was associated with a particular place: 'department store theft'. One of the earliest films, Edwin S. Porter's *The Kleptomaniac* (1905), describes how the visual stimulus of big-city department stores was too much for some people. The people in question were women, and it was in department stores that middle-class women suddenly became common thieves. Kleptomania was also linked to pathological sexual problems, and to menstruation, pregnancy and mental disturbances during the menopause. Kleptomania became a woman's illness which was thus able to explain the irrational behaviour shown by the kleptomaniac.

The female kleptomaniac has always been a subject of great interest, and the fascinating history of middle-class Victorian female shoplifters in the United States has been written by Elaine S. Abelson (1989). Her study shows how shoplifting middle-class women were an illogical and unacceptable threat to prevailing moral values. By explaining this behaviour in medical terms one removed the implication of 'moral chaos', as well as providing the boundaries of class and gender. 'The individual became the focus; the crime was lost. Neither the excesses of the institutions nor consumer capitalism were indicted. The fault lay within the women themselves' (Abelson, 1989: 12).

Towards the end of the century, however, there came a new view which also saw kleptomania as a social phenomenon, with an in-built criticism of the department stores for enticing people to steal. The milieu of the store exposed its customers to temptation, creating a new acquisitiveness and the desire to own things. It is important to remember that the idea of the female kleptomaniac was nevertheless to remain one of the basic approaches to the handling of shoplifting in department stores, although in the EPA context she functioned as a symbol of the unusual shoplifter. Shoplifting became a part of everyday life at EPA, which meant that it could not be regarded as an illness.

Shoplifters and shop-rats

Were women unable to cope with the demands of modernity? Were the sensory impressions of all these tempting and promising articles too much for them? All the things that smelt so new, that lay within touching distance, appeared to exert far too strong an attraction on certain sensitive individuals. Suddenly the intensity of the new way of urban life divided people into those who could control all this and those who yielded to the temptation of their senses. A woman who grew up in the countryside remembers how her mother visited EPA along with a friend. The trip to town was called an 'outing', but her real purpose was to buy a light for the newly renovated sitting room:

> I remember the lamp very well, a round disc of rough glass with three gazelles ground into it. Many people admired it at the time. But Mother was far from happy when she got home with the lamp. When she had been looking at lamps, her friend had gone round on her own, looking at other things. When they were ready to leave, a guard came and picked up her friend! Took her to the office. Mother was horrified. This was where she learned the word shoplifting. Neither the word nor the deed had previously been part of Mother's consciousness. It must

have been a gloomy journey home. I don't remember what the woman had stolen, I just remember that she had put it into her handbag. And that Mother was terribly shaken when she got home that evening.[10]

At EPA, even the most trustworthy person could be transformed into a common thief, a fact that no one – perhaps not even the woman herself – had known before. EPA brought out dangerous and unpredictable characteristics, revealing which people were not equipped with the right virtues for coping with worldly temptations. The mother in the tale became aware not only of how untrustworthy her friend was, but also that shoplifting existed as a word and a deed. Reality made itself felt at EPA.

Let us now look more closely at another type of female shoplifter at EPA, a type that caused the company much more serious problems than ordinary shoplifters. In the early 1940s one could read in *EPA-nytt* how a shop assistant could best catch 'shop-rats' (*butiksråttor*).[11] The shop-rat in question was not an ordinary shoplifter but a person who stole from other customers. She was known as the '1,300 kronor thief', after an incident in 1942 when a female customer lost her handbag containing that amount.[12] Thefts from other customers were regarded as a very unpleasant side-effect of the modern department store idea. For EPA it was important to be found not guilty in these incidents, and not to be blamed for having such crowded stores that they encouraged thefts of this kind. The customers were supposed to feel safe in the store.

One could learn how to recognize a shop-rat by her searching gaze. Unlike the other women, she was not looking at the articles on sale, but at the other customers – at their bags in particular. Shop-rats showed little interest in the counters: 'they tend to stand behind a lady with an easily opened handbag hanging on her arm'. One could see how the shop-rat carefully fingered the catch and then quickly stuck in her hand and fished up a wallet or a purse. The writer of the article also noted with amazement how careless most women were with their handbags. Overwhelmed by the desire to buy, they did not care where they put their bags down, eager as they were to examine the articles on sale. A woman could even leave her handbag at one counter to rush rapturously to another counter when something caught her eye. Here the shop assistants had to be particularly observant and try to rescue the bag before a shop-rat laid her hands on it.

These female bag-thieves thus took advantage of EPA and its public shopping arena. EPA offered a public crowd where physical intimacy combined with psychological anonymity aroused some of the visitors' desires and cravings. These female thieves were regarded as amateur criminals who could not keep their hands to themselves, either out of habit or because of kleptomania. They were not real pickpockets of international class ('who are impossible to stop'), but rather odd personalities who could not resist a crowd of women and a tempting handbag.

The distinction between an ordinary shoplifter and a shop-rat was based partly on gender, and partly on age. The ordinary shoplifter was a young boy, a little rascal, whose behaviour in the store easily revealed what he was

Figure 5.3   *A shop-rat in action*

up to. If the young shoplifter could be saved, the female shop-rat was a hopeless case by comparison; strolling idly around, she showed no interest in the articles on offer, instead taking advantage of enthusiastic and absent-minded women who could not look after their own handbags. Seduced by this new cornucopia of goods, the women were robbed – by other women. The female shop-rats created a sense of insecurity by their behaviour; they became anomalies in a female pattern of modern consumption, and were therefore regarded as mentally unstable individuals or downright kleptomaniacs.

Visiting EPA as a child

I remember especially some of the toys made of that strange, newfangled material – plastic. There were aeroplanes made of speckly brown plastic, cast in one piece, with openings for the cockpit windows; they were models of American bombers (incidentally, one such bomber had recently made an emergency landing at the civil airfield in Halmstad and created a great stir among children and adults alike). There were also small black models of the first Volvo PV 444s which were new then, with axles of steel wire and with white wheels; these toy cars ran very smoothly, and of course they were highly desirable presents in the eyes of a seven-year-old.[13]

This is a man's recollection of how he managed to get into EPA on his own one day in the late 1940s. On one of the counters there were Santa Claus masks with white beards and red caps. That same day, he had found two kronor in a drawer at home and claimed them for himself. He used these two coins to buy a Santa Claus mask, which he proudly showed off to his little brothers when he got home. When his parents learnt what had happened, the boy was given 'a thorough thrashing', and banned from further visits to EPA.

Many people today remember how common it was for children to steal money at home so as to buy a longed-for article. Letting children move freely around a department store was something new at this time. Naturally, this gave children wishes and cravings for things that they had never seen before. Many informants become lyrical when they talk about the new world of things that suddenly lay open waiting for them, and they thought that 'the store in the city was like the whole market-place back home'.[14] Another woman remembers the scents of EPA: 'I can still recall what the smell was like when you came in through the big glass doors. A mixture of plastic and eau-de-Cologne.'[15] Sensory memories like this are common in recollections

Figure 5.4   *'The small customer becomes a big customer . . .'*

of EPA. Sensory memory is a form of storage, and the senses defer the material world by changing substance into memory (Seremetakis, 1993: 4).

> I remember that one of my first purchases was a plastic make-up bag, purple and blue. Through time it got hard and ugly. It contained a lipstick of the 'Mitzi' brand and a light-coloured cream called 'Tokalon', nail varnish, 'Perplex' mascara, a bottle of perfume smelling of lily of the valley. . . .[16]

For young girls the cosmetics department was a place of longing. The stationery department was another enticing place for both sexes. All this writing paper (some of it scented), all the greeting cards, envelopes, pictures of film stars, notebooks, ball-point pens, rubbers, and so on, offered a new range of stationery that school could never match. It was strictly forbidden to use ball-point pens in school, and scented paper was not something girls kept in their school desks.

EPA had other technical novelties to entice young people. One very popular example was the escalator. The first escalator is said to have been installed in 1934 in the newly opened EPA store in Malmö. The escalator is described by most informants as the thing they associate most with EPA at this time. Children often went into EPA just to try it out, and they could ride up and down again and again. Another technical phenomenon was the automatic service in the EPA bar: 'you could push a button on a menu board, and when you got to the top of the queue the plate was waiting for you'.[17] EPA was also first to introduce soft ice-cream to Sweden. Virtually every EPA store had a small kiosk inside the store serving soft ice-cream; a visit to EPA was often synonymous with getting a cone with two flavours of soft ice-cream.

Visiting EPA was not just a way to experience goods but also a chance to have many other experiences at the same time. This was a revolutionary way to consume, with a special effect on children and young people in particular. Since these groups had previously been barred or carefully supervised in small shops, EPA opened the doors to a whole new market of experiences.

'Stealing at EPA, now that's fun!'

> There's no fun at home, my mum and dad only quarrel and scold. We can't be in the hobby-room, because there's an old buff playing the gramophone. You get thrown out if you try to have some fun. GO DOWN TOWN, STEALING AT EPA, NOW THAT'S FUN![18]

This was a letter to the editor of a Swedish evening paper in 1958, and it was published in the EPA staff magazine the same year as a reminder to the sales staff to keep their eyes open.

'You can tell just by looking what they [young shoplifters] have in mind. They can hardly stand still, they get anxious and nervous in front of the counter.'[19] By keeping them under observation for a while and letting them do what they had planned, it was possible to catch them red-handed. It was important to give these first-time offenders 'a proper frightening the first

Figure 5.5 *Modern orality – EPA as a meeting place*

time'.[20] If shoplifting became a habit and they were successful several times, then there was no hope left for these young delinquents. The shop staff had an important function to fulfil here: by being observant and fair, they could lead young people in the right direction. The risk that someone would 'begin with a hairpin and end with a silver bowl', as an old Swedish proverb says, thus seems to correspond well to EPA's view of this problem.

In many ways EPA nevertheless seemed to regard the young shoplifters with some indulgence. They knew that the thefts were not so much criminal behaviour as relatively harmless childish pranks. It was important to make it clear that this could not be tolerated, but the company often chose to overlook it. One man tells how, at the age of 12, he committed his first and only theft during a lunch break at EPA.[21] He left the school along with a friend to go down town 'for a stroll round EPA'. The theft had not been premeditated; 'it just happened' that the two boys each slipped a key-ring into their trouser pockets. They were discovered almost at once, and a man in a white coat gruffly demanded to see what they had in their pockets. When the terrified boys assured him that they had not taken anything, the man contented himself with that (perhaps the key-rings did not cost very much, and he was certain that he had frightened them sufficiently), so the boys were able to leave the store with the stolen key-rings – but also with a firm resolve never to do the like again.

More than any other crime, shoplifting can be compared to a kind of competition, a sporting event which can be repeated over and over again (Katz, 1988: 67). The department store venue is always the same, the challenges are familiar, and the location of the dangers is known. The contestants themselves decide if and when they want to try a more difficult event than any in which they have yet competed. The shoplifters appear to be competing against themselves more than against other shoplifters. One of the security managers at EPA speaks with resignation about the fictitious society humorously referred to as 'The National Association of Shop-lifters'.[22] The shoplifters were always one step ahead, he says. Just as one way of stealing had been discovered, the gangs of shoplifters thought of another one. They swapped hints about good ways to steal, competing against the department store, and at the same time setting themselves the challenge of carrying off the exploit.

Being able to steal something at EPA was synonymous with success in a difficult task, with discovering that something as seemingly tricky as this was in fact quite easy, if only one dared. As Jack Katz writes, 'The excitement of the challenge in the deviant project – an excitement that the acquisition would not have were it not deviant – is experienced as an external provocation that works independently on the self' (1988: 56). Young shoplifters could become aware of themselves in a new and un-accustomed way through the mental stress involved in escaping discovery. By succeeding in a theft they could feel that they had luck on their side and were not mediocrities after all. By managing to conceal a secret, not revealing their true selves, they could gain in self-esteem. For most young shoplifters it was a one-off experience, a confirmation that did not need to be repeated over and over again. For some people, the shoplifting was more or less involuntary, sometimes even done out of sheer necessity. One woman remembers how, in the mid-1960s, her period had started while she was at school and she was too shy to go to the school nurse for a tampon:

> I went to EPA, but I didn't dare ask if I could take the tampons and pay later, which I could do in our little shop, but not in the big department store. So I went to the packets of OB [tampons] and took just *one* OB out of a packet. Then I put that packet at the back of the shelf and hoped intensely that no one had seen me.

I stuck the OB in my pocket and went back to school quickly and headed straight for a toilet.

The next day I had money with me, so we went to EPA during the lunch break, my friend and I, and I picked out my packet which was still at the back of the shelf. Then we went to the cash desk and I paid, and after that I was able to breathe out.[23]

This type of involuntary shoplifting would have been impossible in a small shop, although there it would have been possible to buy on credit. At EPA, however, it was perfectly possible to go in and borrow a tampon from a packet without anyone noticing. The large number of products and the anonymous environment made it possible to take a personal advantage of EPA's new concept for material representation by borrowing from the bank of goods that was available.

EPA and the public sphere

The episode of the 'borrowed' tampon also raises questions about whether or not EPA was a public place. The department store milieu could often give the visitor a sense of being in a kind of open-air marketplace. The new urban landscape offered a multitude of public places for experiences of excitement, pleasure, entertainment, recreation, dining, dreaming and consuming. These were public meeting places for a new type of divided cultural identity-creation. For the upwardly mobile middle class it became important to know at least who one was *not*, in order to be able to get to know oneself (Frykman and Löfgren, 1987). As a place with 'disorganized order', the cells of the city thus become an arena for people from diverse cultural and class backgrounds, reflecting each other in their different needs. An urban life also requires its opposite: the longing for the unfeigned and unaffected. The fascination with 'the exotic Other' has an outlet through the spectacle (Featherstone, 1992).

But most of these places were in fact not public, except for the parks, public beaches, unspoilt nature, marketplaces and city squares. Restaurants, cafés, theatres, cinemas, zoological gardens, swimming baths and department stores were not public places, even if the visitor did feel free and unguarded. The visitor to EPA often regarded the department store arena as a public place. This can be illustrated by an incident in the history of EPA. An example of this was reported in a Swedish evening newspaper in 1971.[24] It concerned a man who had found a gold bracelet on the floor of an EPA store. In a letter to the editor he complains about the handling of this incident. When the man picked up the bracelet from the floor he noticed that the price tag still was on. Because of the high price, the man assumed that it did not belong to the EPA range, so he went to the manager of the store. The manager suggested that he should take the bracelet to the police station, but suddenly he changed his mind and declared that since the bracelet had been found at EPA, the reward belonged to the store. At first the finder refused to hand over the bracelet, but when the manager referred to a section of the law which gave the company the right to act in this way, the man gave up. After the episode, however, he contacted the police, who told him that the manager had already handed in the bracelet, and EPA would get the reward if there was one. The police officer admitted, however, that the reward should rightly fall to the person who found it. In the same evening paper EPA responded to the offended man's letter by citing a law from 1956 confirming their right to act as they had done.

In an interview with the manager in question,[25] he told me that he remembered this event very well, and also that a similar case went to court in 1956, when a ruling in the Supreme Court established a precedent. According to the law on lost property, business premises are not considered as public places. The meaning of this law is that no one is allowed to remove objects found on the premises. Anybody who finds something on the floor of a department store has two options: let it be, or hand it to the nearest shop assistant.

'People think that department stores are public places,' the former manager says, 'but EPA was private property, and we had the right to eject anyone we wanted. A department store is not the same as a street or a square. It is private property. Some people simply couldn't understand this.'

Shop assistants at EPA

Being a shop assistant at EPA was a very attractive job to many women in Sweden. An informant remembers how, as a young girl, she dreamt about being a 'real EPA assistant' because 'the women working there were so beautiful, and they somehow seemed so glamorous'.[26] She got a job there in 1950, at the age of sixteen, starting in the sweets and preserves department. In spite of her youth she soon became chief assistant in the department, a responsible appointment and the highest step of the female career ladder at EPA. She retains a fond memory of her work at EPA, as do many former assistants. 'We had a lot of fun in those days, we loved our work and the sense of community, and I felt a great responsibility for my department. The department was really my own responsibility.'

This feeling for the company and departmental solidarity was a typically feminine emotion (Benson, 1986), and the management of EPA were quick to realize its importance and build it into a system. By making one of the most trustworthy assistants responsible for the daily accounts from her department, the management hoped to reduce the wastage and shoplifting. From the end of the 1940s every chief assistant who had served three years in a row with no discrepancies in the cash balance was rewarded and got her picture in the staff magazine (Ekberg, 1990). Some years later this was extended to those who had only one year with no discrepancies. The chief assistant was thus responsible for ensuring a correct cash balance at her counter, and she could be personally liable to make up any differences out of her own pocket.

The problem of staff thefts was efficiently solved by means of this system for encouraging self-control. The store management knew that dishonest employees were good at finding new ways to appropriate money from the till. One widespread and much-discussed method was to register 1 krona if the customer bought something for 11 kronor. The cashier thus earned 10 kronor, and to mark this she put a pin in the till. If the number of pins rose to ten, they were replaced by a paper-clip. In the evening, when the takings were counted, the assistant knew that she had made 100 kronor (Ekberg, 1990). With the system of personal responsibility for both goods and cash receipts, however, this form of theft became impossible.

Technical equipment such as 'random selection generators' was later installed to control the EPA staff, eliminating all ideas of personal responsibility. This was considered necessary because there were more and more assistants, who came and went at a faster rate. These control instruments were often believed to be more technical than they really were. One episode that clearly shows the faith in new technology comes from the time when EPA had just installed a new surveillance system to detect when the staff tried to take goods out of the store at the end of the working day. The problem was that the management did not have the authority to search anyone unless there were very good grounds for suspicion. They therefore had to select people at random, and even then the selected person could decide whether or not she would let herself be searched.

This particular episode occurred at a recently installed generator, where the passing employees had to push a button as they were leaving the store for the day. If a green light came on, the employee could leave without being searched, but if the red light came on, the employee was expected to permit a search. In this way, no single employee would feel accused of being a thief, since all the decisions were the work of a random selection generator. When a young assistant one day was leaving her work, she stood by the machine for a long time, regarding the green light in wonder. Finally she shook her head and exclaimed, 'Isn't it fantastic what technology can do these days. Just think, this machine can tell thieves from honest people!'[27]

The criminal shoplifter and the shopping detectives

During the late 1950s and the 1960s more parties to the debate on shoplifting were heard. Different investigations of shoplifting were started, and in 1968 an inquiry was carried out at the behest of the Swedish Ministry of Justice. These investigations turned out to be difficult because of the lack of statistical evidence. The figure of 3 per cent wastage turned out to be an assumption with no evidential basis, and the only thing one could be sure of was that 'the real number of shoplifting crimes is substantially greater than the number of discovered cases' (SOU, 1971: 10). The huge number of articles on sale in the department store made it hard for the companies to supervise the flow of incoming and outgoing goods, and the only cases of shoplifting that were discovered were when the shoplifter was caught red-handed. The report also stated that shoplifters who get caught do not necessarily have the same characteristics as the shoplifters who do not get caught. The statistical evidence is even more limited at the next level of analysis: cases reported to the police. Although the department stores showed a greater tendency than other businesses to report shoplifters, it seemed that they followed certain unwritten rules: they did not call the police if the value of the stolen goods was below a certain amount, nor did they report children or old people. The number of cases was thus considerably reduced before they appeared in court.

During the 1960s several security companies were established in Sweden. In order to curb shoplifting and wastage more effectively, the department stores needed help from outside. EPA at this time was the only department store in Sweden that made its own investigations and kept records of its financial losses. It also employed security managers, recruiting ex-policemen for the purpose. These were given the title of 'security consultants' to avoid any speculation among customers or staff. The consultants themselves thought that they had greater potential to intervene – they made no distinction between people of 'high and low' status (judged by appearance), and as policemen they could not let any of the shoplifters slip through the net.[28] The management of EPA were not totally satisfied with the new situation, and some of the managers thought that the new consultants never affected the wastage in the company. 'They didn't have any knowledge about the problems in the retail trade that caused the great wastage' (Ekberg, 1990: 337).

Since the 1960s EPA had also employed female supervisors to keep an eye on customers and staff alike. They were often recruited directly from the home, changing their role dramatically from housewife to spy. They did not generally stay long at EPA, and were soon replaced by new women. Some male students also earned extra money as detectives at EPA, to help to finance their studies. The detectives were instructed to act like ordinary customers, dressed in ordinary clothes, usually unknown even to the sales staff. Their work was far from easy. The Swedish newspapers printed articles and letters about innocently accused customers. The evening paper *Aftonbladet* asked, 'How far can a shop supervisor go?'[27] and went on to report the case of a woman who had been searched in the street 200 metres away from EPA. The woman had felt extremely humiliated when a crowd of curious people had gathered around her in the street, hoping to see the revelation of a real shoplifter. The female detective was looking through her EPA carrier bags, and after finding the receipts which proved the woman innocent, she said: 'You see, we have to check that the assistants register the correct sum!' To many customers it was an unpleasant surprise that EPA cooperated with the police, and even worse was the fact that EPA could not trust its own people.

EPA-nytt in 1967 reported the increasing difficulty in supervising the stores. The main problem was striking a balance between effective crime-prevention measures and creating a pleasant atmosphere for the customers.

By treating shoplifting as a criminal offence, the management of EPA hoped for a deterrent effect, that people might understand the problem as something affecting society as a whole instead of just the department store. In choosing between protecting themselves from financial losses and not causing their customers any discomfort, EPA arranged a surveillance system based on the idea that it should only be visible when a crime was committed. An honest customer should not have the slightest feeling of being controlled or supervised. The detectives had a bad reputation, and the debate reached its climax when a lady cashier at one of the EPA bars was accused of stealing and fired because she had five kronor in the pocket of her working clothes. 'THE SECRET EPA SPIES MUST GO!'[30] and 'EPA'S SPIES FIRED ME!'[31] were some of the headlines in the papers after this encroachment. The lady cashier had been watched by three 'spies' when she put the money in her pocket, something that was strictly forbidden on the department store premises. The money, however, was part of a collection intended for another assistant who was leaving.

Learning to consume

Modern department stores and shoplifting are two phenomena intimately linked to each other. As department stores were established around the world, they automatically brought shoplifting in their wake. The seemingly unlimited range of articles tempts the customer, but this is precisely the point of the aesthetic: to tempt the buyer. However, the temptation of the articles must not make too great an impact on the consumer; longing must not turn into irresistible desire. This is an extremely difficult balancing act in the department store, where everything is within easy reach. Morality and self-control are absolutely necessary companions in the department store, virtues which the customers are assumed to possess before they confront the temptations of the store.

Most of EPA's customers were working-class women who, thanks to the homelike yet public atmosphere, learnt the art of the *flâneuse*. Going to EPA was a way to get away from home for a couple of hours; a harmless occupation and an accepted alibi that did not challenge accepted gender stereotypes (Bowlby, 1985). EPA was also an exciting place for children and adolescents, who had previously been carefully supervised in the small shops. Suddenly they could stroll at liberty around among toys and sweets, touch and look at things they had only seen pictured in the mail-order catalogues. To many people in Sweden the early EPA stores opened a new world, and this world of longing and temptation gave them dreams of being able to acquire some of the articles displayed in such abundance in the EPA stores.

Many informants describe EPA as the arena of their first shoplifting crime, because it was so easy to put something in your pocket when strolling around. Tempting fate by stealing the forbidden fruit was a challenge that most of my informants could not resist. Those who had never pilfered even regarded themselves as peculiar. To the young consumers, shoplifting served as a form of initiation into department store culture. For most of them, though, the first crime was also the last. The management were, as we have seen, well aware of this problem, but seemed to accept the shoplifting as mischievous pranks by young consumers who were innocent at heart. Worse was the problem of adult shoplifters, and especially the female 'shop-rats' who stole from the other customers. This could not be accepted as a natural part of the department store culture; it was instead regarded as a symptom of illness and impossible to cure. However, the worst form of theft was what happened within the company; the shop assistants who tampered with the cash-balance led to the campaign whereby the faultless chief assistants were rewarded. They were to be a model to the other assistants, inspiring them to be diligent and loyal to their own department.

Control systems of different kinds succeeded each other and culminated in the 1960s and 1970s in a spy system whereby detectives were hired to supervise both customers and employees. The supervision, however, was to be invisible so that nobody would feel that he or she was a presumed pilferer. In a way, however, this was the aim of the system, since signs which read 'This department store is under surveillance' were placed in the most prominent places in the store. Unidentifiable and able to see everything, the secret detectives moved around, and because of the knowledge and awareness that you could be observed by one of them, the control worked automatically (cf. Foucault, 1979).

EPA was one of the first department stores to hire security guards and campaign for the criminalization of shoplifting. This must be related to EPA's clientele and the public view of EPA as a 'second-class' department store. EPA did not have any obligations towards its customers, unlike the more sophisticated shops, where it was possible to be indulgent to light-fingered customers. EPA was necessary to many people who could not afford to buy things elsewhere. EPA's shop assistants did not have to bow and curtsy to their customers, and often did not have any personal relationship to them. On the other hand, EPA did make an effort to create an intimate atmosphere of responsibility and solidarity among the staff. In the forty years of the staff newspaper one can see clearly a picture of a united EPA family that was supposed to withstand attacks and threats from the outside. The first accusations concerned the standard-price system, and then followed the recurrent claims about the poor quality of EPA's goods, and finally EPA was accused of spying on customers and employees alike. Many of the employees refer to the shoplifting as a reason why it became unpleasant to work at EPA after the war, but they describe it as an 'attack from the outside' on the company, and not in terms of feeling that they were under surveillance themselves. EPA managed, however, to keep the wastage down to about 1 per cent, and many employees are proud of this fact, for several other chain stores 'were delighted if the wastage once in a while was $2\frac{1}{2}$ per cent' (Ekberg, 1990).

The shoplifter as a cultural category is difficult to define. Today, the shoplifter is invisible (except in the company's wastage figures); nobody seems to know who he or she actually is, and this makes the phenomenon all the more dangerous. From being the pilfering child, the kleptomaniac woman or the pensioner of urban legend (who hides a frozen chicken under his hat and faints at the cash-desk), the shoplifter has become a cultural category that cuts across all boundaries of class, age and gender. The shoplifter has no face, only long fingers, and the temptation to steal seems to pop up inside ourselves when least expected.

Shoplifting as an institution and a cultural category is extremely important in department store culture. As a step in our training to be a good consumer, we need the counter-image of incorrect consumption. Incorrect consumption also legitimates its opposite – the right way to consume. To become a moral and civilized consumer, you must be aware of the negative counterpart, and shoplifting plays a useful role in this conceptual world.

Notes

This chapter was translated by Alan Crozier.

1. This is a fictitious collage of the material I have collected about EPA. It is an attempt to convert meetings, field observations and archival studies into an academic account. I have been inspired in this by the anthropological debate of the 1980s about the representation of the things we study (Clifford and Marcus, 1986).

2. The significance of the *place* for a description is important (Certeau, 1984: 117). Every place has its narratives, but a place is not much more than a limited area, demarcated from other places, until it has become a subject of narratives about things that have happened there. When something happens in a place, it is filled with content and movement, becoming a *arena* for an event or many events. The arena is place as practice. I have also studied other arenas of consumption, such as the flea market (Fredriksson, 1991a, 1996), the living room (Fredriksson, 1990) and the consumption of forest for leisure purposes (Fredriksson, 1991b, 1997).

3. *EPA-nytt*, winter 1932: 1.

4. 'Epa-sytemet och dess följder' ['Epa-system and its consequences'], in *EPA-nytt*, winter 1932: 1.

5. Ibid: 8.

6. The great Swedish fear of becoming 'Americanized' has long been, and continues to be, a typical discourse in Swedish culture (see, for example, O'Dell, 1993).

7. 'Epa-systemet och dess följder', in *EPA-nytt*, winter 1932: 1.

8. *Epa-nytt*, winter 1932: 1.

9. NK (Nordiska Kompaniet) and PUB had been established since the nineteenth century as extravagant department stores based on continental models such as *Le Bon Marché* in Paris (Miller, 1981).

10. Response to questionnaire LUF 195 (LB).

11. *EPA-nytt*, summer 1942: 5.

12. The '1,300 kronor thief' had been arrested at a Grand store (an older sister store of EPA) in Gothenburg.

13. Response to questionnaire LUF 195 (BA).

14. Response to questionnaire LUF 195 (IJ).

15. Response to questionnaire LUF 195 (ES).

16. Ibid.

17. Ibid.

18. *Expressen*, March 1958.
19. *EPA-nytt*, summer 1942: 5.
20. Ibid.
21. Interview with JN, October 1995.
22. Interview with TE, autumn 1994.
23. Response to questionnaire LUF 195 (MC).
24. *Kvällsposten*, 5 June 1971.
25. Interview with EE, 3 October 1994.
26. Interview with MS, 14 October 1994.
27. Interview with TE, 20 April 1995.
28. Interview with TE, 20 April 1995.
29. *Aftonbladet*, 4 October 1965.
30. *Arbetet*, 26 October 1976.
31. *Aftonbladet*, 29 September 1974.

References

Albeson, Elaine S. (1989) *When Ladies Go A-Thieving: Middle-Class Shoplifters in the Victorian Department Store*. Oxford: Oxford University Press.

Benson, Susan Porter (1986) *Counter Cultures: Saleswomen, Managers and Customers in American Department Stores, 1890–1940*. Urbana and Chicago: University of Illinois Press.

Bowlby, Rachel (1985) *Just Looking: Consumer Culture in Dreiser, Gissing and Zola*. New York: Methuen.

Campbell, Colin (1987) *The Romantic Ethic and the Spirit of Modern Consumerism*. Oxford: Basil Blackwell.

Certeau, Michel de (1984) *The Practice of Everyday Life*. Berkeley and Los Angeles: University of California Press.

Clifford, James and Marcus, George E. (1986) *Writing Culture: The Poetics and Politics of Ethnography*. Berkeley and Los Angeles: University of California Press.

Ekberg, Erik (1990) 'Epoker inom EPA-varuhusen samt Fusionen med NK-Åhléns' ['The Epochs of EPA and the Merger with NK-Åhléns']. Unpublished manuscript, Lund.

Featherstone, Mike (1992) 'Postmodernism and Aestheticization of Everyday Life', in Jonathan Friedman and Scott Lash (eds), *Modernity and Identity*. Oxford: Basil Blackwell. pp. 265–90.

Foucault, Michel (1979) *Discipline and Punish: The Birth of the Prison*. New York: Vintage Books.

Fredriksson, Cecilia (1990) 'Ett rum i tiden' ['A Room in Time']. Unpublished manuscript, Lund.

Fredriksson, Cecilia (1991a) 'I varusamhällets utkant – en studie av loppmarknaden' ['On the Periphery of a Consumer Society: A Study of a Flea Market']. *Nord-Nytt, nordisk tidskrift for folkelivsforskning*, 44: 16–24.

Fredriksson, Cecilia (1991b) 'Excuse Me, Where's the Forest?' Paper presented at the 'Land–Life–Lumber–Leisure' workshop, Ottawa, Canada, May 1991.

Fredriksson, Cecilia (1996) 'Loppmarknader och ruiner. Om loppmarknadens estetik' ['Flea Markets and Ruins: The Aesthetics of Flea Markets'], in Ingrid Nordström and Renée Valerie (eds), *Tycke och smak: Sju etnologer om estetik*. Lund: Carlssons. pp. 17–46.

Fredriksson, Cecilia (1997) 'Ursäkta, var är skogen?' ['Excuse Me, Where's the Forest?'], in Katarina Salzman and Birgitta Svensson (eds), *Moderna landskap: Identifikation och tradition i kulturmiljön [Modern Landscapes: Identification and Tradition in Cultural Environments]*. Stockholm: Natur och Kultur.

Frykman, Jonas and Löfgren, Orvar (1987) *Culture Builders: A Historical Anthropology of Middle-Class Life*. Brunswick, NJ: Rutgers University Press.

Katz, Jack (1988) *Seductions of Crime: Moral and Sensual Attractions in Doing Evil*. New York: Basic Books.

Miller, Michael B. (1981) *The Bon Marché: Bourgeois Culture and the Department Store, 1869–1920*. Princeton: Princeton University Press.

O'Dell, Tom (1993) 'Chevrolet . . That's a real Raggarbil! The American Car and the Productions of Swedish Identities', *Journal of Folklore Research*, 30(1): 61–73.

Seremetakis, Nadia C. (1993) 'The Memory of the Senses: Historical Perception, Commensal Exchange and Modernity', *Visual Anthropology Review*, 9(2): 2–18.

SOU – Statens offentliga utredningar [Official Reports of the State] (1935: no. 63), *De svenska enhetsprisföretagen. Utredning av inom handelsdepartementet tillkallade sakkunniga* [Swedish Unit Price Companies. Report of the Expert Committee organized by the Department of Commerce]. Stockholm.

SOU – Statens offentliga utredningar [Official Reports of the State] (1971: no. 10), *Snatteri. Betänkande utgivet av 1968 års brottsmålsutredning* [Shoplifting. The Official Report of Criminal Cases, 1968]. Stockholm.

Synnott, Anthony (1993) *The Body Social: Symbolism, Self and Society*. London: Routledge.

Williams, Rosalind (1982) *Dreamworlds: Mass Consumption in Late Nineteenth-Century France*. Berkeley and Los Angeles: University of California Press.

Zola, Émile (1992) *The Ladies' Paradise*. Berkeley and Los Angeles: University of California Press.

6

SHOPPING IN THE EAST CENTRE MALL

Turo-Kimmo Lehtonen and Pasi Mäenpää

In seventeenth-century London there used to be a popular game in which a ball of boxwood was struck with a mallet in an attempt to drive it through a raised iron ring at the end of a playing alley. Both the game and the playing alley were called pall-mall, or simply mall. Thus, the etymological root of the main arena for the contemporary culture of consumption is found in a field of play, and, as we will argue, the spirit inherent in this root is being revitalized in the nature of the shopping mall.

The official opening of the extended East Centre Mall (*Kauppakeskus Itäkeskus*) in 1992 coincided with the deepest recession in Finland since the Second World War. Moreover, it was built in the middle of the eastern suburbs of Helsinki where the average income was lower than that of the whole city and where, in 1993, the rate of unemployment was 20 per cent and still rising in 1994. The extension, which tripled the floor space of the mall, was financed by a bank that had gone bankrupt a year before the opening because of poor investments and an overly liberal lending policy. In spite of all this, the mall has been a success. How has this been possible? What makes the mall attractive?

In this chapter, we will attempt to analyse how the East Centre Mall succeeds in functioning as a space for consumption by tracing customers' practices in using it and the ways they motivate these practices. The study is based on empirical data gathered by conducting group interviews and participant observation. All in all, thirteen groups of between three and seven people were interviewed between 1992 and 1995. The groups were selected as being representative of various walks of life. They included male and female, teenagers, young mothers, young adults, upper- and lower-middle-class and unemployed people. Geographically, all the data concern the area of Helsinki and its surroundings. Six of the interviews focused on shopping generally, two focused on urban life in Helsinki, and the five most recent interviews focused specifically on the East Centre Mall. The first two samples of interviews have been presented and analysed in an earlier stage of the research project (Lehtonen, 1993, 1994; Mäenpää, 1993).

In the following, we will discuss the ways in which the East Centre Mall is being used by its customers to satisfy what are perceived to be basic needs, but also for having a good time. In order to determine the various uses of the mall we will represent different modes of visiting it as well as modes of talking about it. The aim is to acknowledge the large range of experiences attached to the use of the mall, which vary from the plain and pragmatic to the leisurely and ludic, and to analyse the entanglement of these experiences. For just as the life of the mall is grey, it is also colourful, and we need appropriate conceptualizations to understand its vivacity. These we will try to develop through an analysis of the mall as a spatial setting and by discussing the motives for its use.

We will first begin by elaborating on the nature of the East Centre Mall and on the ways it has affected the general 'shoppingscape' of the city of Helsinki and its surroundings. The idea is to locate concretely the activity of shopping and to see what, in the Finnish context, is the new specificity that the mall has brought about. Then, going through our interview material, we will consider the reasons why shopping in the East Centre Mall, even though it often consists of the everyday purchase of necessary goods, is also seen as an enjoyable activity. The interviews provide the basis, in the final part of the chapter, for a more theoretical reflection on the nature of pleasurable shopping.

The changing scenes of consumption

The new consumer oases

In the 1980s a new type of domestic tourism emerged in Finland. As a function of a growing economy and the consequent rise in spending power, various kinds of enclaves for tourist visits were established. In particular, theme parks for children became popular venues for short trips for the whole family, and modern spas were popular among both elderly people and fitness-conscious adults. The largest petrol stations by the main roads were named 'gates', as they tried to stop passers-by for refreshment within a symbolic threshold between the regions of the country. All these enclaves arose outside population centres, alluring travellers as small tourist sites where one could come for anything between an hour, and a day or two. They are detached from main cities, and are in some respects miniature cities in themselves, with people wandering around and looking around, eating, drinking and shopping. They are like oases: small isolated worlds dedicated to recreation and to the pleasures of the senses.

At the same time, in late 1980s Finland, the retail trade was beginning to concentrate business into huge supermarkets. In addition to the benefit of lower costs for shopkeepers, customers, it seemed, preferred to do their shopping in bulk and for lower prices in stores at a distance rather than in the small store next door. When the completed East Centre Mall was opened in 1992 it seemed to be targeted at the point where these two trends of consumption, the tourist oasis and massive supermarket, meet. The mall is a separate complex of shops, department stores, groceries, services and entertainment, which simultaneously meets all kinds of needs and offers something new.

A special instance of the new tourist sites are the huge ferries that cruise around in the Baltic Sea. The cruises became enormously popular during the 1980s, and accordingly ever bigger and better ferries were built. The ferries leave Helsinki for Stockholm, Tallinn or St Petersburg, but the special hit since 1986 have been the 24-hour cruises that are just round trips, with no other goal than coming back to Helsinki. On these cruises, the main thing is to have a good time with one's fellow cruisers; to eat well, to dance and to do loads of tax-free shopping. The ferries are like moving cities, completely detached from the everyday spheres of home and work and of duties; thus one can buy everything 'duty free'. They are like floating malls with an emphasis on entertaining spectacle and the feeling of a safe adventure. The ferries embody the idea of a city with a 'lively centre' yet without the noise of traffic; what is left is a pedestrian high street with shops, cafés and restaurants and surrounding cabins that provide 'backstages' for privacy. In many people's minds the East Centre Mall came to be a kind of terrestrial counterpart to these ferries, with a similar emphasis on 'feeling good' and the provision of safe entertainment in an imposing atmosphere.

A commodity steamer on dry land

The East Centre Mall is the most important new local shopping scene in Helsinki. It is situated approximately 10 kilometres outside the city centre and is easily reached, with good connections by metro, bus and by car. It is the only mall in Finland that provides easy access not only to full-scale shopping facilities, but also to many public and private services, for example, a library, a branch of the Social Insurance Institution, a cinema, a swimming pool and an amusement park. It is advertised as the largest mall in Scandinavia with a floor span of 80,000 square metres, 170 shops or service points and parking for 2,500 cars. It is visited weekly by nearly 400,000 customers. This is a notable accomplishment, considering that the greater Helsinki area is only inhabited by one million people and that the whole population of Finland is five million, spread over a large area.

The mall is divided into two main sections. The bigger and newer part, called 'Bulevardi' (the Boulevard), consists of a street-like arcade that is in total 16 metres wide and 22 metres high, with shops on three floors; the older part, 'Pasaasi' (the Passage), is slightly narrower and smaller, the total length of the mall being over 400 metres. Together the two spaces form a street-like arcade that is crisscrossed by many smaller routes which are like alleys leading either out of the mall or into shops situated to the side. The simplistic form of a street has two main effects: you get to know the space quickly, and the street keeps you going. The mall is like an enlarged passage, but by passing through it one arrives nowhere. As in the 24-hour ferries, in the mall people have no other destination than the place itself.

The East Centre Mall bears a closer resemblance to the actual city of Helsinki than the ferries. Like the ferries, it puts the image of the lively city centre into practice but in a much more realistic way. Instead of an ideal model, the mall approaches a duplicate of the city centre of Helsinki. This becomes clear when the maps of the two are compared (see Figure 6.1). The floor plan of the East Centre Mall bears a remarkable resemblance to the street plan of an area between the two main department stores in the city centre. Even the relative proportions of the two spaces approximate each other.

The main street-like arcade is equivalent to the main street of Helsinki, 'Mannerheimintie', which leads to the very heart of the city. The smaller arcade corresponds to the main shopping and banking street, 'Aleksanterinkatu'. At the point where these two streets meet is 'Kolmensepänaukio', the liveliest square in the city; as the main meeting point of town dwellers it is like the core of the centre of Helsinki. Correspondingly, in the mall, at this point, there is the information desk with a floor plan, several kiosks selling snacks, bazaar-type street vendors and a large café. Like the original 'Kolmensepänaukio', it serves as a lively starting point from which to meet friends and orient oneself to the space around, and as a place to sit down for refreshment. So, the East Centre Mall is more or less unconsciously familiar to the people of Helsinki from the very first visit and so easy to get acquainted with.

The three department stores, as well as other main stores in the mall, are to be found in their original form in the centre. In fact, there are very few shops in the mall that are not found in the city centre. But then uniqueness is not its aim at all. The aim of the mall is to have more or less everything that the centre has; it is like a commercial city centre compressed into a compact and manageable package, put within easy reach of both private and public transportation. As an interior, it is dry and warm in any season or weather – the cold fact of Helsinki is its nearly arctic location – and the convenience is supported by the lack of actual traffic compared to the city centre. The mall seeks to offer in one convenient space everything that is scattered over a larger area in the city centre.

In this way, the centre of Helsinki can be said to have begun to float and to have drifted 10 kilometres east to a port of convenience. Even if the East Centre Mall stands on dry land, as a reproduction of the city centre of Helsinki, it is a floating image able to sail and anchor anywhere. Whether 'the city' has hereby been moved nearer or further off depends on the place of residence of a city dweller naturally, and, as we will later show, the point of going shopping to the East Centre Mall can lie in both its proximity and its remoteness.

Restructuring the city

Urban culture in Finland is fairly young and the cities are relatively small; Helsinki is often called 'a pocket-size metropolis'. The opening of a huge

(a) The Centre of Helsinki

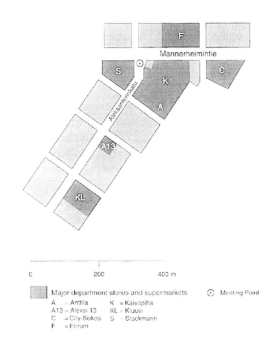

(b) The East Centre Mall

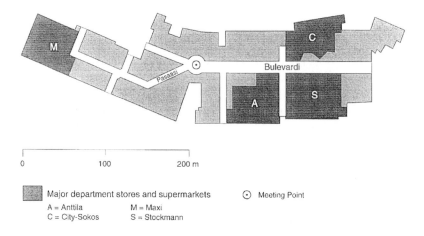

Figure 6.1 *The centre of Helsinki and the East Centre Mall: comparison of plans*

mall in such a small city has significance for the whole of public city life. It is worth asking whether the East Centre Mall has a potential to extend and transform local practices of using and experiencing public space. For a decade, both town planners and citizens have increasingly sought a lively 'European' city culture with pedestrian streets, open cafés, flea markets, street artists, urban happenings and a looser licensing of alcohol sales. Since Finland joined the European Union and Helsinki became a candidate for the title of European cultural capital for the year 2000, the street-level city culture has been very much an issue. The East Centre Mall can be seen as the creation of a new type of commercially centred, shopping-oriented urban space in Finland, where many ideals of the street culture are realized. To town dwellers the mall represents the latest mode of shopping, for other Finns it is a considerable tourist attraction.

The East Centre Mall brings to Helsinki a new cultural layer: as an architectural construction it imitates shopping streets, passages and market-places, but due to the surrounding settlement and the people who use the mall, it manages to generate an image and atmosphere of its own. The East Centre Mall is not just another site for shopping, but something different from other sites. By the same token, following the completion of the mall, the rest of the city is not what it used to be either. The mall affects the structure of the city in two directions, the suburbs and the centre, from the half-way position where it is geographically located.

The old shopping centres built in every eastern suburb of Helsinki in the 1960s have quickly become old-fashioned and even marginalized. A 44-year-old female cook paints a somewhat burlesque picture:

> They are the kind of places you wouldn't like to walk in more than to the store where you're heading, because there are just those people there who go from one bar to another eating sausages. . . . Somehow I can't go and buy food if I have to walk over vomit, and bleeding guys tottering around. When that happens I can't think of anything nice to buy.

In describing how terrible those miserable places are to visit, the interviewee indirectly reveals her ideal of good shopping: walking around without a certain destination and coming up with something nice to buy. This is no longer possible in the old shopping centres. The marginalization of the old shopping centres is usually the outcome of the constant urge to novelty of a modern city development. The consequences are examined by concerned town planners. But looking from the half-way position of the mall in the direction of the centre of Helsinki, the effects seem more favourable and perhaps less predictable. The old age of the suburbs is associated with the sad and impersonal concrete buildings of the 1960s and 1970s, and thus it is bad from the shoppers' point of view. But the out of date look in the centre of the city is more 'authentic' and finer, as the architecture mostly dates from the beginning of the century. Thus, this out of date feel is good in the 'traditional' marketplaces in the centre. The cook ponders the question further:

I don't think you can compare the East Centre Mall to the atmosphere of the Market Square and Market Hall, or to the cafés by the Esplanade [major shopping spaces in the city centre] and how they spread out there. I think there is an original atmosphere which belongs to the buildings there, which are quite different and beautiful, and there's a fundamentally different feeling there. Even if your eyes are closed you can feel how different it is to here [in the mall]. There's a kind of suburban atmosphere here anyway.

It seems that especially now that the mall has come to town, certain spaces in the centre of the city have gained in originality. In the young urban culture of Helsinki, where the mid-nineteenth-century neoclassicist centre is almost the only non-twentieth century architectural entity left, there is a craving for an older built environment. The atmosphere people are looking for is old, hence 'original' and 'authentic'. As a new reference point, the mall paves the way for a more nuanced aestheticization of urban spaces in Helsinki; in negative terms, too, as people now look upon some older shopping centres as being outdated. Going shopping is different in different places, and this can lead to constant differentiation. Hence, at least viewed from inside the phenomenon of shopping, the extending commercialization of city space has differentiating and restructuring effects, instead of merely making the whole town one huge shopping site.

The practices and pleasures of modern shopping

From the functional point of view, a shopping mall seems to be a step further in a certain line of development of modern trading whose starting point can be traced to the passages and department stores of Paris in the middle of the nineteenth century. All of a sudden customers were surrounded by an abundance of purchasable objects and were allowed to look at them and touch them without a counter desk and a salesperson coming between them. In the modern department store the interaction involved in the negotiation of prices was no longer the core of the commercial event. As Rosalind Williams puts it: 'active verbal interchange between customer and retailer was replaced by the passive, mute response of consumer to things' (1982: 67). Commodities and the stable prices attached to them were now to speak for themselves during the 'mute' moment *before* the expected act of purchasing. It marked the beginning of shopping as *being with things* which one might want to buy rather than shopping as interacting with other people.

Gradually, the extension of 'being with things' has generated a specific form of being that has become more and more self-supporting. In a mall, this 'need' for a merely enjoyable state of being is taken very seriously, as it was in the original and archetypal department stores of the nineteenth and early twentieth centuries. The lively atmosphere resembles a fair or a marketplace. The mall is an entertaining spectacle in itself, but it subsumes further spectacles such as buskers, pantomime artists, jugglers, painters, and so on.

Also available are wide assortments of snacks, titbits, sweets and drinks, which are consumed as 'oral side-involvements' of shopping (see Falk, 1994: 29–30). All these pleasures, as well as the architectural details and artistic figures, fuel people's appetites to make looking and strolling pleasurable. In the East Centre Mall the 'being with (purchasable) things' is made the thing itself.

The customers of a modern mall are released from interaction with staff and are therefore freed from having to formulate their wants verbally, and free to move around in space at their own pace, joining the collective rhythm of the people in the mall. This dual freedom – or the urges brought about by astute shopkeepers – contributes to customers' self-orientation and to the subjectivity of the shopping activity. What becomes central is an 'experiential aspect' of the action, instead of an 'expressive aspect' (on these concepts, see Falk, 1994: 62). It is this 'mute response' of the modern consumer, or the activity of passive shopping, so to speak, that we aim to make audible in our analysis of the East Centre Mall.

The definition of shopping

In the following, we will concentrate on some aspects of how and why shopping can be thought of as pleasurable, as something done for its own sake. To begin with, it is useful to take a closer look at the very concept of shopping, in order to understand the variety of meanings attached to the activity. Here, pleasurable shopping is understood as *consumption-oriented movement in a space where one has the possibility of making purchases.* This definition implies that the shopper relates to the environment from the point of view of consumption, even though he or she does not make purchases all the time. In other words, shopping always has something to do with buying, but in a way which allows it to be also plain day-dreaming and the planning of future purchases. Furthermore, shopping is about moving in the city, in malls and shops, that is, in a space that makes purchasing possible and where the openness and plurality of possibilities are fundamental.

In emphasizing the aspect of possibility, it becomes evident that shopping as a pleasurable leisure activity does not necessarily require a great amount of money. This is connected to the fact that, in Finland at least, the unemployed spend more time shopping than the employed (Niemi et al., 1991: 68). By and large, the interviewees criticized high prices very little, with adolescents being the most notable exception. Not even the unemployed complained about their reduced purchasing power. On the contrary, like a decent citizen of liberal capitalism, one unemployed respondent even emphasized that it is each individual's responsibility to create good feelings for oneself in a shopping mall, and that this, according to her, was independent of one's monetary situation. It seems that even with the deep recession of the beginning of the 1990s, most people were wealthy enough to go out and enjoy shopping. Or, to put it more precisely, the question of liking or disliking shopping did not seem to depend primarily on one's wealth, but rather on one's inclination and skill in spending one's time in the mall. With every visit, the mall offers something more than buying-myself-this-and-that-here-and-now. It is not only a place in which to buy the necessary goods, it is also *the place to go*.

In the analysis of the practices of consumption it is useful to make a distinction between two different ways of understanding the concept of shopping. The first, defined and described above, emphasizes the kind of shopping where the important thing is to enjoy oneself, where shopping is a pleasurable social activity in itself. The second sees shopping as strictly the grey and uninteresting purchasing of the necessary means for maintaining and reproducing the modern human being. These ways of understanding the act of shopping can be distinguished from each other as shown in Table 6.1.

These types are seldom distinct in practice. Between them there lies a certain tension. On one side, we have the hedonistic element of consumption, the seeking of new inner or lived experiences (*Erlebnis*; Schulze, 1992). In the other column, the kind of action typified reminds one of the objectifying (Simmel, 1990) or ascetic (Weber, 1978) rationality also characteristic of the social action of modernity. What Prus and Dawson say about their distinction between 'shopping as recreation' and 'shopping as work' is valid here too: 'While offering contrasts, these themes are not mutually exclusive. Not only may shoppers quickly switch from one definitional frame to the other during shopping expeditions, but they may also simultaneously define shopping in both recreational and laborious terms' (1991: 149). In the following, the emphasis is on the pleasurable side. It should be borne in mind, though, that the necessities of buying are never absent from the social form of shopping, although shopping is not only a necessity, a must, that is seen positively. It is the intermingling of these two aspects – necessity and pleasure – that constitutes the shopper's activity.

Table 6.1 *Shopping: pleasure versus necessity*

Shopping as a pleasurable social form	Shopping as a necessary maintenance activity
spending of time	scarcity of time
an end in itself	a means
does not necessarily imply making purchases	always implies making purchases
impulsiveness	planning
dreaminess and self-illusory hedonism	realistic satisfaction of needs
effectiveness unimportant	as effective as possible
pleasure	necessity
outside the routines of the everyday	an everyday routine among others
emphasis on experience	emphasis on rationality
playfulness	seriousness

The tones of the mall

Although it is characteristic of the East Centre Mall to allow for a great variety of possible activities, its *raison d'être* lies in its being a centre for purchasing, and in the turnover created by the daily exchange. 'We [the family] always have some kind of basic need, and we go to find a solution to that demand' (male graduate engineer, aged 37).

At first our interviewees presented their visits to the mall as simple and pragmatic. To ask people how they use the East Centre Mall is to ask how their daily life is constructed. Adolescents go the mall after school, mothers and fathers drop in after work and before going home to make an evening meal. Unemployed people are able to go when the mall is not crowded, and the mother of a small child is taken to the mall by car by her husband after the family lunch, and then brought back home for dinner. People use the mall as part of their own daily and weekly rhythm, and for the fulfilment of their everyday needs. They go to the mall with practical thoughts and leave it again for the sake of other duties elsewhere.

This mundane attitude recurred in the comments the interviewees made on the atmosphere of the mall. The East Centre Mall was regarded as a somewhat ordinary place for the common people of the eastern suburbs and surroundings, like their 'home yard'. It was pointed out that you can go to the mall 'as you are', without thinking much about what you look like. Those who have business there twice a week or more have become acquainted with the shops. For an unemployed man, aged 37, the mall is an alternative to being at home and a place where he can meet his unemployed friends on a daily basis: 'It's a habit of mine to come here and spend time with my friends somewhere and then go somewhere else for the evening.'

A visit to the East Centre Mall usually consists of certain customary chores, and people seem to do what they do without reflecting on it too much. When people are asked simply how they typically use the mall, they emphasize the practicality of the action. Even though this emphasis on practicality in the description of shopping activities seems valid enough, it is the other side of the coin. In addition to the less colourful everyday chores, the shopping phenomenon entails more colour which can either arise from the commonplace or is in any case entangled in it.

In the interviews, people living next to a smaller mall or shopping centre told us they would still rather go to the East Centre Mall – which is what they regularly do. They use either the bus, subway, car or bicycle and feel it is more convenient to come to the mall than to the smaller stores nearby. As a 41-year-old unemployed woman says: 'Even if I counted my money and noticed that I had nothing but fifty marks [about £7] and I should still buy two packets of cigarettes plus food, I'd still come here.' How can this 'convenience' that people feel be explained by the pragmaticism of their behaviour? What makes them prefer the distant mall even when they are short of money and able to buy only a little? There must be more than plain purchasing involved.

When people were asked expressly whether they enjoy shopping in the East Centre Mall and why, they typically said first how easy, convenient, cheap and efficient it is to do the shopping in the huge mall, where everything they need is concentrated under the same sheltering roof. 'There's like everything here, actually. You just come and choose where to go.' 'The shops are so close to each other that you don't have to run from store to store and upstairs, like in the centre of Helsinki.' 'If you want to see everything quickly, it's possible here.' 'You want to compare and buy the best and the cheapest.' The mall is seen as a concentration of shops in one convenient location.

After presenting this rationalistic framework of ease and efficiency the interviewees were inclined to describe what really makes for enjoyable shopping. The cook quoted above found no contradiction in her description of what she does as 'doing business systematically' and 'enjoying new textiles because I like going to art galleries anyhow'. To look for something according to a plan coheres with having fun. Shopping experience is both rational and hedonistic at the same time. However, this paradox is not solved but rather 'acted out' in the practice of shopping – it remains as a source of permanent tension stimulating the activity of shopping.

Perhaps the rationality of the shoppers is not so much turned to a calculation of utility in any narrow sense. Following Gerhard Schulze, one could rather trace here a rationality of inner experiences (*Erlebnisrationalität*). What people seek are inner experiences and good feelings, and in so doing they try to optimize the possibilities of achieving them. As Schulze (1992: 430) says, when, rather than taking the flow of experiences as it comes, one tries to control and regulate it, one acts in accordance with a rationality of experience.

The main point here is that ease and efficiency form the basis of a pleasurable shopping event. If the act of purchasing is not simple and quick, the shopping experience as a whole cannot be entertaining and leisurely. Or seen the other way around: beyond every dreamy and distant occasion for 'being with things' the shopper must be able to see a simple act of purchasing, of 'taking' the article 'in' without disturbance or delay. Ideal shopping is carefree and light-hearted, and the mall works hard to offer this utopia to its customers. The main questions are how and under what social conditions does this dream come true. The concepts of tourism, social form and play can usefully be applied in discussing this phenomenon.

Tourism in the everyday world

Pleasurable shopping and tourism bear a close relationship. Both of them take place outside the everyday spheres of home or work, where a controlled adventure is possible (on their metonymical relationship, see Falk, Chapter 8, this volume). What is fascinating in both is the encounter of the new and the unexpected and the experience of being 'somewhere else'. In both tourism and shopping, the central aspect is the experience of movement and the special relationship with the environment. This is also the basis for the special way in which a shopper can see the everyday environment, as if with the eyes of a tourist. The relation between tourism and shopping is close also because shopping constitutes a very important part of being a tourist. Often the consumers *are* tourists as well as being *like* tourists. They have an aesthetic relation to their environment, and the core of their pleasure is the encounter with the new and the exotic, and the attempt to assimilate it in terms of what is known and familiar.

The image of the East Centre Mall seems to be a complex one as far as its cultural characteristics are concerned. In the interviews, people characterized the mall as at once Finnish, European and American, suburban, provincial and urban, familiar and exotic. This perplexing mixture of familiarity and otherness could be seen merely as the quality of a culturally manifold artefact. But seen from the point of view of users' experiences, it can be taken more seriously as a central aspect of shopping in the mall. Arising from the interviews, there are several other points which lead to the same idea of the mall as a space for exploring the boundary of the familiar and the unknown. It seems that this very liminality gives the East Centre Mall its intensities and makes the whole enterprise work.

To begin with, the exciting tension between the familiar and the unknown can be seen in the 'Restaurant World' of the East Centre Mall. Most of the restaurants of the mall are concentrated in this area. This makes it easy for the shoppers to compare the range of possible alternative cuisines. Generally, what one eats in the mall differs from what one eats at home. The food and the restaurants are slightly exotic; they connote with places far away and unusual tastes. And yet the idea is not to offer something really strange or foreign or new, but something that is familiarly exciting and dangerous, to offer experiences with a controlled degree of novelty and controlled adventures of taste with a predictably happy ending. This border between the familiar and the exotic is reflected in the names of the enterprises in the 'Restaurant World': 'Manhattan Steak House', 'Döner Kebab', 'Napoli Express', 'Finnish Restaurant Jagellonica', 'Fonda del sol, Mexican Restaurant', 'Europa Café' and 'Europa Pub', 'McGrouse', 'Greek Pizzeria-restaurant Rodos' and 'House of Sheng, Chinese Restaurant'. Finnish cuisine exists comfortably alongside the others but it, also, is made somewhat exotic by reference to a historical event in its name.

As an experience, going to the mall means having a trip 'somewhere else', where the real world is constantly challenged by the possible world, and where the shopper can sway between the two. This *oscillation* between 'what is' and 'what could be' seems to predominate in the life of the mall. The oscillation was recognized also in the contradiction of the commonplace and the festive. As has been noted above, when interviewed, people tended to repeat how practically they behave when the issue was that of their own visits to the mall. But when talking about what they like in shopping in the mall the attitude changed. This happened when, by way of concluding the interview, they were asked to cut pictures and texts from magazines and use them to compose a collage with the title 'A Visit to the East Centre Mall'. An unemployed woman, aged 48, presented her collage, which she named 'Spending payday in the mall':

> You go and do a bit of shopping, take a look at some clothes, and then of course go for a beer in between. Then some perfumes and things like that. And then at some point we eat and have some goodies. . . . When I want to go with my friends or with my sister, when we want to give ourselves a treat then we go shopping like this. We eat well somewhere and have drinks and so on. Then I don't actually think about the cost.

To represent the atmosphere at the East Centre Mall, most of the interviewees used pictures of exotic and sunny environments, luxury products, beautiful smiling people and words like 'happiness', 'unusual', 'just for fun', 'sensation' and 'celebration'. All of a sudden the whole scheme of the practical satisfaction of needs was gone. If these oppositional standpoints, prosaic and sensual or commonplace and joyous, are a reliable reflection of the action that really takes place, they prove the variety of the ways people use the mall. In the same way as there are styles of talking about the mall, there are styles of using it. Between luxurious spending on a payday and twenty minutes in the grocery store there are visits that could be labelled 'Saturday shopping with the whole family', 'Busy mother finally having her own time', 'An unemployed man spending the whole day meeting others', or 'Shopping date with a friend, sister, mother or grandmother'. In all these one can see an aspect of personal transcendence, or, rather, putting distance between the subject and the everyday chores of home and work.

We wish to argue, namely, that it is not so much the vertical variation of festive and commonplace, as in carnival, but rather the horizontal oscillation between proximate and distant that makes the world of the mall go round. Whereas the carnival is an exaltation of the flesh and carnal pleasures, playing with the 'high' and the 'low' (cf. Bakhtin, 1968; Stallybrass and White, 1986), what is essential in pleasurable shopping is romantic dreaming and the aestheticization of the environment. Distances and social gaps are closed and transgressed in the traditional carnival, whereas in shopping one actually removes oneself further from one's own environment and everyday life. Carnival is the same place upside down; it is a dream come true in the here and now, whereas dreaming in the mall takes you to places far away. There is an inherent paradox in visiting the familiar mall, because one knows perfectly well where one is, but can simultaneously be lost in the dream worlds provided by the surrounding goods.

A tourist or a tripper?

In discussing shopping in the mall, it would seem more appropriate to talk about *trippism* rather than about tourism. Obviously, 'tourism' refers to the verb 'to tour', which etymologically means travelling around or making a circuitous journey. Also 'The Grand Tour' of the sons of the European aristocracy and gentry during the period between 1600 and 1800 – which the studies of tourism usually refer to as one origin of modern tourism – was especially circuitous travelling from town to town. Although the present-day meaning of the verb *to tour* merges into *to make a trip*, the latter expresses more accurately the phenomenon that is involved here, because the noun *tour* means travelling around from place to place or a long journey including visits to a number of places in sequence, whereas the noun *trip* is a more general word, indicating going to a place at any distance and returning. In the case of the mall, and perhaps of other recreational enclaves as well, it is necessary to focus on the idea of going to only one distinct place and returning again, because this is the clue to the primary concept of the mall as a place of buying and selling.

As has been noted above, the *differentia specifica* of the East Centre Mall from the customers' point of view is that everything is under one roof. The pragmatic idea behind this – which is also utilized in the advertising of the mall – is that in order to shop, there is no more need for tiresome and stressful tours between distant points. All kinds of stores, boutiques, public and private services and amusements are gathered together in one point of sale, so to speak. After further scrutiny, this is revealed to be false, of course, because the movement between shops is only transposed inside the mall and reduced in scale. The circular wandering is something which is experienced holistically and not as divisible into shopping first for this and then for that. The mall has internalized the circuitous movement from outside of the action of shopping to inside, transforming its burden to pleasure. Thus, 'tourism', understood as circular movement, describes rather the mode of the shopping action itself, whereas with 'trippism', understood as making a trip, the totality of the experience from the beginning to the end can be indicated more clearly.

This way, talking about trippism referring to the whole action of leaving home or work and returning also paves the way for emphasizing that the idea in shopping – at least in the case of the East Centre Mall – signifies not only a touristic orientation inside the mall, but also that the journey itself, as movement from one place to another, has a specific bearing on the experience of going shopping. As we pointed out above, the interviewees preferred the distant mall to stores nearby. If the transportation is comfortable, the following becomes true: the further you go shopping, the more pleasant it is. In everyday shopping this sounds like a paradox, but in the sphere of tourism, it is a truism.

Significantly, then, it seems that the East Centre Mall prospers not only due to its position at the heart of the populous eastern suburbs of Helsinki, but even more because it is distant and different enough to be a place 'somewhere else', while still sufficiently easy to reach. This effect of a separate, distant place is strengthened by its inner-directedness. The East Centre Mall stands on wasteland like an island surrounded by a network of traffic routes: roads, a bus station and subway. The mall opens inwards – a characteristic that Anne Friedberg (1993) thinks generally defines malls – to its own arcade, and coldly turns its back on the world outside. As an architectural composition it does not communicate with the landscape or the buildings nearby. The East Centre Mall forms a closed arena for shopping, with symbolically unspectacular and modest entrances that open up towards different routes: towards streets outside, the bus and subway stops, and, probably most importantly of all, towards the parking places. The passages that lead in are actually gateways made only for the purpose of getting inside. If you are not in the mall, you are out, nowhere.

Even if shopping usually takes place on the way home after work, since the East Centre Mall is a world of its own, it captures customers for quite a while. Moreover, one can say without exaggeration that something in people's experiences of the mall justifies the connotation of a trip as a state of euphoria induced by drugs. The idea of being hooked on shopping in the mall emerged also in the interviews. When you have a trip in the mall you leave your normal, perhaps worried state of being for a while in a way that can even lead to more or less compulsive behaviour. As a male accountancy manager, aged 30, saw it, the mall is like 'a carnivore' or 'a huge joyful octopus' with groping tentacles reaching out from all around to catch you.

The social form of shopping and the play form

An interviewee in her thirties, a mother of small children who works as an accountant, uses shopping as a break from the routines of work and home:

> I enjoy shopping. When you go there alone and you don't have to care about others, you can have a look at things in peace, see what to buy. You feel it's your own time when you go shopping [laughs].

For her, shopping can be an occasion to enjoy herself and have her own time when this might otherwise be difficult. The bustle of the mall gives one an ideal sense of independence and autonomy – one is not expected to do or to be anything, and one can be alone without feeling lonely. While shopping one can feel that one does not have to be responsible for anything else other than oneself:

> You sometimes go just because it's fun, you've got free time, you think of what to do and decide you'll go to the East Centre, there are loads of shops. Even if you don't need anything it's fun just to walk around and have a look at what there is, and maybe sit down for a coffee at some point. Yeah, it's fun.

She wants to go shopping by herself, because she 'can't stand' having anyone else with her. For her the world of goods is there all the time to be entered, but it does not impose itself on her. One can distance oneself from it by going to have a cup of coffee, for instance. Moving around and looking at things is pleasurable in itself, even without making any purchases. The shoppers are not just at the mercy of the object world. Rather, by their interpretation they create a space where they feel free. This space is not independent of given social determinants, but the process of its creation allows for certain degrees of freedom.

The sociality of shopping

The pleasures of shopping not only derive from the possibility for autonomy. On the contrary, often the enjoyable aspect of going shopping is the special sociality attached to it. This sociality can be both unpronounced interaction and a conscious, verbalized end in itself. Shopping can often be a way to spend time together, and at the same time it makes possible the shared creation of taste and style. In other words, it provides a means for the creation and maintenance of social relations, and in this way it affects the process of social identification (on shopping with companions, see also Prus, 1993). Workmates, for instance, can go shopping together after work. Also, many interviewees reported that they do the shopping for the weekend together with their spouses. For elderly people shopping can be an important means of meeting people and having contacts which are possibly otherwise rare. For some people, to go shopping can even be a hobby, like for a young interviewee and her boyfriend; they go out every Saturday to shop and spend time together in the city:

> My boyfriend and I have made it a habit to go to the centre of town during the weekend. We don't take the car, we use public transport so that we can walk around in town, go to shops, see what there is, and then maybe go for a pint before carrying on, or get something to eat. It's fun going around like that, you're not in a hurry to be anywhere at any particular time. It's like leisure time when you go shopping. It's not the main thing that you've bought anything. You've just spent time and seen people and things.

The sociality of shopping was very much stressed by another interviewee, a mother of two daughters in their teens. She usually goes shopping with one of the daughters, and this is an occasion for both of them to discuss the important things in life. As she herself expresses it, shopping is for her 'a social form'; it allows for a specific kind of sociability. In this case, the fun of shopping does not derive from buying or wanting or desiring objects; rather, shopping is a convenient way of being together, enjoying oneself and the company of another person while at the same time doing the necessary shopping. 'It's just communicating and being together.'

While shopping, being together can be built on the shared action, which supports the continuity of the social occasion; the sociality does not have to be pure or intensive. Shopping creates a safe and convenient framework for relaxing together. The sociality or the intercourse can go on while people do their shopping. The communication can even be the main thing, but it does not need to rely on itself. The objective of the action, the things and people that can be looked at and discussed, comes as a mediating force between the actors, giving them distance from each other, although it is this very same objective that also unites people who go shopping together. The pleasures of shopping come from the ability to be alone or to be together or just to spend time as a tourist would, without any hurry or necessity to buy anything, to be outside of home and work with the freedom from responsibilities. But what is common to these pleasures? One answer can be sought from the relative stability of the ways that actual shopping takes place, from the routines of shopping.

In the interviews, it became clear that shopping is usually seen as a recurring part of everyday life, although its meanings vary from one occasion to another. Shopping is closely integrated into the rhythm of the day, and as such it is a routine among other routines. And the routines one deals with at home affect the routines of shopping, so that skills like cooking and cleaning call for the skills of shopping for good food and proper equipment, and vice versa.[1]

In the study of shopping, the generality and stability of the action can be approached using Simmel's concept of *social form* (see especially Simmel, 1992: 13–41), where a form is the interaction between elements that are its contents, interaction that causes these elements to become a unity. The contents can be individual interests, drives, desires and goals, for instance. A social form thus mediates between changing and varying contents. The form is autonomous, because it cannot be derived from external explanatory factors. It can be both an end in itself as well as a means for various ends. Shopping can be seen as a social form through which one can acquire daily necessities, have time just for oneself or share time with others.

The social form is what makes action socially meaningful. As such, it comes close to the notion of ritual. Rituals are coherent sequences of action that create and organize our experience. As Lakoff and Johnson put it: 'In performing them, we give structure and significance to our activities, minimizing chaos and disparity in our actions' (1980: 234). Besides helping us make sense of our environment, rituals are means of communication and expression. A ritual can be a habitualized form of interaction, and hence unplanned and unconscious (cf. Goffman, 1967). Even as such it is charac-terized by intensive and active participation in the roles that are re-created and reproduced through it. Rituals are important for us, because they help us to have coherent views of both the social environment and ourselves. One of the most frequently occurring everyday rituals in the modern Western world is shopping (on the rituality of consumption, see also Douglas and Isher-wood, 1980; Rook, 1985).

As with other rituals, shopping expresses and reproduces social distinctions of time and space. This is amplified by the position shopping has between the spheres of 'home' and 'work'. In fact, shopping as a social form and ritual is often between or outside these two spheres; it mediates between them and helps to make the distinction between the orientations that these spheres imply. First, many people who work near the shopping centres may spend a large part of their lunch break shopping. In this way people separate the working day into two and detach themselves from the sphere of work. Second, many people go shopping after work on the way home. One really enters the sphere of home only after the shopping is done. Third, the biggest shopping of the week is often done on Friday or Saturday. In this way, shopping functions as part of the change of orientation from the weekday and worktime to weekend and leisure. Despite the recent tendencies of shops to remain open twenty-four hours a day and the resulting freedom to move from one sphere to another at any given time, these kinds of ritual changes of orientation are not only private, they are shared. This sharing is evidently reflected in the rush hours of the malls. As a rule of thumb, the retailers in Finland count on making half of their weekly turnover on Friday and Saturday.

The shopping ritual organizes both individual and shared time by marking the differences between different spheres. Following Durkheim (1965), it could be thought that in the idea of ritual there is an element of connecting people, and the heightened form of this connection is sacredness, an expression of togetherness. Obviously, there is nothing really sacred in shopping either as a necessity or as a pleasurable activity. Émile Benveniste (1974; cited in Agamben, 1989: 88–9) has, however, suggested a connection between ritual and play which may be fruitful here. According to Benveniste, a ritual is always connected to a myth, when it has to do with the sphere of sacredness. But when the myth is taken away from the ritual, only an empty form is left. This form is thus transformed into play, something done for its own sake, not because of its sacred connotations. In a similar manner, a myth without a ritual is transformed into a story told for its educational and entertaining functions. And as Giorgio Agamben (1989: 89) adds, this applies also to everything in the practical–economic sphere. It is a question of appropriation and transformation of the objects 'originally' used for purposes other than play. This connection can, in effect, tell us something very fundamental about shopping as a leisure activity: it is playful when its practical purposes lose their dominance. Moreover, these two spheres, the practical–economic and playful, are not exclusive of each other; rather, they are intermingled, and as such they constitute the totality of the action.

The concept of play

The concept of play needs to be briefly analysed here. To distinguish play and games from the rest of the social world is not easy. This was already recognized by Johan Huizinga in his famous history of *Homo Ludens* (1955). While emphasizing the natural playfulness of the human being, Huizinga ended up considering play to be the constitutive basis of culture itself. Georg Simmel, a representative of the classical period of sociology, considered social games from the point of view of the constitution of society. 'The more profound, double sense of "social game"', Simmel wrote, 'is that not only the game is played in society . . . but that, with its help, people actually "play society"' (1950a: 50). Roger Caillois, in his taxonomic study of play, defined play as free, separated, unproductive activity, which is governed by rules. Furthermore, the result of play is always uncertain and mentally it is based on the logic of make-believe, which means that it is 'accompanied by a special awareness of a second reality or of a free unreality, as against real life' (Caillois, 1961: 9–10).

For present purposes it is sufficient to state, in accordance with Huizinga (1955), that play is free activity standing quite consciously outside the realm of 'ordinary' life as being 'not serious', but at the same time absorbing the player intensely and utterly. This definition should, though, be supplemented with Simmel's emphasis on the fact that play should not lose all of its connection to the 'serious', if it is to remain interesting and not become 'empty play' (1950a: 43). Play is an autonomous, imagined sphere *in* reality which aims at joyfulness and entertainment. It is an artificial world inside the world. Play is capable of capturing one's main attention for a period of time, and when the play is at its most intense, the player's action and thoughts are inseparable, as the player is drawn into the 'flow' (Csikszentmi-hályi, 1975) of the game.

It seems to us that the phenomenon of going shopping can form an autonomous and autotelic activity that surpasses the commonplace sphere of 'real' reality – with 'real' understood here as something that has to do with the seriousness of everyday constraints and necessities. Shopping as a pleasurable activity is in many ways a kind of action that transcends the everyday routines, it is a kind of 'semi-routine or a kind of routinised non-routine' (Urry, 1990: 10). In pleasurable shopping the serious parts of the action become secondary, and the freedom, lightness and enjoyment come to the fore. The playfulness of shopping is always connected with public spaces, both in cities and in large malls. Shopping as a social play form is ruled by certain ways of being with others, even when one seemingly 'plays' only by oneself. It is central to pleasurable shopping that it always *takes place* in public space.

Playful practices in public spaces

Shopping arenas are placed either in the inner city or in separate shopping centres or malls. In fact, the centre of the city is often defined by the intensiveness of its commercial function. Lively shopping areas are always significant parts of the public urban sphere; the commercial spaces are public or semi-public and in principle open to everyone, gathering people together as anonymous crowds. As Richard Sennett puts it, the 'city is a human settlement in which strangers are likely to meet' (1978: 39). Seen from this perspective, the mall is a city both simulating and reproducing the city centre in the outskirts.

The contemporary city space is a public social setting which (in orderly circumstances) respects personal space and individual integrity. In streets and marketplaces everyone is seen by everyone else, and every abnormality is potentially noticed by more or less inquisitive eyes. However, you are able to wander around in your own thoughts because a mutual respect for 'privacy' prevails in the urban public space. The other side of this 'alone-ness' is that it implies a sense of insecurity: you cannot expect anyone to come to you in case you suddenly need help. Feeling that you do not have to care about anyone else and no one cares about you can give you the utmost sense of freedom unless you begin to feel lonely. Alienation, people becoming strange to others and themselves as well, is certainly a main theme of urban discourse in social criticism. But, it is the sunny side of the 'Street of Indifference', which has seldom been analysed as a possible source of the joy, entertainment and particular togetherness characteristic of all public spaces with large crowds.

After Baudelaire's analysis of the *flâneur*, Simmel was one of the first to recognize the ways in which the modern metropolis as a huge community of anonymous urbanites gives its members positive freedom to adjust to the continuous flow of impulses in their own personal way. Nevertheless, freedom in the form of anonymity and privacy does not signify freedom of expression. Thus, in the liveliest shopping street, where alluring windows with reduced price-tags and swarming crowds overflow, facial expressions are uniformly nonchalant, gestures unaffected and bodily movements highly predictable. Simmel (1950b) thought of these manners as symptoms of certain mentalities – becoming blasé, cynical or generally indifferent – which urbanites are forced to compose in order to adjust themselves to the hectic life of the modern metropolis. But there is also scope for another kind of interpretation, more in the spirit of Goffman's analysis of city life: the indifferent and non-striking manners can be taken merely as masks proper to the social situation, not as stable mentalities.

The question remains: what happens behind the mask? Naturally, the 'civilized' urbanites, hard-boiled in the melting pot of the city, select what to 'take in' from the flow of impulses they experience. But in the mall they are supposed to enjoy everything around them. They are bombarded with signs of things which are there only to please them, and they find themselves under siege from the promises of enjoyment those signs suggest. What the shopper senses in the mall is the pleasurable *abundance*. Now it seems that in the economy of the shopper the income of the impulses is overflowing, but the mask of calm indifference that the public street-play requires as a rule prevents the natural outcome, that is, the expressive behaviour. What could be the result of the constant reception of impulses if not expressive interaction?

What happens in this setting of manifold impulses is that *the reactions of the urbanites turn in on themselves*. Instead of expression, there are *impressions* with which to play in one's imagination. The anonymity provided by the crowd gives one freedom, even pushes one to orient oneself to one's inner world. Behind the silent mask there is a private world of the imagination which has become sensitive to the perpetual flow of stimulation. Simmel's man of the metropolis and Campbell's (1987) self-illusory hedonist merge into a hedonistically oriented urbanist who begins to fulfil him- or herself upon entering into the playground of imaginary pleasures. The public city space is a social world of fantasizing individuals who share the seen reality while having private inner worlds of dreams and private associations of images. They refrain from actual interaction, but use others and the signs they transmit for purposes of inner-directed pleasurable contemplation.

It is precisely in these lively public places – where one cannot expect anyone else to be kind to oneself and where others' personal impressions are not reached – where people stay just to spend time and to watch the swarming crowd. When urban people like to rest and relax they choose the busiest corner to sit down. It is here that people have their meeting points, sit down under a statue or have a cup of coffee in a street café. As one interviewee put it: 'Sometimes I like just to sit and watch people, not any special types of people. I just generally like watching what they busy themselves with.' At the same time, everybody is aware of being an object of others' gazes, as part of the momentary sociable community of people just passing the time and watching.

In the architecture of the East Centre Mall attention has been paid to the need for liveliness in public spaces. 'Bulevardi', the bigger and newer part of the East Centre Mall, is designed to function at once both as a street and as a square. People walk mainly along the alleys, which are a couple of metres wide, on both sides of the street-like space. Between these traffic flows there are sections of emptier space of approximately 10 to 20 square metres, which are usually framed by small trees or benches, or both. Whereas the floor of the pathways is made of rock, in the middle area it is wooden. In one of these sections there is a café, or pizzeria, in another a stage. These arenas stop people for a while to relax and to have a look around before they join the flow of shoppers again. To sit down is not to retreat entirely from the bustle of the mall but to become a spectator of the surrounding moving images.

The flow of people shopping and of objects is similar to both television and cinema: private and predictable yet indeterminate action, where 'what we go to see, to experience over and over again, is our own desire' (Barry, 1981/2: 21). The connection between cinema and shopping is also made by Bowlby (1985) and Friedberg (1993). The difference between watching television or films and the activities of shopping and walking about in the city is in the possibility of joining in the bustle of moving images. Whether sitting or walking, in public places like the East Centre Mall one is both subject and object (see also Shields, 1994).

Street sociability

The particular public form of sociality, of being at once both interested and yet indifferent and anonymous, we term *street sociability*. Street sociability is entertaining the sharing of public places with strangers, with whom one is in eye contact and with a bodily closeness that is discreetly played down, but without directly addressing them by voice. There is an atmosphere of sharing the fact of 'being present together', where there is the *possibility* for reciprocal communication, even if it only rarely really occurs. It is worth emphasizing that this notion of street sociability does not seek to define the totality of the experience of being in the city space. One should not forget the restless hurry, chaotic traffic jams, rush hours, sweaty queues, feelings of insecurity and other unpleasant sides of the city or the mall. Street sociability is only a name for the entertaining community of strangers, the exciting tension of a controlled incalculability, with emphasis on the aleatory elements of the street. It is a case of observing the surrounding phenomena privately but in public. Street sociability has no other aim than entertainment, thus it is autotelic and very much like play – *street play*, no less.

Every now and then the playfulness of street sociability is explicit, both conceptualized and ironized by city dwellers. In the interviews there emerged three kinds of play that people entertain themselves with. The first of these concentrates on imagining: one searches for interesting people and tries to guess who they are and what their life histories are like. Second, one tries to find familiar faces, either those of celebrities or those of friends – like an ornithologist spotting birds. The third play is called *palloilu* in Finnish. Verbatim it means 'playing ball'. It is an expression with which adolescents and young adults verbalize their act of having fun wandering around in the city, especially when it is full of people and action. 'Playing ball' means bouncing like a ball from one place to another without any particular goal or purpose.

The point here is the general principle lying behind these kinds of play. It is the *aleatory* nature of street-life. The playful excitement of street sociability is based on the possibility and chance that something special and unusual could happen. This is what one looks forward to when one 'goes out'. For Goffman (1967) the public city space is 'where the action is' and this action is always connected with chance, with the possibility that something unexpected might happen. Analogously, for Baudelaire's *flâneur* the modernity of the boulevards of Paris was *le transitoire, le fugitif, le contingent* – in a word: unpredictable.

We argue that the aleatory or serendipitous character predominates over the pleasure-seeking experience of urban life, the typical experience of the people who go and spend time in the East Centre Mall. The lively city environment, or the mall as its modification, is a playground for games of chance, a continuous flow of intensifying and expiring tensions of lottery. While in the city, you cannot foresee whom you are going to meet or what seductive commodities you are going to encounter. But when you believe in encountering someone or something interesting, it becomes more likely to happen. It is a self-fulfilling prophecy.

As we write this chapter, the East Centre Mall is marketing itself with a campaign entitled 'Lucky Days'. It is based expressly on the idea of aleatory play. The mall regularly conducts campaigns like this to keep itself in people's minds as the place to go. During the spectacle of four 'Lucky Days', there are different games of chance arranged along the arcade in which anyone can participate for free. For example, there is a wheel of fortune, and a game called 'Floor Lottery' in which people make a bet on a number by standing in a certain spot on the floor. Games of chance are introduced to the culture of the East Centre Mall continually. Located centrally at the crossroads of 'Bulevardi' and 'Pasaasi', there is a casino with roulette, black jack and slot machines in the continental atmosphere of a darkened room. Right at the centre of the square, at the very heart of the mall, there is a kiosk with two desks: one is for information, and the other for the state-owned lottery and betting agency.

Shopping as part of the play

The culture of street sociability is born out of the tension of anonymity and intimacy, the tension in which encounters are dictated by chance. The excitement of the mall comes from an anticipatory enjoyment of possibly coming across something one might find pleasant, something one might desire. Desire is attached to objects that stand out against a grey and indifferent mass, objects that somehow are something new and exciting, and yet something familiar, surprisingly appropriate to the experienced desire. The most delightful experience for a city shopper is to encounter something that one has somehow anticipated or longed for, but of which one has had only a faint idea. The state of mind of the shopper is dominated by longing for something one does not know yet, but which one is disposed to recognize as belonging to oneself.

This romantic, unspecified longing predominates both over the experience of street-life and the experience of pleasurable shopping. When the entertaining longing for things becomes an end in itself, shopping also begins to take the shape of autonomous play as a social frame. Things bought are just part of the experiences of enjoyment and amusement. These experiences are born in a social frame of the urban public world of the mall, where street sociability is the entertaining element. It is autotelic, because the pleasure is not reducible to purchasing.

The phenomena of *expectation* and *anticipation* play a central role in shopping. While wandering around in malls and in shopping streets, people have two different kinds of expectations that might even co-exist. First, they are searching for something particular, something specific which they expect to find, for instance the daily groceries, new shoes or a certain new record. Second, there is an openness to everything and anything, endless curiosity for something new, an openness that could be seen as a pure form of anticipation, because it is never determined by content, something particular and exact that one would hope to find. Still, the new things the shopper searches for should not be disturbingly new, but rather they should be easy to enclose in the familiar. Usually, it is not a question of revolutions in taste, but rather of sudden and small impulses. If waiting without any promise of redemption can feel good, then in a lot of shopping the pleasure comes from enjoying the state of expectation itself.

In this state of mind anything can be interesting for the shopper. In this way, the shopping mood is constituted as a certain kind of dreaming, but none the less in open relationship to the world around where one is sensitive to the contingent and sudden impulses of the environment (Campbell, forthcoming; cf. also Campbell, 1987: 77–95). Dreaming is a condition for the awakening of desire and for the wish to buy on impulse. Characteristic of shopping as a leisure activity are spontaneity and impulsiveness, the ability and willingness to change plans on the spur of the moment, susceptibility to changes in direction and route – a general swaying hither and thither. For many people, the most enjoyable purchases are surprising discoveries, something they have not deliberately gone to look for. As one of the interviewees says: 'Impulse buys, they're lovely.'

Shopping mood: relaxed restlessness

Someone doing participant observation in the East Centre Mall will soon be puzzled: how can the shoppers seem to be at once both very relaxed, unconcerned and calm, and, at the same time, somehow restless, moving all the time, heading in directions that seem to change every minute? Somehow shoppers seem to be at once totally satisfied and in a perpetual state of desiring something new. It is the same duality of peace and tension as in relaxing in a street café in the midst of liveliness. This paradox corresponds to the conclusion of Pasi Falk's theory of consumption, where he states that in the end, the lack and the desire are the same thing (Falk, 1994: 143). This paradox can be approached by sketching a dynamics of action with overlapping characteristics.

At one level, the shopper is very alert and tuned for basic openness, expecting to encounter something new. It is a question of a similar anticipatory expectation as in games of chance: something *might* happen. And this is the basic mood in the game of shopping. At another level, the shoppers are very relaxed and calm. The safety and peacefulness are found in the anonymity of the crowd, in the privacy, where one is freed from the imperatives of acting authentically and from all responsibilities. One can just concentrate on receiving and feeling impulses and impressions. At a third level, there is a restlessness that pushes the shoppers to find new directions for their quests. They are bound to follow all their sudden impulses. They are in the mood of relaxed strolling but constantly susceptible to anything desirable. This state has been taken advantage of in pedestrian streets and in the East Centre Mall. Shops tend to open on to streets and narrow the path shoppers walk on. It is made as easy as possible to fall for the surrounding goods. As a metaphor for this shopping mood, there are two artistic figures or sculptures in the main street of the East Centre Mall: a flying seagull and a fountain made from tall steel rods, over the surface of which water flows down. Flying and flowing are the ideal moods for the shoppers.

Playing with identity

Shopping seen as the enjoyable wandering around in shops and in malls means playful activity in the inner world of the shopper. Shoppers use things and people as stimulants to their imagination, searching for inner experiences. In the mall one is surrounded by a plenitude of seductive objects, and the feeling that there are endless possibilities of choosing something for oneself is enjoyable. Personal independence and autonomy in the crowd make possible the realization and creation of a personal taste. In the anonymity of the crowd it is easy to try on new things and styles, and the aggregation of choices slowly transforms oneself as a person.

Because of the shelter that anonymity brings, shoppers can explore and try on things and role-models previously strange to them. In the social sphere of the mall the feeling of anonymity, a sense of being no one in particular, is supported by the feeling of being 'somewhere else'. The sense of not being the self restrained in everyday life even urges one to open to the surrounding world of goods. The objects are both dreamed of and felt. Would this be right for me? Does it suit me? Do I suit this? It is a question of a play with images, of individual *mimicry* (see Caillois, 1961: 19–23). The relationship between the 'I' and some object is felt, probed and tried on, and the pleasure is born of playing the possessor of, or being clothed by the object, if only for the moment.

In going to shops, one 'gets ideas'. Shopping means fantasizing about oneself as someone else. It is imagining oneself being in a new way, as one pushes the limits of the image of the self in a desired direction. The mall is a theatre of longing, inventing and testing roles which lifestyles and styles of performing oneself formulate. It is the crowd and the public street sociability that create the setting of anonymity and a looseness of the bindings of everyday constraint. The sense of being not quite oneself, but being more or less no one – which is bound to happen in a crowd – is conducive to the illusion that one can be any self one happens to desire. This implies not that the shoppers are like chameleons changing their identities voluntarily, but, rather, that they are like children playing roles. Fundamental to the shopping experience is the pleasure and excitement arising from the potential opening and removal of the self's boundaries.

With the problem of self-building through consumption in mind, it seems essential to emphasize that the logic of transforming oneself through shopping is ludic in character. One does not go and buy a new identity. One enters the playground of the mall with open senses and endless longing, letting it all mingle in the mind to make up something new. The playfulness of shopping is above all in the mimicry of the performances that shoppers play to themselves in their private fantasy worlds. Shopping is a mental process whereby the most desired of aleatorily oncoming images of surrounding objects are selected, and the shopper uses them as probes for new styles of clothing, furnishing, eating, and so on. It is reasonable to assume that the course of the individual trajectories of self-building through shopping are highly predictable, and that the changes made are small. Still, we find it necessary to stress that lying at the core of the ideal shopping experience is the feeling of freedom from restraints of the self fixed to everyday life and a becoming aware of the open world around.

As a social form, shopping is made possible by the emergence of a modern subject with a strong inner world, a subject with a tendency for romantic dreaming; acting someone else, being present for oneself in an 'as-if' setting (Campbell, 1987: 189). But another condition is the social frame of street sociability, where one can operate in one's world of imagination without being disturbed by others. Hedonistic fantasizing presupposes an autonomy of play, which rests on being anonymous among other anonymous people. The crowd is both a mirror and a shelter in the creation of individuality and in the hiding behind masks that being part of a crowd requires.

Mother mall

Besides the fascination of the unpredictability of public street-life we have discussed thus far, there is always a chance that something unwanted might happen. Even though we emphasize unpredictability as the key to playful street sociability, it is important to note that this entertaining aspect of uncertainty relies on mutual trust between the 'players'; one must be sure that all the others play in accordance with the rules too. If the implicit rules of street sociability are not followed, the aleatory element, the feeling that 'something unexpected might happen', starts to generate fear. In the dark side of the streets and crowds there is fear of violence and robbery. An ideal shopping space is one with the advantages of open public place and without its disadvantages. This is what the East Centre Mall tries to optimize, as it tames the unexpected to become entertainment. It is a transparent space for commodity spectacles, where the whole space is so well lit that there are no dark shadows, and hence no threatening places.

Crime-rates in Helsinki are comparatively low, but the fear of crime still has a significant role in the experience of the city space (Karisto and Tuominen, 1993). In contrast, in the East Centre Mall people feel safe, a point emphasized by the interviewees. It is reasonable to assume that the sense of physical safety in the mall signifies more a calm atmosphere than actual security. Somewhat surprisingly, the East Centre Mall is not felt to be a place of hectic chaos of buying and selling, but a rather serene place. As we have stated above, the basis of relaxed shopping lies in the social condition of street sociable play, where everyone's inner life is sheltered and nourished by the anonymity of the crowd. This social order of the civilized public street is transplanted inside the East Centre Mall. It is supported by the romantic names of the two arcades of the mall – 'Bulevardi' and 'Pasaasi' – which refer to a time and place far away, in the golden age of Baudelaire's Paris. With no local connotations, the names amplify the touristic effect of a place 'somewhere else' and serve as icons of pleasurable, cultivated street-life. As a semi-public, controlled interior the mall has managed to tame the unexpectedness of city-life even better than Haussmann's boulevards did in Paris.

In addition to safety, the mall has other ways of taking care of the customers and caring for them. The taming of the unexpectedness that the presence of unknown people generates has a kind of counterpart in the sphere of goods. When one enters the mall, there is the exciting uncertainty of what kind of an article you will meet with next, but there is also confidence of the coming satisfaction. Once you know you are part of the community of consumers, the community of money, you know that your needs will be taken care of.

> *A male graduate engineer, aged 30*: When you walk here [in the mall], or actually before you come here, you know that if you need a certain article, you'll find it here for sure, without leaving the building.

> *A female teacher, aged 44*: Yes, it's a kind of positive feeling, and when you get through here, then everything is just fine.

> *A male accountancy manager, aged 30*: You don't have to know exactly what you want, only roughly.

In the tranquil playground of the mall the anxiety of not knowing what you want and how to get it fades. Instead, as soon as you enter the mall, there is a peaceful horizon of fulfilment, of desires acquiring their shape and dreams coming true. The tranquillity is both manifested and supported by the slower pace of walking. Once again: if you are in the mall, you are at your destination already. There is no hurry any more, because you are not going anywhere. You are doing what you came to do, wandering freely with open eyes in your 'own' world.

Needless to say, the situation is different during the Friday and Saturday rush hours. Naturally, the mall is crowded at these times and busy enough to irritate customers. It would be mistaken to argue that all the shopping in the East Centre Mall is nice and fun. Quite often it is troublesome and unpleasant, but this is not the general experience that the interviewees had of the mall. The mall is unpleasant when relaxed shopping does not succeed, when the idea of the mall does not work. As we have stated, the primary conditions for pleasurable shopping are ease and simplicity. A shopper wants to make an ideal shopping trip, but if there are too many people doing the same thing, they all fail. Therefore, the unemployed people and housewives interviewed were eager to take advantage of the quiet hours before midday.

While the mall is felt to offer everything one needs, as the commercials proclaimed and our interviewees confirmed, it also takes care to set the boundaries. The graduate engineer continues:

> It's nice that the assortment remains quite reasonable, so that I don't need to choose from an enormous range, because then it would be hard to decide. Someone has already thought it over for me, and I can choose one from the more appropriate assortment.

The mall opens customers' eyes to the multiplicity of things, but simultaneously it sets limits to their desires. The mall shows that these things here are everything you are to choose from, in order to stay in a reasonable and manageable world. A larger assortment would make you confused and unable to rationally handle your shopping, which is what pleasurable shopping requires. Many interviewees stressed the importance of being able to compare articles and prices between shops as the basis of their shopping. The aim is to get a general view of the supply by checking all the appropriate stores, and then, after comparing the articles, to choose the best one and buy it.

Here, some of the interviewees themselves referred to the metaphor of play. For the teacher quoted above, 'to purchase is always a kind of gambling', because one must be aware of the prices to be able to win, that is, to choose the cheapest and most advantageous option. But it is not like winning a game of chance, because in order to win one has to work by searching and comparing. The opposite way to win the game is not to buy at all, but to resist all the groping tentacles of the octopus. Self-discipline, overcoming oneself and leaving the mall with empty hands can also produce pleasure. A woman in her forties, working as an assistant financial inspector, explains: 'When there are the ''Crazy Days'' at Stockmann's, I go through the whole shop, from the top floor down. And it's such a wonderful feeling when you get out and haven't bought anything.' The mall takes care that your daily needs will be experienced as pleasurable desires, and that these vague desires then take the shape of reasonable wants you can put into practice. It works like a mother opening up the world for her eager children to conquer, but simultaneously restricting it to be small enough to be manageable without fear of chaos and confusion.

Encountering the self and the others in the mall

We have sought to analyse shopping activities in their natural surroundings in the East Centre Mall as part of urban life in Helsinki in the 1990s. Let us bring this attempt to an end by first summarizing the argument and then concluding with a notion of the shopper's relation to the community of the mall.

We began the analysis by stating that 'being with things' is the action itself when shopping in the mall. Then the action was shown to have both pragmatic and pleasure-seeking dimensions, which become intermingled with each other in the practice of shopping. Pleasure found in shopping was first connected with tourism, or, as we preferred to call it, *tripp*ism. Crucial here was the idea of the leisurely spending of time, of going 'somewhere else', either alone or together, away from the spheres of home and work in order to be freed from duties and in order to enjoy oneself. After these empirically based discussions, we elaborated more theoretically the nature of the shopping activity. We discussed the ways the mall generates possibilities for both sociality and the feel of independence. The pleasurable aspects of shopping activity were conceptualized with the notion of *play*, autotelic social action, which has a close connection with the more general concept of *social form* that is helpful when one tries to understand the shared nature of all shopping activity.

These two concepts were useful in the analysis of the role played by the urban surroundings in the activity of shopping that is situated in the midst of crowds and the *street sociability* inherent in public and semi-public spaces. The concept of play was utilized to analyse the separate and autonomous reality of enjoyable urban scenes which governs the social order and the orientation of urbanites in social situations. Central to the pleasurable shopping experience was the aleatory element of unexpectedness and novelty. But if the implicit rules of street sociability are not followed, the aleatory element, the feeling that 'something unexpected might happen', starts to generate fear. Thus, the mall flourishes when it is able to channel this aleatory element into excitement.

The success of the East Centre Mall is based on the way it sets up a free pleasurable game of chance as a shopping-oriented street-sociable field. The ideal of the light-hearted and carefree shopping seems to be reached in the social condition of play. We have pointed out the playful logic of transforming identity through shopping as a process involving the self and the possible self. The essential role of anticipation in the middle of numerous possibilities was also discussed. Playful trial and anticipatory longing postulate two simultaneous and interdependent worlds: the familiar one that is and the unknown one that could be. In the playful street sociability, in the freedom and looseness of its anonymity and in the touristic disengagement from everyday life, can be detected an autonomous and autotelic, trance-like aspiration reaching out from the demanding self and towards other people.

Note

1. This connection between domestic work and shopping skills has recently been emphasized by Colin Campbell (1995). What is distinctive in our interviews, compared to consumption studies conducted elsewhere than Scandinavia, is that, at least in principle, most families we interviewed claimed that the responsibilities for housework and shopping are shared by male and female equally; thus, the category of 'housewives' does not seem to be as central here as it is, for instance, for Daniel Miller's (1995) analysis of shopping.

References

Agamben, Giorgio (1989) *Enfance et histoire: Dépérissement de l'expérience et origine de l'histoire*. Paris: Éditions Payot.
Bakhtin, Mikhail (1968) *Rabelais and his World*. Cambridge, MA: MIT Press.
Barry, Judith (1981/2) 'Casual Imagination', *Discourse*, 4: 4–31.
Benveniste, Émile (1947) 'Le jeu comme structure', *Deucalion*, 2.
Bowlby, Rachel (1985) *Just Looking: Consumer Culture in Dreiser, Gissing and Zola*. London: Methuen.
Caillois, Roger (1961) *Man, Play and Games*. New York: Free Press.
Campbell, Colin (1987) *The Romantic Ethic and the Spirit of Modern Consumerism*. Oxford: Basil Blackwell.
Campbell, Colin (1995) 'Learning to Shop'. Paper presented at the Fifth Interdisciplinary Conference on Research in Consumption, Lund University, 18–20 August.
Campbell, Colin (forthcoming) 'Shopping, Pleasure and the Context of Desire', in Gosewijn van Beek and Cora Govers (eds), *The Global and the Local: Consumption and European Identity*. Amsterdam: Spinhuis Press.
Csikszentmihályi, Mihály (1975) *Beyond Boredom and Anxiety*. San Fransisco: Jossey-Bass.
Douglas, Mary and Isherwood, Baron (1980) *The World of Goods: Towards an Anthropology of Consumption*. Harmondsworth: Penguin.
Durkheim, Émile (1965) *The Elementary Forms of Religious Life*. New York: Free Press.
Falk, Pasi (1994) *The Consuming Body*. London: Sage.

Friedberg, Anne (1993) *Window Shopping: Cinema and the Postmodern.* Berkeley and Los Angeles: University of California Press.

Goffman, Erving (1967) *Interaction Rituals. Essays on Face-to-Face Behaviour.* Garden City, NY: Anchor Books.

Huizinga, Johan (1955) *Homo Ludens.* Boston: Beacon.

Karisto, Antti and Tuominen, Martti (1993) 'Kirjoituksia kaupunkipeloista' [Writings on Urban Fears]. Helsinki: Proceedings of the Information Management Centre no. 8.

Lakoff, George and Johnson, Michael (1980) *Metaphors We Live By.* Chicago: University of Chicago Press.

Lehtonen, Turo-Kimmo (1993) 'Shopping as a Meaningful Activity'. Paper presented at the Fourth International Conference on Consumption, Amsterdam, 8–11 September.

Lehtonen, Turo-Kimmo (1994) 'Shoppailun sosiaalinen muoto' [The Social Form of Shopping], *Sosiologia*, 31(3): 192–203.

Mäenpää, Pasi (1993) 'Niin moni tulee vastaan' [You Come Across So Many People]. Helsinki: Proceedings of the City Planning Office no. 14.

Miller, Daniel (ed.) (1995) *Acknowledging Consumption: A Review of New Studies.* London: Routledge.

Niemi, Iris, Pääkkönen, Hannu, Rajaniemi, Veli, Laaksonen, Seppo and Lauri, Jarmo (1991) 'Vuotuinen ajankäyttö, Ajankäyttötutkimuksen 1987–88 taulukot' [Annual Time Use: The Tables of the Time Use Survey 1987–88]. Research reports 183b. Helsinki: Statistics Finland.

Prus, Robert (1993) 'Shopping with Companions: Images, Influences and Interpersonal Dilemmas', *Qualitative Sociology*, 16(2): 87–110.

Prus, Robert and Dawson, Lorne (1991) '"Shop 'Til You Drop": Shopping as Recreational and Laborious Activity', *Canadian Journal of Sociology*, 16(2): 145–64.

Rook, Dennis W. (1985) 'The Ritual Dimension of Consumer Behavior', *Journal of Consumer Research*, 12: 251–64.

Schulze, Gerhard (1992) *Die Erlebnisgesellschaft: Kultursoziologie der Gegenwart.* Frankfurt am Main: Campus Verlag.

Sennett, Richard (1978) *The Fall of Public Man: On the Social Psychology of Capitalism.* New York: Vintage Books.

Shields, Rob (1994) 'The Logic of the Mall', in Stephen Harold Riggins (ed.), *The Socialness of Things: Essays on the Socio-Semiotics of Objects.* Berlin and New York: Mouton de Gruyter. pp. 203–29.

Simmel, Georg (1950a) 'The Metropolis and Mental Life', in Kurt H. Wolff (ed.), *The Sociology of Georg Simmel.* Glencoe, IL: Free Press. pp. 409–24.

Simmel, Georg (1950b) 'Sociability. An Example of Pure, or Formal, Sociology', in Kurt H. Wolff (ed.), *The Sociology of Georg Simmel.* Glencoe, IL: Free Press. pp. 40–57.

Simmel, Georg (1990) *The Philosophy of Money.* 2nd edn. London: Routledge.

Simmel, Georg (1992) *Soziologie: Untersuchungen über die Formen der Vergesellschaftung.* Frankfurt am Main: Suhrkamp.

Stallybrass, Peter and White, Allon (1986) *The Politics and Poetics of Transgression.* London: Methuen.

Urry, John (1990) *The Tourist Gaze: Leisure and Travel in Contemporary Societies.* London: Sage.

Weber, Max (1978) *The Protestant Ethic and the Spirit of Capitalism.* London: George Allen & Unwin.

Williams, Rosalind (1982) *Dream Worlds: Mass Consumption in Late Nineteenth-Century France.* Berkeley and Los Angeles: University of California Press.

7

SHOPPING, PLEASURE AND THE SEX WAR

Colin Campbell

This chapter is an attempt to interpret the main findings of a research project aimed at studying people's attitudes to 'shopping'.[1] The data concerned were obtained through group interviews with both men and women between the ages of 25 and 45 and drawn from socio-economic groups A, B, C1, C2 and D. They took place on the premises of a market research agency in Leeds between October 1991 and May 1992. Analysis of the interview transcripts suggested that the central findings were (a) a wide variation in the extent to which individuals expressed a positive attitude toward this activity, and (b) that this variation correlated with gender more than with any other single variable. The main aim of this chapter is to attempt to suggest a satisfactory explanation for these findings.

The results

When asked to express their general attitude toward shopping the responses of individuals ranged from declaring that they 'loved it', through those who professed comparative indifference, to those who said that they absolutely 'hated it'. Interestingly only a minority of respondents claimed indifference, the majority falling into one of the other two categories. Of course, 'shopping' is not an undifferentiated activity and some respondents frequently modified their responses by indicating a positive attitude towards one kind of shopping but not others. The dimensions along which such discrimination was most commonly made included the contrasts food versus non-food, regular versus occasional, and corner-store shopping versus a shopping 'trip' to the city centre. In addition, some interviewees also indicated that they felt positive about shopping under certain circumstances but not others; for example, when they had money to spend, were unaccompanied by children, felt in a good mood, or were buying clothes for themselves. These variations are clearly important and any comprehensive attempt to understand what determines whether people find shopping enjoyable or not would require that they are taken into account. However, they will be ignored here, for far more marked than such qualifications was the very noticeable pattern in the interview data linking a general predisposition to evaluate shopping positively or negatively with gender.

Essentially the results suggest that women were much more likely to express positive attitudes toward shopping than were men, and correspondingly that men were far more likely to express negative attitudes toward shopping than women. What is more, women were far more likely to express a strong positive attitude – that is, to say that they 'loved' shopping rather than that they merely 'liked' it. Correspondingly, men were far more likely to express a strong negative attitude – that is, to say that they 'hated' it rather than merely 'disliked' it. In addition, women were more prone to express positive attitudes toward a range of different kinds of shopping, whilst when males expressed a positive attitude it was more likely to be toward a very product-specific form of shopping (for example, shopping for records, computers or electrical goods). Finally, women were also much more likely than men to express a preference for shopping above other forms of leisure-time activity, such as watching a film or eating in a restaurant.

Interpretation

Consumption as a 'feminine' activity?

These data clearly confirm earlier research suggesting that 'shopping' in a modern industrialized, Western society is a thoroughly 'gendered' activity (Lunt and Livingstone, 1992; Oakley, 1976); and that it is widely perceived as closely linked with one gender rather than associated equally with both – specifically that it is regarded as linked with the female role and thus is itself seen as in some degree a 'feminine' activity. Consequently when children are socialized into their gender roles, they presumably learn, in the process of acquiring their identity, that shopping is basically part and parcel of the activities which help to define the female role, and especially of that distinctive sub-role of housewife, which is in turn seen as associated with the more general status-complex of wife and mother. By contrast, the adult male role is defined in terms of paid employment outside the home, that is, as a 'breadwinner' rather than a 'homemaker', and hence is identified in terms of activities quite unconnected with shopping. Indeed, since it has been suggested that, at root, the male–female dichotomy in modern societies is little more than a direct correlate of the more general contrast between production and consumption (as Gardner and Sheppard put it, 'traditional wisdom has it that men produced whilst women consumed', [1989: 46]), the feminine nature of shopping could be seen as a special instance of that equation. In reality such a claim seems too over-generalized as notions of masculinity and femininity would appear to be defined in terms of differences which apply to the spheres of both production and consumption. What one can state with confidence, however, is that there is a marked difference in those predominant activities which typify each sex's preferred pattern of consumption. Thus whilst 'drinking' and 'watching sport' constitute popular male forms of consumption, it would seem that 'shopping' is the preferred female mode of consumption par excellence. There is certainly ample evidence to show that shopping is a predominantly female activity, for not only do women constitute a majority of shoppers, but they also spend more time shopping than men, generally visiting more retail outlets and purchasing more products (see, inter alia, Gronmo and Lavik, 1988).[2]

It seems more than probable that it is this close identification of shopping with one gender which explains why the men in our sample were much less enthusiastic about the activity than were the women. If they perceived shopping to be a 'female' activity, then they would have a good reason for refraining from endorsing it; for they might feel that to do so could put their own masculinity in question. This interpretation is supported by other evidence which suggests that many men do indeed perceive shopping to be 'effeminate'. For as Oakley noted, 'There are husbands who will not go in shops, [and] husbands who will go in shops but who will not carry the shopping for fear of being labelled "effeminate"' (1976: 93). There are also comments from our interviewees which suggest that some men who, if they do admit to enjoying shopping when in the company of other men, seem to feel the need to accompany such a declaration with a 'disclaimer' of some kind.[3] Indeed it is possible that, for some men at least, this public expression of distaste for the activity is seen as a confirmation of their manhood.

Implications

If we accept that the association between shopping and femininity is as intimate as suggested here, then this has certain definite implications for the choices which face males in our society. For this would suggest that men are confronted with the stark choice of either avoiding the activity as much as possible, and thereby preventing any possibility of a threat to their masculinity, or of engaging in it and running the risk of being perceived as being 'effeminate'. The first alternative, that of complete avoidance, does appear to be an option favoured by some of the men in our sample; a tactic made feasible either by the exclusive use of mail order – which has the advantage of rendering one's shopping activity invisible to others – or by simply delegating it to their partner. Some men appear to have delegated not only all household shopping to their female partner but also all decisions concerning the purchase of items for their own personal use. As many as one-third of the women spoke of buying their partner's clothes for them, whilst only one or two women referred to their men buying clothes for them in return, and these items were usually gifts such as lingerie, and not the 'everyday' clothes that the women typically bought for their menfolk. However, total avoidance is hardly a realistic option for most men, if only because they do not all have partners willing or able to shop on their behalf, in which case an alternative tactic of 'distancing' seems to be employed. This involves the individual in making comments which, while indicating that they do shop, still serve to manifest a reluctant or less than complete involvement in the activity. Hence men attempt to distance themselves by remarking that they only do it 'when they must', and that they try to 'do as little as they can' or endeavour to 'get it over with as quickly as possible'. By thus indicating that they are not really committed to this 'feminine' activity, they thereby seek to limit any threat which it might pose to their gender identity. Yet the fact remains that many men do visit shops and not always under the pressure of dire necessity or with manifest reluctance. Some even indicated a degree of enthusiasm for the activity. So obviously not all men appear to feel that by behaving in this way they are thereby posing a threat to their sexual identity. How can this be explained?

Male and female ideologies of shopping

It would seem that an important factor that enables males to shop without endangering their masculine image is the presence in the culture of a male 'philosophy' of shopping, or more properly an 'ideology'; that is, a system of beliefs and attitudes which serve to define and justify the activity in ways that are consonant with masculine ideas and attitudes and hence can function to counter its popular and widespread feminine image. Men who shop are thus able to invoke this ideology in order to distinguish what they are doing from the 'feminine' form and thereby protect their gender identity. In other words, it is not just a question of there being a gender difference in the evaluation of the activity of shopping with women liking it and men disliking it. There would appear to be another, if less marked, contrast in the way in which shopping is itself defined, with both a male and a female version of what the activity involves.

Not surprisingly, perhaps, this contrast is formulated in terms of the instrumental versus expressive dichotomy, with men inclined to see shopping as a purely purchase-driven activity related to the satisfaction of need, whilst women are more likely to view it as a pleasure-seeking activity related to the gratification of wants or desires. That is to say, men presume that shopping only takes place when the existence of a 'need' has been established and they typically see no intrinsic value in the activity itself, judging it to possess worth purely as means to the end of acquiring goods. Women, on the other hand, whilst also aware of the value that shopping possesses as a means to this end, are also inclined to see the activity as possessing value in itself, independently of whether goods are purchased or not. Consequently they do not regard it is as an activity that is only justified by the presence of an unsatisfied 'need', but as also having an intrinsic 'recreational' value.[4]

This contrast is best illustrated in terms of the different attitudes expressed toward 'browsing' and the respective comparative valuations accorded to the 'costs' of time and money.

The male view of shopping is, in essence, one in which a 'need' (or needs) is (are) identified, an appropriate retail outlet is visited, and a suitable item purchased, after which the shopper returns home. As one of our interviewees expressed it, men like to 'go, buy it and come out'. Browsing or 'window-shopping' is not seen as having an essential part to play in this process, being seen as a waste of the precious commodity of time, whilst adding little or nothing to the success of the activity itself. Hence although male shoppers would not claim to be indifferent to price, and some do indeed place a high value on bargains, there is a sense in which the male philosophy can lead to a higher value being placed on time than money. Consequently if 'shopping around' means literally visiting many retail outlets, then it may well be rejected in favour of paying a higher price in order to keep the overall shopping time to a minimum. In this respect men closely resemble 'convenience shoppers' (Bellenger and Korgaonkar, 1980), and, perhaps paradoxically, the 'economic shopper' first identified by Stone (1954).

The female view, by contrast, regards browsing as an essential part of the activity of shopping, whether undertaken within or between retail outlets (for a discussion of 'browsing', see Bloch et al., 1989). It is seen as essential not just because it is the only means of obtaining information about the full range of items available for purchase, but also because it is recognized that it is only through direct exposure to the items for sale that the experience of 'desire' which generates 'wanting' can occur. However, in addition to this, women speak of the pleasure that can be gained from the activity of shopping whether any purchases are made or not. They refer, for example, to the pleasure to be had in 'just looking round', or in 'being able to wander and look at things' in a way which suggests that a fundamentally aesthetic and expressive gratification is involved. In fact, women are much more likely than men to refer to shopping in terms which imply an enjoyable leisure-time activity in its own right, on a par with tourism for example, as when they speak of a shopping 'trip'. Consequently women often look forward to going shopping and, in sharp contrast to the men, often embark on a trip without any very specific idea of what they intend to buy. Thus while men typically refer to the need to 'go shopping for X', women simply say that they are 'going shopping'. In addition, women are much more likely than men to combine a shopping trip with such other pleasurable activities as 'having a gossip' with a friend, or having a coffee or a meal, or indeed combining the two. Finally, since the activity has its own intrinsic satisfactions, women are fully prepared to invest time and effort in 'shopping around'; that is, in the direct physical sense of visiting a range of retail outlets. This is a significant fact because it means that women effectively acquire information about products and retail outlets 'cost-free' as it were, a mere by-product of enjoying their leisure time. By contrast, for those men who dislike shopping, acquiring such information is only possible at considerable 'cost'.

One way of looking at this marked gender difference in attitudes towards shopping is to regard males as effectively attempting to assimilate shopping to a 'work frame' while females assimilate it to a leisure one (at least as far as non-food shopping is concerned). This is to suggest that males, either because of their socialization or because of their traditional greater involvement in the world of paid work, are predisposed to see shopping as an activity that falls under the general heading of 'work', even if in their eyes this is qualified by the addition of the adjective 'women's'. Consequently not only do they not expect it to be enjoyable but they presume that the appropriate standards for evaluating it are those typically applied in the world of work, that is, rationality and efficiency. This leads to the tendency for men to emphasize the importance of first clearly defining a 'need', then the identification of an appropriate retail outlet where this need can be satisfied through purchase, followed lastly by the least expenditure of effort and money in finding and purchasing a suitable item. By contrast, women tend to apply a leisure frame when viewing non-food shopping, especially perhaps clothes shopping, regarding this as essentially recreation, sharply distinguishing it from 'work' whether of the paid or 'house' variety. It follows that they are necessarily inclined to define the activity as enjoyable and to reject any purely instrumental or utilitarian frame of reference. Like all recreation, they assume that the appropriate values are those of enjoyment and the indulgence of wants and desires in the legitimate pursuit of pleasure.

It is intriguing to speculate as to whether the application of these contrasting definitions is a consequence of the fact that women enjoy shopping more than do men, or whether it is the application of contrasting definitions that itself causes women to find it pleasurable while men do not. The suspicion must be that it is the latter of these two possibilities and that women find it easier than men to obtain enjoyment from shopping (especially for clothes), for two reasons. First, because female fantasies tend to revolve around what they look like much more than is true of males (see Singer, 1966) and hence can be more easily related to clothes and adornment generally; and, second, because females and not males are socialized into being the aesthetically skilled gender and hence find it easier than males to appraise and assess aesthetically significant goods.

These two ideologies serve to legitimate each gender's shopping style whilst belittling that of the other. This is achieved by presenting each style as the 'natural' and, above all, the 'rational' way to shop. Thus the male ideology not only offers men a way of engaging in shopping without undermining their own sense of gender, but also supplies them with arguments with which to portray the feminine mode of shopping as 'irrational', thereby re-enforcing the general male stereotype of women as prone to impulsive and irrational conduct. By employing the male model as a standard men are able to criticize women for (a) spending too long over the activity, (b) visiting too many shops, (c) being unable to make up their minds between alternative products, and (d) ending a tour of various shops by buying the item they first saw. In effect, as our respondents expressed it, women are presented as 'taking ages' and generally being 'too picky'.

In response women also employ their conception of shopping as an ideology; one that functions both to justify their own conduct and to deny legitimacy to the male one. However, unlike the men, it is not clear that women would have any great need to legitimate their conduct were it not the subject of criticism by males. Hence theirs could be seen as a predominantly defensive ideology. Women typically complain that men (a) don't spend long enough over the activity, (b) try to restrict their visit to only one or two shops, (c) don't know what they like (as opposed to what they need), (d) often buy the first thing they see in their haste to get out of the shop, and (e) are not knowledgeable about products or sensitive enough to variations in price. From the female viewpoint, therefore, men are not so much 'irrational' as simply poor shoppers, and as a consequence wasteful and 'uneconomic' in their purchases. Essentially this is because they are reluctant to shop around, both in order to discover the full range of items which are on offer related to any given need, but also in order to evaluate them and establish their price before making a purchase. As one of our respondents expressed it, 'men don't understand that it is necessary to compare, to look around to see if you see anything better at the other shops', consequently they 'don't appear to care about money'. Finally, men are also seen by women as 'unsophisticated' shoppers in the sense that they find it difficult to articulate their 'taste'.[5]

It is important to enter a caveat at this point. For although it is clear that men and women do commonly articulate very different attitudes toward shopping, their actual behaviour may not correlate too closely with the opinions and attitudes that they express. Apart from the fact that there is a considerable literature in the social sciences to suggest that there is commonly a gulf between accounts and actions (see Gilbert and Mulkay, 1984; Heritage, 1983), one would not expect beliefs that serve as an ideology to be an accurate representation of reality. So it is in this case, and there is evidence to suggest that the contrast in male and female shopping styles is not actually as marked as the expressed rhetoric would lead us to believe. For example, as indicated earlier, there is a form of shopping more favoured by men than women and in respect of which men quite clearly 'browse' rather than limit their time to the minimum. It is hard to categorize, but it was variously described by the male respondents as 'electronics, computers and things', 'gadgets, computers and electronics', 'technology', 'anything electrical' or 'electrical goods'; whilst the women respondents referred to it as 'do-it-yourself shopping', or 'car shopping'. Perhaps a suitable general term for this category would be 'technology shopping' since this is its main item, although it does also appear to include books, records and videos. The memorable phrase used by one man to describe it was '[videos] or stuff like that, something that you don't have to pull over your head'. As this last phrase suggests, this form of male-dominated shopping is commonly contrasted with clothes shopping, which is regarded as very much a female domain. However, 'technology shopping' is also often not seen by men as 'shopping' at all, but regarded, rather like buying a car or even a house, as a serious economic transaction. By carefully defining what constitutes shopping in this manner men are able to maintain their general representation of this activity as feminine despite their own extensive involvement in it.

There is also a degree to which women, although commonly celebrating their skill and prowess in shopping, may in reality acutely dislike some features of the activity and consequently attempt to minimize their involvement in it. In these contexts they behave more like men, trying to restrict the time and reducing the number of retail outlets visited. This is most likely to be the case with food shopping, which many of our female respondents disliked, seeing it as part of the 'job' or 'work-role' of housewife. Interestingly, although most women did see this as a kind of 'shopping', they tended to differentiate it from 'real shopping' by referring to buying groceries as 'doing the shopping' (thus demonstrating its affinity to 'doing the housework'), while buying clothes was referred to as 'going shopping' (thus revealing its affinity with the pleasant activity of 'going out'). Hence both men and women could be said to be redefining what constituted shopping in line with their more general ideological positions.

Conclusion

By developing a distinctive male view of shopping, in contradistinction to the prevalent female one, men can be seen to be doing two things. First, they are providing a rationale which enables them to shop without compromising their gender identity. Second, they are articulating an ideology which serves to condemn and belittle women's conduct in a sphere in which they manifestly predominate. By so doing men avoid having to acknowledge the fact that women not only perform this critical consumption task, but also manifest superior expertise in the process. By employing the male ideology as a basis for a critique, women's expertise and skill in this sphere is effectively discounted, and hence their conduct represented as confirming the less than flattering male stereotype of women that is often articulated by men with respect to other areas of social life. In this way, women's dominance and competence in this field – which could otherwise be seen as a threat to male societal and cultural dominance – is thus successfully 'neutered'. However, it would appear that one consequence of the male endorsement of this ideology is that they necessarily come to regard shopping in such a way that the activity itself can rarely become a source of pleasure.[6] One suspects that the female ideology of shopping functions not only to legitimate women's shopping style as opposed to that favoured by men, but also to justify women in excluding males from this activity. The ability to present males as effectively 'incompetent' at shopping enables women to argue that men should not be allowed to engage in the activity and hence to volunteer (sometimes with a mock show of reluctance) to do their shopping for them. Thus, although the fact that the majority of men's clothes are still bought by women could be seen simply as evidence of the widespread male aversion to shopping, it could also be seen as evidence of the extent to which females have 'taken over' an activity that males might otherwise have undertaken by themselves, a 'take-over' that one suspects is facilitated by an argument something along the lines of 'you only make a mess of it; you'd better leave it to me'.

Equal but different?

If gender is indeed as closely associated with contrasting shopping ideologies as is suggested here, then it is interesting to speculate on what happens when couples engage in cooperative or 'joint shopping'. By 'joint shopping' or 'joint purchasing' is meant those occasions when both partners feel it necessary to participate in the purchase process, as is most likely to happen when the couple are contemplating buying an expensive consumer durable, such as a bed, cooker, sofa or even a car. These shopping events are of special interest as they would appear to present considerable difficulties.[7] For, if the previous analysis is correct, then such joint shopping would be a context in which the conflict of shopping styles should generate considerable strain and conflict. After all, it is clearly not possible to both 'shop around', examining every variety of suitable product on sale, and at the same time keep the time spent shopping to the minimum needed to go to one shop and purchase a suitable product. It would seem that when a man and woman go shopping together somebody has to abandon their favoured shopping style and adopt (or at least accommodate themselves to) the style favoured by their partner. In view of this it is unsurprising to discover that many of our respondents – of both genders – indicated that they 'hate' to shop with their partner and reported that they were simply unwilling to go shopping with them. It must be said, however, that, in general, the men seemed to be less accommodating in this respect than the women. On the other hand the interviewees did report occasions on which 'joint shopping' took place, suggesting that the two ideologies might not be totally incompatible. Indeed, although the male and female shopping ideologies appear to have been formulated in opposition to one another and are employed by each gender to legitimize its own conduct and denigrate that of the other, it is not clear that they are necessarily opposed. They could even function as complementary dispositions. The most obvious way in which this might work in practice would be through a simple division of labour designed principally to relieve the male of the 'chore' of browsing. Thus a wife, for example, in her capacity as 'browser', may visit a variety of shops to establish the range of products on offer before returning with her husband so that they may jointly make a final choice from a predetermined short-list. However, in other situations there may be a truly complementary division of labour in which each partner makes a distinctive yet different contribution to the process of selecting and purchasing the item concerned. Thus, the male may well have been given the task of drawing up the technical specification of need relevant to such a purchase; perhaps involving a visit to a retail outlet, perhaps merely collecting brochures or making telephone calls, whilst the female is delegated to make any 'aesthetic' decisions, such as those concerning colour, style or texture. This complementary form of shopping can often be witnessed at the point of sale. Such a complementarity does not, of course, necessarily mean that each accords equal respect to the contribution made by the other, but it could provide the basis for a mutual recognition of the advantages offered by the preferred shopping mode of the other.

The future is female?

The identification of male-related shopping attitudes as focused on a rhetoric of 'need', in contrast to a female one centred upon a rhetoric of want and desire, has some interesting implications in the light of prevailing theories of the 'postmodern' consumer society. For since these characteristically present a concentration on the satisfaction of needs with a 'traditional' or premodern consumer milieu, while presenting the modern (or postmodern) mode as one that is centred on the gratification of wants and desires (Campbell, 1987; Featherstone, 1991), then it follows that men are 'old-fashioned' consumers while women are modern and sophisticated consumers. If one assumes that such a trend will continue, with more and more emphasis placed on recreational consumption and with shopping envisaged as an enjoyable and essentially leisure-time activity akin to tourism and other 'expressive' forms of entertainment (Campbell, 1995), then this could mean that men are faced with the choice of either becoming more and more 'feminine' (perhaps along the lines of the much-heralded 'New Man') or of being increasingly marginalized in the emerging 'postmodern' consumer society.

Notes

This chapter is based on a paper presented at the Conference on Consumption, Risk, Pleasure and the State in Contemporary Capitalism, Helsinki, Finland 14–19 June 1993. It was written with the assistance of Paul Hewer.

1. Shopping is taken to mean any activity which involves the treatment of products as potential objects of acquisition through purchase – especially by means of visits to retail outlets.

2. Interestingly, whilst research undertaken by social scientists also suggests that they have tended to equate shoppers with women, they have not to date fully explored the implications of this gender bias for theories of consumerism.

3. It is worth observing in this connection that whilst the principal basis for this shopping = feminine assumption appears to be the close association of shopping with the role of 'housewife', there are other dimensions involved. It would appear, for example, that there is a widespread perception among men that retail outlets are 'women's spaces', ones which they may even be reluctant to enter, as Oakley (1976) notes. Commonly staffed by women, tastefully decorated, warm, quiet and comfortable, with piped music and pleasant perfumes, many shops are perceived by men as possessing a fundamentally 'female ambience'.

4. This distinction resembles others which have been proposed, notably the 'recreational' versus 'convenience' or 'economic' shopper typology proposed by Bellenger and Korgaonkar (1980). It is not identical, however, as the instrumental/expressive contrast is essentially an analytic dichotomy arising out of a theoretical schema (see Parsons, 1951). For the use of the instrumental/expressive dichotomy in relation to shopping, see Brusdil and Lavik (1989).

5. There is evidence in the transcripts of the interviews to suggest that men have difficulty making judgements of taste. Possibly this is because they have less sensitivity to fashion than women. If this is true it would explain the fact that some men either try to avoid aesthetic decisions altogether or operate with simple (and unchanging) rules, such as 'I always choose black', or 'I always go for plain jumpers', etc.

6. It could be that male recreational shoppers were under-represented in our sample because it did not accurately reflect the population as a whole. One obvious omission concerned young males, who do have something of a reputation for browsing in groups – albeit usually in such a restricted milieu as record or computer shops. It could also be that males from the professional classes (again rather under-represented in our sample) would be less likely to endorse the somewhat restricted conception of masculinity which seems to prevail among lower status males.

7. Of course, these shopping ideologies may bear little relationship to real conduct. In which case conflict may not occur on these occasions. There is in fact some evidence to suggest that the shopping behaviour of males may not accord with their ideology as they do indeed 'browse', albeit in a restricted context.

References

Bellenger, Danny N. and Korgaonkar, Pradeep K. (1980) 'Profiling the Recreational Shopper', *Journal of Retailing*, 56(3): 77–92.

Bloch, Peter H., Ridgway, Nancy M. and Sherrell, Daniel L. (1989) 'Extending the Concept of Shopping: An Investigation of Browsing Activity', *Journal of the Academy of Marketing Science*, 17(1): 13–21.

Brusdil, Ragnhild and Lavik, Randi (1989) 'Shopping Becomes More than Buying – On the Trace of the Future Consumer'. National Institute for Consumer Research, Lysaker, Norway.

Campbell, Colin (1987) *The Romantic Ethic and the Spirit of Modern Consumerism*. Oxford: Basil Blackwell.

Campbell, Colin (1995) 'The Sociology of Consumption', in Daniel Miller (ed.), *Acknowledging Consumption: A Review of New Studies*. London: Routledge. pp. 96–126.

Featherstone, Mike (1991) *Consumer Culture and Postmodernism*. London: Sage.

Gardner, Carl and Sheppard, Julie (1989) *Consuming Passion: The Rise of Retail Culture*. London: Unwin Hyman.

Gilbert, G. Nigel and Mulkay, Michael (1984) *Opening Pandora's Box: A Sociological Analysis of Scientists' Discourse*. Cambridge: Cambridge University Press.

Gronmo, Sigmund and Lavik, Randi (1988) 'Shopping Behaviour and Social Interaction: An Analysis of Norwegian Time Budget Data', in Per Otnes (ed.), *The Sociology of Consumption: An Anthology*. Oslo: Solum Forlag. pp. 101–18.

Heritage, John (1983) 'Accounts in Action', in G. Nigel Gilbert and Peter Abell (eds), *Accounts and Action: Surrey Conferences on Sociological Theory and Methods*. Aldershot: Gower. pp. 117–31.

Lunt, Peter K. and Livingstone, Sonia M. (1992) *Mass Consumption and Personal Identity*. Buckingham: Open University Press.

Oakley, A. (1976) *Housewife*. Harmondsworth: Penguin.

Parsons, Talcott (1951) 'Toward a General Theory of Action', in Talcott Parsons and Edward Shils (eds), *Toward a General Theory of Action*. New York: Harper & Row. pp. 209–18.

Singer, J.L. (1966) *Daydreaming*. New York: Random House.

Stone, Gregory P. (1954) 'City Shoppers and Urban Identification: Observations on the Social Psychology of City Life', *American Journal of Sociology*, 60(1): 36–45.

8

THE SCOPIC REGIMES OF SHOPPING

Pasi Falk

Overture

The following will be a preliminary speculation on the different scopic registers (Lacan, 1991) and regimes (Metz, 1983) involved in the activity of shopping. My aim is to locate the visual dimensions of shopping within the broader context of the urban experience and to relate them to other kinds of public places and ritual sites such as movie theatres, cafés, shopping sites, museums, art galleries and chapels – the two last mentioned acting as paradigmatic reference cases for my speculation on the mystery of shopping. All these places and sites mould and support a specific scopic regime and all of them are linked to the *street* scene, the public space par excellence.

The street, in a more general sense, is not only a linear space of transportation (the traffic) but a complex of dynamic spatiality (or spatial dynamics) constituted as an *experience* through the movement of the body and the eyes – of the passers-by: *flâneurs*, (potential) shoppers, and so on. As an experiential space the street is created in the very act of the walking and seeing bodies filling the street with a web of routes, including all the freely chosen turns and halts. And even if the freedom of movement is more or less restricted by certain boundaries – one cannot walk through a wall and one should not walk against a red light – it nevertheless opens up a realm of 'walking rhetorics' (Certeau, 1984: 100–2); the possibility of composing individual routes as spatial 'narratives'.[1]

Furthermore, the street has an ambiguous character in terms of the topological distinction between inside and outside. On the one hand the street is *the* public space inside the city – concretized in the city walls of a premodern town. On the other hand, even though the street is a physical exterior (the open air), it borders on the walls of the buildings, thus making the street into a corridor or 'gallery' (according to the etymological roots of the world) – without a roof. Now, in the case of (relatively) pure residential areas in which the (house) walls of the street function as boundaries dividing the space into public (outside) and private (inside), the interior-like character of the street remains marginal.

However, when moving 'down town' to the sites of shopping and (other) urban leisure activities the spatial configuration looks different. The distinction between outside and inside tends to be dissolved, first, due to the fact that the wall of the building/street does not demarcate the distinction of public/private and, second, due to the physical marginality of the 'wall' in between. At the street level – which is the level of the scopic register of the pedestrian[2] – the glass doors are open for free access and the glass walls visually penetrable. The endless row of shop, café, gallery (and so on) windows[3] and the open doors transform the street scene into an experiential character of the street. Moving from in front of a shop window to the interior of the shop does not actually cross any significant boundaries – neither between the public and private nor between the inside and outside. The classical 'monument' (cf. Foucault) to the overcoming of the inside/outside distinction is, of course, the shop arcades (or galleries or passages) which may be conceived of either as interiors opened up at both ends or as covered (pedestrian) streets.

Now, it may appear that I am losing the shopper somewhere in the crowd, in the stream of passers-by in the street. In a certain respect this is actually my intention, that is, to place the shopper in the wider context of 'street life' and the various scopic registers it involves. Then again, the activity of 'recreational shopping' (Hewer and Campbell, Appendix, this volume) hardly exists in a pure form. It is usually intertwined with other 'narrative' moves in and out of other places such as cafés, cinemas or perhaps even art galleries – more seldom into a chapel, which will be the topic of the next section.

The chapel

Menaggio is a small town by Lake Como in northern Italy. Although it is a kind of centre for tourism in that area it has somehow maintained the atmosphere of an Alpine health and holiday site of the late nineteenth century, with a few classic hotels (especially the Grand Victoria Hotel, in which I stayed for some days in July 1992) and the Strand Boulevard with small numbers of casually but traditionally dressed elderly guests slowly passing by. Menaggio seems to lack all the signs of modern industrial tourism and somehow its temporal coordinates lag about one century behind. But of course the town has its shopping street, not only for the tourists mostly travelling through but also for the locals.

There is, however, something else in the same street: a small chapel in the same row with the shops. It is a dark inward-looking hole between two outward-looking lighted shop windows. Menaggio has of course also a 'real' church, one which 'stands out' in its vertical structure reaching up to heaven.

So people are walking on the shopping street and looking at the shop windows. The tourists move slower due to their double orientation as tourist shoppers, that is, 'gazing' both at the whole milieu (cf. Urry, 1990) and the small-scale attractions, especially the shops and the objects they offer for display. The locals are moving somewhat faster and in a more goal-directed manner, taking the milieu for granted and looking primarily for (and at) possible novelties in the shop windows. Both locals and tourists may occasionally pop into the shop to have a closer look, occasionally proceeding to the realm of contact senses: touching, trying on (a shirt), smelling (a perfume) and tasting (a slice of cheese).

The locals tend to shop more instrumentally, focusing primarily on everyday necessities, while the tourists are more probably engaged in a pure form of recreational shopping – again due to the double orientation: being inside a double liminal space of a tourist site and the leisure realm of shopping.

These two shopper groups differ also in terms of their relationship to the *camera obscura* and the *camera lucidas*, that is, to the chapel, which in this respect may be conceived of as an inversion of the shop. The chapel is almost exclusively visited by the locals. It is too small to be recognized as a tourist *sight* worth *seeing* and thus only those 'outsiders' suffering from excessive curiosity – such as myself – end up stepping inside this tiny anti-shop to make an observation; two or three people spending their silent moment apart from the more or less noisy street-life.

Then again, the contrast between the small chapel and the shops is not really that obvious after all. Assuredly the chapel is dark in contrast to the bright shops and a silent space devoid of the noise of the street and the voices (speech) near the shop windows and inside the shops. But if one focuses on the aspects of *movement* and *looking* – or moving the body and the eyes – the contrast turns out to be less obvious. Both the chapel and the shop halt the moving (walking) body for few minutes and in both cases the eyes are fixed on a stable object, at least for a while. Both function, though in different ways, as spaces of pause and as an escape from the flow of the street. Both offer an opportunity to rest one's eyes: stopping the movement of the eye by fixing it, for a while, on a specific object or sight which could be characterized as the small-scale visual attractions of a cityscape.[4]

But there is also a difference in the character of the small pause and the 'eyes' rest'. The chapel promotes a kind of inward meditative look as an aspect of a peace-seeking mind while the shop invites a more extroverted and active look which possibly leads to closer contact with the objects, from the shop window to the shop interior and from looking to touching, and so on. One could say that this difference of the implied looks corresponds to the ways in which these two spaces open up towards the street: the dark entrance of the chapel invites only those with an intention to enter while the shop with its bright lights and the exhibiting openness (the shop window) is constructed to catch the potential shopper's look, to stop her/his motion, to get her/him inside in the hope of a purchase.

Nevertheless, even if we disregard the shopkeepers' interests, both the shop window and the shop interior offer an opportunity for an unforced and legitimate pause not only for shoppers but for anyone in the street. The 'show window' gives – as Baudelaire noted – 'the flâneur somewhere to rest his eyes' (cited in Barry, 1982: 14), but it also acts as a legitimate stop for a private detective keeping a proper distance from, and avoiding eye contact with, the one tailed in the street (a familiar scene found in the detective film genre).

Interlude

Certainly this is only a part of the urban tale. The urban space offers a whole range of natural opportunities for shorter or longer halts involving different types of scopic regimes. Unlike cars in traffic, where the movement is determined by traffic lights and rules giving priority to an instrumental scopic regime ('the industrial gaze'; see Lesemann, 1982; 80)[5], pedestrians have wider room for manoeuvre. People do not just move through the street channel from point A to point B. They wander and look around – the *flâneur* with 'his voyeuristic, aestheticizing gaze' (Potter, 1986) – also offering themselves to be looked at (the 'exhibitionist' dandy); stop to have chat with someone they meet in the street; pop into a pub for a beer while looking out at the flow of the street-life; join the 'audience' of a street café (in Paris) with the chairs facing the street stage; rest for a while on a park bench allowing the eyes to wander over everything between the clouds in the sky and the endless flow of passers-by; or perhaps waiting for someone at the street corner.

However, if someone hangs around a street corner too long, perhaps also violating the unwritten scopic code by looking too intensively (staring, gazing) at the others, he or she runs the risk of being interrupted with charges of 'loitering', an offence defined in the municipal ordinance. Thus not only movement (the simple case: do not cross the street on a red light) but also non-movement in the urban public space has certain boundaries defined by explicit or implicit rules – the latter of which apply also to the definition of the proper use of the scopic register in the same way there are certain (culturally relative) unspoken rules concerning the proper interactive distances between people who know or do not know each other (from absolute strangers to symbiotic lovers).[6] Nobody is sued due to impolite gazing at others. Nevertheless, the boundaries of normalcy are endangered. The behaviour is 'inappropriate in the situation', as the phrase goes (cf. Goffman, 1966: 3).

The bi-directionality of looks – the 'chiasm of looks' as Merleau-Ponty (1981) puts it – between strangers in the urban (street) scene is expected to respect the code of transient eye contact. A prolonged look – a *gaze* – which disregards the counter-look is experienced by the 'object' as offensive, provided that it does not lead to an unspoken agreement of reciprocity (mutual flirt, or perhaps 'love at first sight').[7]

Thus the scopic regime of reciprocal looks in the street and other public spaces is usually realized according to the principle of role switching. One may look, even intensively, at the other from a certain distance until the other looks back. At this moment the first one should turn his/her eyes elsewhere in order to avoid an awkward situation. The avoidance of prolonged eye contact is, however, supported by the dynamic character of street life. Due to the rapid pace of moving bodies, heads and eyes, and due to the relative short distances between people in the crowded street scene, reciprocal looks are structured into a serial switching of looks, oscillating between the roles of a voyeurist and an (in)voluntary exhibitionist (cf. Sennett, 1978), as it were.

In other words, most of the reciprocal looks are not simultaneous but *serial*: looking at the other when he or she is not looking at you, in a way anticipating and avoiding the possible counter-look. This seriality of quick looks supports a scopic regime which gives priority to the *glance*. And so also does the occasional transient eye contact which 'normally' should not last longer than a fraction of a second.

The eyes do not actually rest in the dynamics of reciprocal looks between urbanites (although longer distances allow a more restful mode of people watching while cancelling the effect of a counter-look). Thus the visual regime of reciprocal looks could be seen as an aspect of '(over)stimulating' urban life, a topic that was much discussed in the late nineteenth century, more systematically in psychological and sociological discourse. The phenomenon was evaluated from poetical–positive (Charles Baudelaire) through the theoretical–neutral (Georg Simmel) to the pathologizing–negative (George Beard).

However, despite the differences there seemed to be a shared understanding of the factors causing (over)stimulation: the hectic pace of urban life in general, the noise and the expanding field of visual 'stimulation' – especially in the urban public realm. For George Beard (1869) these were among the factors causing 'neurasthenia' or nervous exhaustion, while for Georg Simmel (1950) the overload triggered a defence reaction which he called 'blasé-attitude' – a kind of psychological filter softening the constant flow of stimulation. In the case of human encounters in the public space this implied the creation of a psychological distance compensating for the lack of physical distance (for example, rush hour in the underground).

Then again, above I focused primarily on the scopic registers in which the object of the look is another live human being, that is, a configuration in which the look is met by an actual or potential counter-look.[8] This is, however, only one aspect of the 'stimulative' urban milieu. The major visual stimulation in the urban scene is realized in settings in which the object of the look is a material thing, an image, an event – or, better, some kind of synthesis of these 'objects': the world of goods, moving or static printed pictures, advertising, spectacles, and so on. Actually the scenes of shopping – from small boutiques to department stores and shopping malls – are primary spaces for a scopic regime in which the object of the look does not have eyes and thus does not look back. Or, to be more precise, even if the 'thing' or image (a photograph of a person 'looking at you') looks at you it does not *really* see you.

This configuration implies another kind of (urban) scopic regime which allows a variety of more or less prolonged looks – gazing, watching and staring – furthermore opening up the possibility of resting one's eyes. Watching a movie is, from a technical point of view, something like a two-hour stare (as a rule, lacking a counter-look), nevertheless it does not exemplify a stronger sense of an 'eyes' rest'; it catches the spectator's attention, fixing his/her eyes on the screen and simultaneously locating the dynamic flow in the moving pictures. The same applies also to other spectacles in which the movement of the spectator is replaced by the mobile performance. So it seems that we have to look elsewhere for situations in which the halts of the body and eyes and prolonged looks can be realized as individual choices, and, furthermore, where the things/images looked at are more or less immobile. Such settings are found, for example, in institutions such as museums, exhibition halls and art galleries, the latter of which will be my second case on the way to the shopping sites.

The art gallery

Some weeks after Menaggio I stayed for two days in New York collecting impressions from a 'real' urban milieu and spending half a day visiting some of the art galleries. It was not my first experience of an art gallery but what inspired me to some reflection was the specific contrast between the inside (the gallery) and the outside (the street), a contrast somewhat reminiscent of the one I experienced in the street chapel of Menaggio. Leaving behind the fleeting impressions of the street, I wandered slowly through the silent rooms of the gallery stopping in front of the 'things' of art – mostly immobile, even the 'mobiles' – and resting my eyes for a shorter or longer moment.

The art gallery is inhabited with things and images to be looked at but not to be touched (as a rule). The space is constructed for uni-directional gazing, rendering a marginal role for possible reciprocal looks – even in the case of performance art involving live human bodies. A great number of the art exhibitions function, of course, also as 'shops' offering the works of the artists for sale and hoping to attract potential customers, not only those who are 'just looking' (cf. Bowlby, 1985). Anyway it may be presumed that a vast majority of visitors belong to the latter group.

In distinction to the chapel the art gallery promotes an outward look, perhaps even one searching for new aesthetic 'stimulation'. In this respect it is not that far from the scopic regime of shopping. On the other hand, these two regimes differ in the way the look is related to the moving body and the other senses. In the art gallery the distance to the object is (usually) maintained while in the shopping context it may lead to close encounters and to the use of contact senses (cf. above). Thus the 'shopping gaze' (cf. Turo-Kimmo Lehtonen and Pasi Mäenpää, Chapter 6, this volume) is reminiscent of the approaching gaze of a hunter who 'eats' the anticipated quarry with his eyes before it is caught and (later) actually eaten (Mattenklott, 1982).

Finale

Then again, when dealing with recreational shopping, in which the necessity of purchase – and purchasing necessities – has a marginal role, a hunter's gaze taken to its realization (the purchase) is a mere potentiality. It is occasionally realized but the sense of shopping is not reduced to it. This implies that we still have to keep in focus the other experiential dimensions of shopping, which, in terms of the scopic regimes, has many common characteristics with the cases dealt with above. The activity of shopping involves, besides the 'hunting gaze', other kinds of visual pleasures which have practically nothing to do with the possibility of purchase and much in common with 'just looking' in art galleries. After all, where else in the city does one find places in which self-reflection[9] through things and images is made possible as an individually autonomous movement through space, including the freedom to create one's own routes with all the small pauses, halts, looks and touches one chooses?

In a paradoxical way the shopping sites, from department stores to shopping malls, act not only as elements in the (over)stimulative urban milieu but also as places for escape from the 'rapid and uninterrupted fluctuation of external and internal impression' (Simmel, 1950) in the street, as sanctuaries offering an ordered space for the eyes to rest and the hands to touch. And then, there are other, more specific pleasures (and pains) of shopping already dealt with in the preceding chapters of this book.

Notes

1. The spatial narratives could even be transformed into actual mini-scale travel accounts ('first I went to x, then I saw y and we stayed for a while in z . . .') or structured in the form of a treasure map ('take five steps in x direction then turn right and follow y until you see z . . .'), which is something other than the non-narrative topographical map.

2. While staying as a visiting scholar in Cambridge some years ago I discovered a simple scopic indicator which distinguished tourists from the locals: the tourists tend to look (gaze) vertically, on a large scale, at the buildings, façades and sites while the locals applied a horizontal scopic register which operates primarily on a small scale: glancing at others, stopping in front of shop windows to have a look, etc. – at the street level. Then again, the tourist operates on both large-scale and small-scale scopic registers (looking at people, shop windows, etc.). This makes the tourist into a kind of super-shopper (cf. the text below) and the home town shopper into a small-scale tourist. However, it should be noted that the relationship between these two is metonymical rather than metaphorical – or not only analogical but also homological, in the biological sense of the word.

3. The function of these 'windows' is actually an inversion of those of private/closed spaces (home, office, etc.). In the latter the light flows from the outside to the inside and the looks flow in the opposite direction. In the former the flows are inverted: the looks are mainly directed from the outside to the inside and the light flows in the opposite direction – especially in the case of shop (show) windows. In the case of, say, a Parisian boulevard café these flows are more balanced (looking in/out, light in/out). In a way the brothel 'shop windows' in the red light district of Amsterdam represent a kind of voyeuristic synthesis of these two window functions: looking from the outside into the intimate space of the bedroom which could be your 'own' for a while (with the curtains drawn).

4. The large-scale attractions of the cityscape – corresponding to the scale of the (romantic) landscape – have a central role in the scopic regime of the tourist (cf. Culler, 1981; Urry, 1990).

5. The institution of 'cruising' actually fights against this type of scopic regime by foregrounding the more interactive principle of reciprocal looks (to see and to be seen) from a slowly moving car. Cruising is, however, an exception to the rule, frequently considered by the police as a violation of the traffic regulations.

6. Edward T. Hall (1966) revealed the cultural variations of the appropriate distances in different types of interactive situations. However, it may be argued that the growth of urban complexes has in itself a homogenizing effect on the forms of coexistence and interaction in the city which overrides to a certain extent the cultural differences. Consequently the interpretations of urban conduct analysed, for example, by Simmel in 'The Metropolis and the Mental Life' (1950) and by Erving Goffman in 'Behavior in Public Places' (1966), 'Interaction Ritual' (1967), and 'Relations in Public' (1972), have relevance beyond the specific city cultures of their 'home towns'.

7. For an urban poetic soul such as Baudelaire the crossing of looks may also be the ecstatic 'shock' experience of 'love at *last* sight', according to Walter Benjamin's reading of Baudelaire's poem 'À une passante'. The transitory moment of the chiasm of looks creates an (imaginary?) shared experience of a possible love which is never realized. Interestingly, Benjamin compares Baudelaire's deep look to the one depicted in young Stefan George's poem (included in George's 'Hymnen: Pilgerfarten'). In a similar situation the latter turns his longing look away, not daring to 'drown in your eyes' (Benjamin, 1939). To trivialize the difference for the present purposes: Baudelaire takes the risk of prolonged chiasm of the looks while George withdraws his look according to the scopic code. Anyway, both cases confirm Richard Sennett's (1978) characterization of the city as 'a place where strangers can meet' – and remain strangers or turn, for example, into lovers.

8. This scopic configuration includes also the marginal case of the 'panoptical eye' – paradigmatically represented by Bentham's panoptical prison (Foucault, 1979) – which excludes the other's possibility of looking back at the 'surveyor': Orwell's 'Big Brother . . . watching you'. This forced uni-directionality of the gaze is an aspect of a 'subject-objectifying' power technology formulated by Foucault (already present in his earlier concept of the 'clinical gaze' [Foucault, 1976]), but from a wider perspective the negative character (danger and violence) of a look *which cannot be returned* may be traced back to the idea of the 'evil eye' which lies outside one's (scopic) control. The evil eye (*mal occhio*) never looks into your eyes and thus you never know when it will hit you. Something of this evil or panoptical eye is still present in the modern city, not only as a constant awareness of the possibility of being watched – the anxious constellation analysed by Sartre (1966: 340–400) – but also in the more concrete street scene in the form of a passer-by wearing dark sunglasses, especially those acting as one-way mirrors.

9. In this context 'self-reflection' should also be understood literally. I am not referring merely to the abundance of actual mirrors in the (clothing) shops but more generally to the glass walls of a shopping street showing (off) the world of goods and functioning simultane-ously as mirrors collapsing 'the images of the gazing spectator onto the displayed items' (Barry, 1982: 19). The same applies to the sites of reciprocal looks such as in 'Tom's Diner', Suzanne Vega's song (1982), which depicts a scene as follows: 'There's a woman/ On the outside/ looking inside/ Does she see me? /No she does not/ Really see me/ Cause she sees/ Her own reflection . . .'

References

Barry, Judith (1982) 'Casual Imagination', *Discourse*, 4: 4–31.
Beard, George M. (1869) 'Neurasthenia, or Nervous Exhaustion', *Boston Medical and Surgical Journal*, 80: 245–59.

Benjamin, Walter (1939) 'Some Motifs in Baudelaire', in Hanna Arendt (ed.), *Illuminations*. London: Fontana Press. pp. 152–96.

Bowlby, Rachel (1985) *Just Looking: Consumer Culture in Dreiser, Gissing and Zola*. London: Methuen.

Certeau, Michel de (1984) *The Practice of Everyday Life*. Berkeley and Los Angeles: University of California Press.

Culler, Jonathan (1981) 'Semiotics of Tourism', *American Journal of Semiotics*, 1(1–2): 127–40.

Foucault, Michel (1976) *The Birth of the Clinic: An Archaeology of Medical Perception*. London: Tavistock.

Foucault, Michel (1979) *Discipline and Punish: The Birth of the Prison*. Harmondsworth: Penguin.

Goffman, Erving (1966) *Behavior in Public Places*. New York: Free Press.

Goffman, Erving (1967) *Interaction Ritual: Essays on Face-to-Face Behavior*. New York: Allen Lane and Penguin.

Goffman, Erving (1972) *Relations in Public. Micro-studies of the Public Order*. New York: Harper & Row.

Hall, Edward T. (1966) *The Hidden Dimension*. New York: Doubleday & Co.

Lacan Jacques (1991) *The Four Fundamental Concepts of Psycho-analysis*. Harmondsworth: Penguin.

Lesemann, Klaus (1982) *Sanieren und Herrschen*. Giessen: Verlag Hans Huber.

Mattenklott, Gert (1982) *Der übersinnliche Leib*. Hamburg: Rowholt.

Merleau-Ponty, Maurice (1981) *Phenomenology of Perception*. London: Routledge.

Metz, Christian (1983) *Psychoanalysis and Cinema: The Imaginary Signifier*. London: Macmillan.

Potter, Daniel L. (1986) *Finding a City to Live in: Metaphor and Urban Subjectivity in Baudelaire and Mayakovsky*. Vol. 29. Stanford Honors Essay in Humanities, Stanford: Stanford University Press.

Sartre, Jean-Paul (1966) *Being and Nothingness*. New York: Washington Square Press.

Sennett, Richard (1978) *The Fall of Public Man: On the Social Psychology of Capitalism*. New York: Vintage Books.

Simmel, Georg (1950) 'The Metropolis and Mental Life', in Kurt Wolff (ed.), *The Sociology of Georg Simmel*. New York: Free Press. pp. 409–24.

Urry, John (1990) *The Tourist Gaze: Leisure and Travel in Contemporary Societies*. London: Sage.

APPENDIX
RESEARCH ON SHOPPING – A BRIEF HISTORY AND SELECTED LITERATURE

Paul Hewer and Colin Campbell

A BRIEF HISTORY OF RESEARCH ON SHOPPING

The following does not claim to be a comprehensive overview of all those discourses on modern shopping which might be considered relevant from a research point of view – either as insightful descriptions or as more systematic accounts of some aspects of the phenomenon. Consequently this excursus has a certain focus which is defined by the following two criteria. First, it focuses on systematic research on the topic which involves theoretically grounded procedures of interpretation, and, second, it deals with research that understands shopping as an object of research – as a social and cultural complex of practices – which is reducible neither to a mere part of the economic system nor to a field of manipulative intervention. According to these criteria, this brief history of research on shopping could also be called a brief history of the sociology of shopping, provided that the term 'sociology' is understood in a broad sense.

Typologizing shoppers

There has long been a small but significant literature on the history of shopping in general (Adburgham, 1964), whilst, in the 1980s, historians turned to studying the development of the department store in particular (Benson, 1986; Miller, 1981; Williams, 1982). At the same time, market researchers, geographers and town planners have long shown an understandable interest in the retail environment (Gardner and Sheppard, 1989; Goss, 1993). Until very recently, however, sociologists have all but completely neglected the phenomenon.

Yet, in fact, the origins of the sociology of shopping can be traced back to the 1950s and an article entitled 'City Shoppers and Urban Identification' by the American Gregory P. Stone (1954). This formed what was part of Stone's Master's thesis for the University of Chicago in which he sought to assess the implications of Louis Wirth's outline of the character of urban life. For Wirth, the critical feature of city life was that although contacts between people were face to face they were nevertheless 'impersonal, superficial, transitory and segmental' (1964 [originally 1938]: 70). Stone, however, was less than convinced that the character of city life was nothing but a mass of depersonalized relationships (Wirth, 1964: 42), believing, instead, that it contained activities which could be seen to foster the seeds of personalization. So he decided to analyse shopping to see if it did indeed facilitate this form of social integration.

Consequently Stone interviewed over one hundred women, asking them about their attitudes toward shopping, focusing in particular on their reasons for choosing one kind of retail outlet rather than another. Stone then used the answers to these questions on retail patronage to identify four basic orientations toward shopping. These were: the 'economic' shopper whose primary considerations are price and quality; the 'personalizing' shopper, who rates such economic criteria as of secondary importance when compared to the opportunity for interaction which the experience offers; the 'ethical' shopper, who claims to employ moral considerations in the choice of retail outlet; and finally the 'apathetic' shopper. who conducts this activity simply out of necessity.

Gregory Stone's typology has had a significant influence upon subsequent research on shopping, although the issues of urban sociology which first caused him to focus on this phenomenon have not, as yet, been pursued by subsequent investigators. Rather, those who came after him were more interested in the possible commercial benefits which his typology seemed to offer. Thus Ronald Stephenson and Ronald Willett (1969) attempted to correlate the manner in which shoppers purchase goods with the number of stores they are likely to frequent; whilst William R. Darden and Fred D. Reynolds (1971) similarly sought to link Stone's shopping orientations with the purchase of products, in this case cosmetics, concluding that the economic shopper will use cosmetic products which are 'socially visible' whereas the personalizing shopper tends to use products that 'aid elementary hygiene' (1971: 507). Then, also building on Stone's work, George P. Moschis (1976) suggested a classification of shopping orientations constructed around the different kinds of information which individuals employ in selecting products. Shoppers are thus classified on the basis of whether they are brand or store loyal, or whether they are problem-solvers (that is, they resemble Stone's 'economic' shopper) or psycho-socializers, which is to say that they are inclined to emulate the consumer behaviour and choices of others.

Other researchers have gone on to see how far Stone's typology can be applied to specific subsections of the consumer population. Thus Louis E. Boone et al. (1974) compared the shopping orientations of Mexican-Americans living in Texas with middle-class Anglo-Americans from Oklahoma. Their main findings were that the Mexican-Americans were more likely to be 'economic' shoppers, whereas the Anglo-Americans were more personalized in their shopping orientations. William G. Zikmund (1977), in his analysis of the grocery shopping behaviour of the black population of Oklahoma, reduced Stone's scheme to just three types of shoppers: the 'comparative', the 'neighbourhood' and the 'outshopper'; a classification based primarily on the distance individuals are willing to travel, the frequency of their shopping trips and the use they make of shopping lists. Finally, Robert Williams et al. (1978) refined Stone's typology in their study of grocery shoppers, identifying four main types – convenience, price-oriented, apathetic and involved.

As already noted, little of this research displays much of the sociological awareness which marked Stone's original essay, being motivated more by the specific needs of consumer research. None the less, some of this work can be of interest to sociologists, especially since in recent years some consumer researchers have begun to break free of the rather narrow concerns which commercial considerations dictate (see Belk, 1995). Thus Bellenger et al. (1977), although starting with a Stone-type typology, go on to identify the important category of the 'recreational' shopper. Unlike the 'convenience shopper' (who basically resembles 'economic man'), the recreational shopper gains satisfaction from the act of shopping itself. This point is also made by Williams et al. (1978), who identify a category of shoppers who are distinctive in gaining pleasure from the process. Their claim is also that the act of shopping can provide recreational benefits in itself quite separate from any gains which may be obtained through the process of exchange. Then, in a later article, Bellenger and Korgaonkar (1980) add to the description of this kind of shopper, claiming that such shoppers will spend more time shopping, are more likely to shop with others, are less likely to know what they want, and are inclined to continue with the activity even after they have made a purchase. They also provide data which suggest that such shoppers are more likely to be women than men (see Campbell, Chapter 7, this volume), and to be from white-collar rather than blue-collar households.[1]

Despite this tendency for shopper typologies to increasingly incorporate some reference to the experiential aspects of shopping, it is still largely the case that the buying aspect of shopping is foregrounded. To that extent research still tends to be constructed with the interests of market and consumer research in mind rather than those of sociology. To this extent and despite Stone's pioneering work, the construction of shopper typologies has yet to break clear of this legacy. Shopping is still predominantly viewed as a means–end activity centring on the exchange of money for goods. But then of course this tendency is one which the market research perspective shares with neoclassical economics (Hollis and Nell, 1975), economic psychology (van Raaij, 1988) and both rational action and rational choice theory (Coleman and Fararo, 1992; Elster, 1986), all of which unproblematically equate shopping with buying. However, these other perspectives also tend to regard shopping as necessarily constituting a series of decisions taken by individuals who are blessed with both clear knowledge of their own needs and wants and perfect information about the market. Consequently there is a tendency to present the shopper as both an information-processor, a problem-solver and a rational maximizer of utility. Yet the limitations of such a model have long been known. Apart from the a priori nature of the assumptions that they contain, such perspectives ignore all the evidence which shows, as George Katona (1953: 312) has argued, that problem-solving behaviour is a relatively rare occurrence, and that habitual behaviour is a far more common feature of consumer behaviour.

Instrumental and recreational shopping

If it is accepted that shopping is not reducible either to information-processing, decision-making or indeed even buying, then it has to be accepted that the reason why people go shopping cannot be simply equated with a desire to experience the satisfactions to be obtained from the purchase and use of goods. In which case, why do people shop? This was the very question that Edward Tauber (1972) posed in his short but seminal article. Tauber asked thirty men and women why they went shopping, and, from the responses he received, identified a range of motives which had little to do with the act of buying. These ranged from role-playing, diversion from the routine of daily life, self-gratification, learning about new trends and ideas, physical activity, sensory stimulation, social experiences outside the home with friends, communication or gossip with others, peer group interaction, enjoying status and authority, and finally the pleasures of haggling.

Subsequently Westbrook and Black's (1985) research provided broad support for Tauber's findings, but also added two further motivations: first, the motivation of choice optimization, or finding exactly what one wants; and, second, the anticipated utility derived from a new product.[2] In retrospect Tauber's article can be seen to be important because by finally freeing the shopping motive from the buying motive he succeeded in indicating something of the wider social significance of the act of shopping. In particular he opened the way for shopping to be viewed as a form of leisure.

In an article entitled 'Women, Shopping and Leisure', Myriam Jansen-Verbeke (1987) claims that this is indeed how shopping should be viewed – as a form of leisure in its own right – and not simply as a mundane and routine aspect of people's daily lives. She illustrates this point by listing the range of activities which her analysis of shopping in the Netherlands suggests is covered by the term 'shopping'. This includes eating and drinking in cafés and bars, sight-seeing, visiting museums or markets, being with one's friends, and simply walking around. In a sense this should not have been such a revelation for earlier studies had intimated that shopping was more than simply the buying of goods. As early as 1963 Stuart U. Rich had indicated something of the importance of browsing, a point subsequently taken up by Peter Bloch et al. (1989). In their article they define browsing as a 'search activity that is independent of specific purchase needs or decisions' (Bloch et al., 1989: 13). Freed of this necessity, the shopper gains pleasure through the process of 'just looking' (Bowlby, 1985; see Falk, Chapter 8, this volume), which, although it involves obtaining information about products, can also be enjoyed as an end-in-itself. All of which strongly suggests that shopping should perhaps be understood as constituting a distinctive form of experience, one with its own peculiar activities, pleasures and satisfactions, rather than being treated as simply a means to an end.

But then it is useful to reflect on what is actually known about the practice of shopping, as there is a tendency in some contemporary (postmodern?) discourses for speculation about the 'consumer society' to be illustrated by anecdote rather than supported by references to research data. To begin with there is the apparently simple question of how much time people spend shopping. Although such data are scarce it would seem that, according to the Henley Centre (1991), the average person in Britain spends 4.6 hours per week shopping for essential and other items. Naturally this figure masks a number of important differences. For example, while employed men spend 3.3 hours; employed women spend 4.2. hours; whilst for the unemployed, men spend 3.1 hours and women spend 5.1; differentials which are consistent with those found by Gershuny and Jones in 1987. Hawes (1987, 1988), meanwhile, found that 'Americans spend three to four times as many hours a year shopping as their counterparts in Western European countries' (Schor, 1992: 107). All of which suggests that shopping is indeed an important component of most people's 'free time'.

However, this does not imply that shopping has turned into mere leisure, which as such could be defined as an unambiguous activity pattern. Shopping 'for' is not simply transformed into shopping 'around', that is, looking around, but rather these different modes of interacting with the world of goods – involving purchase or not – become actually intertwined and thus structured into various constellations. Consequently one can note that 'shopping' is not an undifferentiated activity. Indeed, as Robert A. Westbrook and William C. Black (1985) observe in their critique of shopper typologies, shopping for groceries cannot properly be compared with shopping for cosmetics or indeed with shopping in a department store.

Thus, if one is to understand the phenomenon of shopping, it is probably as important to differentiate between types of shopping as it is to discriminate between types of shopper. Hence these figures, unless broken down into more meaningful sub-divisions, probably tell us very little. The most significant division would seem to be that between regular grocery shopping, or 'provisioning', and other forms of shopping (mainly, it would seem, for clothes), this latter form being exemplified in the 'shopping trip' (Campbell, forthcoming). This is a distinction which most shoppers themselves recognize as significant, overlapping as it often does with the contrast between shopping viewed as a labourious or as a recreational activity (Prus and Dawson, 1991; Lehtonen and Mäenpää, Chapter 6, this volume).

None the less, there is little doubt that many people do obtain great pleasure from shopping – or at least from some kinds of shopping – and that shopping is a leisure-time pursuit that has increased in importance in recent decades. However, it is not entirely clear what exactly constitutes the source of the pleasure. Campbell has argued that the pleasure to be derived from shopping is related to the extent that it is self-determined, with the activity understood as an 'autonomous field of action' (forthcoming) in which the pleasure is correlated to the extent to which individuals are able to undertake it as they please. In addition, Campbell links the experience with the ability to want goods, arguing that such desire is not programmed but rather occurs as the by-product of pleasurable 'self-directed browsing' (ibid.). On the other hand, Pasi Falk (Chapter 8, this volume) has emphasized the different kinds of scopic pleasures which shopping can provide, pleasures which are quite independent of the act of purchasing, but stem directly from the freedom which the shopper has to engage in 'just looking' as well as employing the other sensory registers (touching, trying on, and so on) (p. 185).

Shopping as a gendered activity

In so far as there are good grounds for discriminating between types of shoppers then the contrast that is of the greatest significance is not one which featured either in Stone's typology or indeed in any of those derived from it. For research suggests that the critical fact about shopping is the extent to which it is a gendered activity. Now, as noted, Stone only interviewed women and in this respect his research embodied the common wisdom of his day, which was that shopping was a predominantly female activity. This assumption was so taken-for-granted in the consumer research and marketing worlds that it has only been in comparatively recent years that men as well as women have been included in the samples of shoppers chosen for study. This fact in itself reveals the one sense in which shopping is 'gendered', which is to say that it is (or at least, it has been) popularly regarded as mainly a 'female' activity, in effect a sub-role of the status of 'housewife' (Lunt and Livingstone, 1992; Oakley, 1974). The second and closely related sense in which it is gendered is revealed in the data suggesting that men and women have differing shopping styles and shopping habits (Campbell, Chapter 7, this volume).

Indeed, if gender is applied to the typologies outlined earlier it is found that men are more likely to be convenience or apathetic shoppers, whilst women are more likely to be recreational shoppers (see Bellenger and Korgaonkar, 1980; Tatzel, 1982). Several studies support this view, confirming that when it comes to shopping men are largely apathetic, preferring non-participation to involvement; a fact which causes Fischer and Arnold to comment (in the course of their analysis of Christmas shopping) that 'men enact their masculinity through more limited involvement in the event' (1990: 354).[3] More recently, Lunt and Livingstone's (1992: 92) research has further confirmed this view, suggesting that men are more likely to be 'routine' shoppers than women, whilst women are more likely to be 'leisure' shoppers. Other work has suggested that the gendered nature of this activity extends to the commodities which men and women are likely purchase when they do go shopping (Pahl, 1989, 1990; see also Peters, 1989).

Of course, if shopping is perceived by men to be a 'female' activity, then it is hardly surprising that they approach it in a different spirit from women, attempting to limit their involvement as far as possible. In this respect one would expect these differential patterns of shopping activity to be mirrored by their different attitudes and beliefs, and research in this field has indeed suggested that this is the case. For Campbell (Chapter 7, this volume) has shown that men and women tend to endorse contrasting 'ideologies' of shopping, systems of belief which, whilst legitimating that style practised by their own sex, tend to denigrate that associated with the other. Hence while men seek to devalue the activity, denying that it has recreational potential and insisting that it is a purely instrumental act to be completed as quickly as possible, women regard it as an important activity, one requiring skill as well as time, energy and commitment, but also one which offers significant recreational awards. Despite claims that these differences are diminishing in contemporary society, there are as yet no data to determine whether this is the case or not.

Given the considerable gender differences in both shopping behaviour and attitudes it is naturally intriguing to wonder how couples manage to undertake this activity jointly. As yet the data available are limited, despite the fact that Elizabeth Wolgast's pioneering article 'Do Husbands or Wives Make the Purchasing Decisions?' first appeared in 1953. Wolgast's data revealed that while women tended to dominate in the purchasing of household appliances, men were more likely to have influence in the choice of the family car. Subsequent research has confirmed this pattern of differential influence for a range of products. This includes research on cars (Cunningham and Green, 1974; Jaffe and Senft, 1966; Newman and Staelin, 1972; Sharp and Mott, 1955; Wolgast, 1953); household appliances from 'white' to 'brown' goods (Jaffe and Senft, 1966; Woodside and Motes, 1979); homes (Kelly and Egan, 1969); and basic foodstuffs.

However, it is not clear that asking couples who made the decision to buy a given consumer good is a very sensible question to ask, for, as Scott (1976) observes, both parties will tend to claim different levels of control. Indeed Woodside and Motes (1979) criticize such analyses on the grounds that they place too much emphasis upon the purchasing decision. They argue that this act needs to be broken down into a series of micro-states, ranging from initially suggesting the idea, to deciding upon the style, type, size or brand of item. In addition, there is the question of who visits the store (and indeed who decides which store to visit) as well as who ultimately makes the actual purchase. Finally, one may note that here, too, studies have tended to presume that shopping equals decision-making and buying and hence have generally failed to examine how couples cope with their differential expectations and experiences of this activity when undertaking it together.

Notes

1. This tendency to construct typologies is still a dominant feature in studies of shopping behaviour. Thus, very recently, two social psychologists have included one in their study of consumption. Peter K. Lunt and Sonia Livingstone in their book *Mass Consumption and Personal Identity: Everyday Economic Experience* (1992) present four categories of shoppers: those with 'careful', 'routine', 'thrifty' and 'alternative' orientations.

2. Sigmund Gronmo (1984: 18) presents an alternative case when he suggests that consumer behaviour can be compensatory or conducted to assuage an individual's lack of esteem in other areas of their daily lives, such as the loss of self-esteem through unemployment.

3. Ann Oakley (1974: 93) writes of men who will not carry the shopping bags for the fear of being labelled effeminate.

References

Adburgham, Alison (1964) *Shops and Shopping, 1800–1914: Where, and in What Manner the Well-dressed Englishwoman Bought her Clothes.* London: Allen and Unwin.

Belk, Russell (1995) 'Studies in the New Consumer Behaviour', in Daniel Miller (ed.), *Acknowledging Consumption: A Review of New Studies.* London: Routledge. pp. 58–95.

Bellenger, Danny N. and Korgaonkar, Pradeep K. (1980) 'Profiling the Recreational Shopper', *Journal of Retailing*, 56(3): 77–92.

Bellenger, Danny N., Robertson, Dan H. and Greenberg, Barnett A. (1977) 'Shopping Centre Patronage Motives', *Journal of Retailing*, 53(2): 29–38.

Benson, Susan Porter (1986) *Counter Cultures: Saleswomen, Managers, and Customers in American Department Stores, 1890–1940.* Urbana and Chicago: University of Illinois Press.

Bloch, Peter, Ridgway, Nancy M. and Sherrell, Daniel (1989) 'Extending the Concept of Shopping: An Investigation of Browsing Activity', *Journal of the Academy of Marketing Science*, 17(1): 13–21.

Boone, Louis E., Kurtz, David L., Johnson, James C. and Bonno, John A. (1974) 'City Shoppers and Urban Identification Revisited', *Journal of Marketing*, 38: 67–9.

Bowlby, Rachel (1985) *Just Looking: Consumer Culture in Dreisen, Gissing and Zola*. London: Methuen.

Campbell, Colin (forthcoming) 'Shopping, Pleasure and the Context of Desire', in Gosewijn van Beek and Cora Govers (eds), *The Global and the Local: Consumption and European Identity*. Amsterdam: Spinhuis Press.

Campbell, Colin (1995) 'The Sociology of Consumption', in Daniel Miller (ed.), *Acknowledging Consumption: A Review of New Studies*. Routledge: London. pp. 96–126.

Coleman, James S. and Fararo, Thomas J. (eds) (1992) *Rational Choice Theory: Advocacy and Critique*. London: Sage.

Cunningham, Isabella, C.M. and Green, Robert T. (1974) 'Purchasing Roles in the U.S. Family 1955 and 1973', *Journal of Marketing*, 38: 61–8.

Darden, William R. and Reynolds, Fred D. (1971) 'Shopping Orientations and Product Usage Roles', *Journal of Marketing Research*, 8: 505–8.

Elster, Jon (ed.) (1986) *Rational Choice*. Oxford: Basil Blackwell.

Fischer, Eileen and Arnold, Stephen J. (1990) 'More than a Labor of Love: Gender Roles and Christmas Gift Shopping', *Journal of Consumer Research*, 17: 333–45.

Gardner, Carl and Sheppard, Julie (1989) *Consuming Passion: The Rise of Retail Culture*. London: Unwin Hyman.

Gershuny, J. and Jones, S. (1987) 'The Changing Work–Leisure Balance in Britain, 1961–1984', in J. Horne, D. Jary and A. Tomlinson (eds), *Sport, Leisure and Social Relations*. London: Routledge and Kegan Paul. pp. 9–50.

Goss, Jon (1993) ' "The Magic of the Mall": An Analysis of Form, Function, and Meaning in the Contemporary Retail Built Environment', *Annals of the Association of American Geographers*, 83(1): 18–47.

Gronmo, Sigmund (1984) *Compensatory Consumer Behavior: Theoretical Perspectives, Empirical Examples and Methodological Challenges*. Oslo: University of Oslo.

Hawes, Douglass K. (1987) 'Time Budgets and Consumer Leisure-Time Behavior: An Eleven-Year-Later Replication and Extension (Part I – Females)', *Advances in Consumer Research*, 14: 543–7.

Hawes, Douglass K. (1988) 'Time Budgets and Consumer Leisure-Time Behavior: An Eleven-Year-Later Replication and Extension (Part II – Males)', *Advances in Consumer Research*, 15: 418–25.

Henley Centre (1991) *Leisure Futures*. London: Henley Centre for Forecasting.

Hollis, Martin and Nell, Edward J. (1975) *Rational Economic Man: A Philosophical Critique of Neo-Classical Economics*. Cambridge: Cambridge University Press.

Jaffe, Laurence J. and Senft, Henry (1966) 'The Role of Husbands and Wives in Purchasing Decisions', in Lee Adler and Irving Crespi (eds), *Attitude Research at Sea*. Chicago: American Marketing Association. pp. 95–110.

Jansen-Verbeke, Myriam (1987) 'Women, Shopping and Leisure', *Leisure Studies*, 6: 71–86.

Katona, George (1953) 'Rational Behavior and Economic Behavior', *Psychological Review*, 60(5): 307–18.

Kelly, Robert F. and Egan, Michael B. (1969) 'Husband and Wife Interaction in a Consumer Decision Process', in Philip R. McDonald (ed.), *Marketing Involvement in Society and the Economy*. Fall Conference Proceedings. Chicago: American Marketing Association. pp. 250–8.

Lunt, Peter K. and Livingstone, Sonia M. (1992) *Mass Consumption and Personal Identity: Everyday Economic Experience*. Buckingham: Open University Press.

Miller, Michael B. (1981) *The Bon Marché: Bourgeois Culture and the Department Store, 1869–1920*. London: Allen and Unwin.

Moschis, George (1976) 'Shopping Orientations and Consumer Uses of Information', *Journal of Retailing*, 52(2): 61–70.

Newman, Joseph W. and Richard Staelin (1972) 'Pre-Purchase Information Seeking for New Cars and Major Household Appliances', *Journal of Marketing Research*, 9: 249–57.

Oakley, Ann (1974) *The Sociology of Housework*. Bath: Martin Robertson.

Pahl, Jan (1989) *Money and Marriage*. London: Macmillan.

Pahl, Jan (1990) 'Household Spending, Personal Spending and the Control of Money in Marriage', *Journal of the British Sociological Association*, 24(1): 119–38.

Peters, John F. (1989) 'Youth Clothes-Shopping Behavior: An Analysis by Gender', *Adolescence*, 24: 575–80.

Prus, Robert and Dawson, Lorne (1991) '"Shop 'Til You Drop": Shopping as Recreational and Laborious Activity', *Canadian Journal of Sociology*, 16(2): 145–64.

Rich, Stuart U. (1963) *Shopping Behavior of Department Store Customers: A Study of Store Policies and Customer Demand, with Particular Reference to Delivery Service and Telephone Ordering*. Boston: Harvard University Press.

Schor, Juliet (1992) *The Overworked American: The Unexpected Decline of Leisure*. New York: Basic Books.

Scott, Rosemary (1976) *The Female Consumer*. London: Associated Business Programmes.

Sharp, Harry and Mott, Paul (1955) 'Consumer Decisions in the Metropolitan Family', *Journal of Marketing*, 21: 149–59.

Stephenson, Ronald P. and Willett, Ronald P. (1969) 'Analysis of Consumers' Retail Patronage Strategies', in P.R. McDonald (ed.), *Marketing Involvement in Society and the Economy*. Chicago: American Marketing Association. pp. 316–22.

Stone, Gregory P. (1954) 'City Shoppers and Urban Identification: Observations on the Social Psychology of City Life', *American Journal of Sociology*, 60: 36–45.

Tatzel, Myriam (1982) 'Skill and Motivation in Clothes Shopping: Fashion-Conscious, Independent, Anxious, and Apathetic Consumers', *Journal of Retailing*, 58(4): 90–7.

Tauber, Edward (1972) 'Why Do People Shop?', *Journal of Marketing*, 36: 46–59.

van Raaij, Fred W. (1988) 'Information Processing and Decision-Making Cognitive Aspects of Economic Behaviour', in Fred W. van Raaij, Gery M. van Veldhoven and Karl-Erik Warneryd (eds), *Handbook of Economic Psychology*. Dordrecht: Kluwer Academic Publishers.

Westbrook, Robert A. and Black, William C. (1985) 'A Motivation-Based Shopper Typology', *Journal of Retailing*, 61(1): 78–103.

Williams, Robert H., Painter, John J. and Nicholas, Herbert R. (1978) 'A Policy-Oriented Typology of Grocery Shoppers', *Journal of Retailing*, 54(1): 27–43.

Williams, Rosalind (1982) *Dream Worlds: Mass Consumption in Late Nineteenth-Century France*. Berkeley and Los Angeles: University of California Press.

Wirth, Louis (1964) 'Urbanism as a Way of Life', in Albert J. Reiss (ed.), *Louis Wirth on Cities and Social Life*. Chicago: University of Chicago Press.

Wolgast, Elizabeth (1953) 'Do Husbands or Wives Make the Purchasing Decisions?', *Journal of Marketing*, 23: 151–8.

Woodside, Arch and Motes, William (1979) 'Perceptions of Marital Roles in Consumer Decision Processes for Six Products', in Beckwith et al. (eds), *American Marketing Association Proceedings*. Chicago: American Marketing Association. pp. 214–19.

Zikmund, William (1977) 'A Taxonomy of Black Shopping Behavior', *Journal of Retailing*, 53(2): 61–72.

RESEARCH ON SHOPPING – SELECTED LITERATURE

The following selected bibliography of research on shopping is provided to give the reader a demonstration of the diversity and richness of current research on this topic. Here the books and articles are divided – for reasons of clarity – on the basis of the following disciplines: economics, geography, history, literature, marketing, psychology and sociology. However, the disciplinary categorization should not be taken too strictly due to the fact that a number of the references fall between disciplines and could actually appear in more than one category. The final two sections provide a list of journals which have had special issues on consumption topics and a list of existing bibliographies in the field.

Economics

Fine, Ben and Leopold, Ellen (1993) *The World of Consumption*. London: Routledge.

Friedman, Monroe (1988) 'Models of Consumer Choice Behaviour', in Fred W. van Raaji, Gery M. van Veldhoven and Karl-Erik Warneryd (eds), *Handbook of Economic Psychology*. Dordrecht: Kluwer Academic Publishers. pp. 332–57.

Hollis, Martin and Nell, Edward J. (1975) *Rational Economic Man: A Philosophical Critique of Neo-Classical Economics*. Cambridge: Cambridge University Press.

Katona, George (1953) 'Rational Behavior and Economic Behavior', *Psychological Review*, 60(5): 307–18.

Mittal, Banwari and Lee, Myung-soo (1989) 'A Causal Model of Consumer Involvement', *Journal of Economic Psychology*, 10(3): 363–89.

Oumlil, A. Ben (1983) *Economic Change and Consumer Shopping Behavior*. New York: Praeger.

Scitovsky, Tibor (1976) *The Joyless Economy: An Inquiry into Human Satisfaction and Consumer Dissatisfaction*. New York: Oxford University Press.

Scitovsky, Tibor (1986) *Human Desire and Economic Satisfaction: Essays on the Frontiers of Economics*. Brighton: Wheatsheaf.

van Raaji, Fred W. (1988) 'Information Processing and Decision-Making Cognitive Aspects of Economic Behaviour', in Fred W. van Raaji, Gery M. van Veldhoven and Karl-Erik Warneryd (eds), *Handbook of Economic Psychology*. Dordrecht: Kluwer Academic Publishers. pp. 74–106.

Warneryd, Karl Erik (1988) 'Economic Psychology as a Field of Study', in Fred W. van Raaji, Gery M. van Veldhoven and Karl-Erik Warneryd (eds), *Handbook of Economic Psychology*. Dordrecht: Kluwer Academic Publishers. pp. 3–40.

Geography

Butler, R.W. (1991) 'West Edmonton Mall as a Tourist Attraction', *The Canadian Geographer*, 35(3): 287–95.

Fairbairn, Kenneth J. (1991) 'West Edmonton Mall: Entrepreneurial Innovation and Consumer Response', *Canadian Geographer*, 35(3): 261–8.

Goss, Jon (1993) ' "The Magic of the Mall": An Analysis of Form, Function, and Meaning in the Contemporary Retail Built Environment', *Annals of the Association of American Geographers*, 83(1): 18–47.

Hallsworth, Alan G. (1994) 'Decentralization of Retailing in Britain – The Breaking of the Third Wave', *Professional Geographer*, 46(3): 296–307.

Hopkins, Jeffrey S.P. (1991) 'West Edmonton Mall as a Centre for Social Interaction', *The Canadian Geographer*, 35(3): 268–79.

Jackson, Edgar L. (1991) 'Shopping and Leisure: Implications of West Edmonton Mall for Leisure Research', *The Canadian Geographer*, 35(3): 280–7.

Jackson, Edgar L. and Johnson, Denis B. (1991) 'Geographic Implications of Mega-Malls with Special Reference to West Edmonton Mall', *The Canadian Geographer*, 35(3): 226–32.

Johnson, Denis B. (1991) 'Structural Features of West Edmonton Mall', *The Canadian Geographer*, 35(3): 249–61.

Jones, Ken (1991) 'Mega-Chaining, Corporate Concentration and the Mega-Mall', *The Canadian Geographer*, 35(3): 241–9.

Sack, Robert (1988) 'The Consumer's World: Place as Context', *Annals of the Association of American Geographers*, 78: 642–64.

Shields, Rob (1989) 'Social Spatialization and the Built Environment: The Case of the West Edmonton Mall', *Environment and Planning D: Society and Space*, 7(2): 147–64.

Simmons, Jim (1991) 'The Regional Mall in Canada', *The Canadian Geographer*, 35(3): 232–40.

Smith, P.J. (1991) 'Coping with Mega-Mall Development: An Urban Planning Perspective', *The Canadian Geographer*, 35(3): 295–305.

History

Adburgham, Alison (1964) *Shops and Shopping, 1800–1914: Where, and in What Manner, the Well-dressed Englishwoman Bought her Clothes*. London: Allen and Unwin.

Appleby, Joyce (1993) 'Consumption in Early Modern Thought', in John Brewer and Roy Porter (eds), *Consumption and the World of Goods*. London: Routledge. pp. 162–73.

Benson, Susan Porter (1986) *Counter Cultures: Saleswomen, Managers, and Customers in American Department Stores, 1890–1940*. Urbana and Chicago: University of Illinois Press.

Bradley, Harriet (1989) *Men's Work, Women's Work: A Sociological History of The Sexual Division of Labour in Employment*. Cambridge: Polity Press.

Bradley, Harriet (1992) 'Changing Social Structures: Class and Gender', in Stuart Hall and Bram Gieben (eds), *Formations of Modernity*. Cambridge: Polity Press. pp. 178–226.

Breen, T.H. (1993) 'The Meaning of Things: Interpreting the Consumer Society in the Eighteenth Century', in John Brewer and Roy Porter (eds), *Consumption and the World of Goods*. London: Routledge. pp. 249–60.

Brewer, John and Porter, Roy (eds) (1993) *Consumption and the World of Goods*. London: Routledge.

Davis, Dorothy (1966) *A History of Shopping*. London: Routledge and Kegan Paul.

Fine, Ben and Leopold, Ellen (1990) 'Consumerism and the Industrial Revolution', *Social History*, 15(2): 151–79.

Horowitz, Daniel (1985) *The Morality of Spending: Attitudes toward the Consumer Society in America, 1875–1940*. Baltimore: Johns Hopkins University Press.

Laermans, Rudi (1993) 'Learning to Consume: Early Department Stores and the Shaping of the Modern Consumer Culture (1860–1914)', *Theory, Culture & Society*, 10: 79–102.

Leach, William R. (1984) 'Transformations in a Culture of Consumption: Women and Department Stores, 1890–1925', *Journal of American History*, 71(2): 319–42.

Leach, William R. (1993) *Land of Desire. Merchants, Power, and the Rise of New American Culture*. New York: Pantheon.

Lears, T.J. Jackson and Fox, Richard Wrightman (1983) *The Culture of Consumption: Critical Essays in American History, 1880–1980*. New York: Pantheon.

McKendrick, Neil (1974) 'Home Demand and Economic Growth: A New View of the Role of Women and Children in the Industrial Revolution', in Neil McKendrick (ed.), *Historical Perspectives: Studies in English Thought and Society*. London: Europa. pp. 152–210.

McKendrick, Neil, Brewer, John and Plumb, J.H. (1982) *The Birth of a Consumer Society: The Commercialization of Eighteenth-Century England*. London: Europa.

Miller, Michael B. (1981) *The Bon Marché: Bourgeois Culture and the Department Store, 1869–1920*. London: Allen and Unwin.

Mukerji, Chandra (1983) *From Graven Images: Patterns of Modern Materialism*. New York: Columbia University Press.

Plumb, J.H. (1982) 'Commercialization and Society', in Neil McKendrick, John Brewer and J.H. Plumb, *The Birth of a Consumer Society: The Commercialization of Eighteenth-Century England*. London: Europa. pp. 265–334.

Porter, Roy (1990) *English Society in the Eighteenth Century.* Harmondsworth: Penguin.
Porter, Roy (1993) 'Consumption: Disease of the Consumer Society', in John Brewer and Roy
    Porter (eds), *Consumption and the World of Goods.* London: Routledge. pp. 58–81.
Reekie, Gail (1992) 'Changes in the Adamless Eden: The Spatial and Sexual Transformation
    of a Brisbane Department Store 1930–1990', in Rob Shields (ed.), *Lifestyle Shopping: The
    Subject of Consumption.* London: Routledge. pp. 170–94.
Reekie, Gail (1993) *Temptations: Sex, Religion and the Department Store.* St Leonards: Allen
    and Unwin.
Thirsk, Joan (1978) *Economic Policy and Projects: The Development of a Consumer Society in
    Early Modern England.* Oxford: Clarendon Press.
Vickery, Amanda (1993) 'Women and the World of Goods: A Lancashire Consumer and her
    Possessions, 1751–81', in John Brewer and Roy Porter (eds), *Consumption and the World of
    Goods.* London: Routledge. pp. 274–301.
Weatherill, Lorna (1986) 'A Possession of One's Own: Women and Consumer Behaviour in
    England, 1660–1740', *Journal of British Studies*, 25: 131–56.
Weatherill, Lorna (1988) *Consumer Behaviour and Material Culture in Britain, 1660–1760.*
    London: Routledge.
Wendt, Lloyd and Kogan, Herman (1952) *Give the Lady What She Wants: The Story of
    Marshall Field and Company.* Chicago: Rand McNally.
Williams, Rosalind (1982) *Dream Worlds: Mass Consumption in Late Nineteenth-Century
    France.* Berkeley and Los Angeles: University of California Press.

Literature

Bowlby, Rachel (1985) *Just Looking: Consumer Culture in Dreiser, Gissing, and Zola.*
    London: Methuen.
Bowlby, Rachel (1987) 'Modes of Modern Shopping: Mallarmé at the Bon Marché', in Nancy
    Armstrong and Leonard Tennenhouse (eds), *The Ideology of Conduct: Essays on Literature
    and the History of Sexuality.* London: Methuen. pp. 185–205.
Bowlby, Rachel (1993) *Shopping with Freud.* London: Routledge.
Leigh, Hunt (1903) 'Of the Sight of Shops', in his *Essays*, ed. with an introduction by Arthur
    Symons. London: Walter Scott Ltd. pp. 20–35.
Mitchell, Wesley C. (1950) *The Backward Art of Spending Money and Other Essays.* New
    York: Augustus M. Kelley.
Woolf, Virginia (1994) 'Street Haunting – A London Adventure', in her *The Crowded Dance
    of Modern Life. Selected Essays: Volume Two*, ed. with an Introduction by Rachel Bowlby.
    Harmondsworth: Penguin.
Zola, Émile (1992) *The Ladies' Paradise.* Berkeley and Los Angeles: University of California
    Press.

Marketing

Alba, Joseph W. and Hutchinson, Wesley J. (1987) 'Dimensions of Consumer Expertise',
    Journal of Consumer Research, 13(4): 411–54.
Bellenger, Danny N. and Korgaonkar, Pradeep K. (1980) 'Profiling the Recreational Shopper',
    Journal of Retailing, 56(3): 77–92.
Bellenger, Danny N., Robertson, Dan H. and Greenberg, Barnett A. (1977) 'Shopping Centre
    Patronage Motives', *Journal of Retailing*, 53(2): 29–38.
Bellenger, Danny N., Robertson, Dan H. and Hirschman, Elizabeth C. (1978) 'Impulse Buying
    Varies by Product', *Journal of Advertising Research*, 18(6): 15–18.

Bloch, Peter H., Ridgway, Nancy M. and Dawson, S.A. (1994) 'The Shopping Mall as Consumer Habitat', *Journal of Retailing*, 70(1): 23–42.

Bloch, Peter H., Ridgway, Nancy M. and Sherrell, Daniel L. (1989) 'Extending the Concept of Shopping: An Investigation of Browsing Activity', *Journal of the Academy of Marketing Science*, 17: 13–21.

Boone, Louis E., Kurtz, David L., Johnson, James C. and Bonno, John A. (1974) 'City Shoppers and Urban Identification Revisited', *Journal of Marketing*, 38: 67–9.

Cunningham, Isabella C.M. and Green, Robert T. (1974) 'Purchasing Roles in the U.S. Family 1955 and 1973', *Journal of Marketing*, 38: 61–8.

Darden, William R. and Ashton, Dub (1974) 'Psychographic Profiles of Patronage Preference Groups', *Journal of Retailing*, 50(4): 99–112.

Darden, William R. and Dorsch, Michael J. (1990) 'An Action Strategy Approach to Examining Shopping Behavior', *Journal of Retailing*, 21(3): 289–308.

Darden, William R. and Reynolds, Fred D. (1971) 'Shopping Orientations and Product Usage Roles', *Journal of Marketing Research*, 8: 505–8.

De Grazia, Sebastian (1964) *Of Time, Work, and Leisure*. New York: Anchor Books.

Dichter, Ernest (1964) *Handbook of Consumer Motivations: The Psychology of the World of Objects*. New York: McGraw-Hill.

Dickson, Peter R. and Sawyer, Alan G. (1990) 'The Price Knowledge and Search of Supermarket Shoppers', *Journal of Marketing*, 54: 42–53.

Feinberg, Richard A., Sheffler, Brent, Meoli, Jennifer and Rummel, Amy (1989) 'There's Something Social Happening at the Mall', *Journal of Business and Psychology*, 4(1): 49–63.

Firat, Fuat A. (1991) 'The Consumer in Postmodernity', *Advances in Consumer Research*, 18: 70–6.

Fischer, Eileen and Arnold, Stephen J. (1990) 'More than a Labor of Love: Gender Roles and Christmas Gift Shopping', *Journal of Consumer Research*, 17: 333–45.

Fischer, Eileen and Arnold, Stephen J. (1994) 'Sex, Gender Identity, Gender Role Attitudes and Consumer Behavior', *Psychology and Marketing*, 11(2): 163–82.

Fischer, Eileen and Gainer, Brenda (1991) 'I Shop Therefore I Am: The Role of Shopping in the Social Construction of Women's Identities', in Janeen Arnold Costa (ed.), *Gender and Consumer Behavior*. Salt Lake City, UT: Association for Consumer Research. pp. 350–7.

Francis, Sally and Burns, Leslie D. (1992) 'Effect of Consumer Socialization on Clothing Shopping Attitudes, Clothing Acquisition and Clothing Satisfaction', *Clothing and Textiles Research Journal*, 10(4): 35–9.

Gainer, Brenda and Fischer, Eileen (1991) 'To Buy or Not to Buy? That is Not the Question: Female Ritual in Home Shopping Parties', *Advances in Consumer Research*, 18: 597–602.

Gardner, Carl and Shepherd, Julie (1989) *Consuming Passion: The Rise of Retail Culture*. London: Unwin Hyman.

Grossbart, Sanford, Carlson, Les and Walsh, Ann (1991) 'Consumer Socialization and Frequency of Shopping with Children', *Journal of the Academy of Marketing Science*, 19(3): 155–63.

Gutman, Jonathan, and Mills, Michael K. (1982) 'Fashion Life Style, Self-Concept, Shopping Orientation, and Store Patronage: An Integrative Analysis', *Journal of Retailing*, 58(2): 64–86.

Hallsworth, Alan G. (1988) 'Analysis of Shoppers' Attitudes', *Psychological Reports*, 62: 497–8.

Hawes, Douglass K. (1987) 'Time Budgets and Consumer Leisure-Time Behavior: An Eleven-Year-Later Replication and Extension (Part I – Females)', *Advances in Consumer Research*, 14: 543–7.

Hawes, Douglass K. (1988) 'Time Budgets and Consumer Leisure-Time Behavior: An Eleven-Year-Later Replication and Extension (Part II – Males)', *Advances in Consumer Research*, 15: 418–25.

Hawks, Leona and Ackerman, Norleen (1990) 'Family Life Cycle Differences for Shopping Styles, Information Use, and Decision-Making.' *Lifestyles*, 11(2): 199–219.

Hirschman, Elizabeth C. (1991) 'A Feminist Critique of Marketing Theory: Toward Agentic–Communal Balance', in Janeen Arnold Costa (ed.), *Gender and Consumer Behavior*. Salt Lake City, UT: Association of Consumer Research. pp. 324–40.

Hirschman, Elizabeth C. (1993) 'Ideology in Consumer Research, 1980 and 1990: A Marxist and Feminist Critique', *Journal of Consumer Research*, 19: 537–55.

Hirschman, Elizabeth C. and Holbrook, Morris B. (1982) 'Hedonic Consumption: Emerging Concepts, Methods and Propositions', *Journal of Marketing*, 46: 92–101.

Holbrook, Morris B. and Hirschman, Elizabeth C. (1982) 'The Experiential Aspects of Consumption: Consumer Fantasies, Feelings, and Fun', *Journal of Consumer Research*, 9: 132–40.

Jaffe, Laurence J. and Senft, Henry (1966) 'The Role of Husbands and Wives in Purchasing Decisions', in Lee Adler and Irving Crespi (eds), *Attitude Research at Sea*. Chicago: American Marketing Association. pp. 95–110.

Jansen-Verbeke, Myriam (1987) 'Women, Shopping and Leisure', *Leisure Studies*, 6: 71–86.

Kelly, Robert F. and Egan, Michael B. (1969) 'Husband and Wife Interaction in a Consumer Decision Process', in Philip R. McDonald (ed.), *Marketing Involvement in Society and the Economy*. Fall Conference Proceedings. Chicago: American Marketing Association. pp. 250–8.

Kerin, Roger A., Jain, Ambuj and Howard, Daniel J. (1992) 'Store Shopping Experience and Consumer Price–Quality–Value Perceptions', *Journal of Retailing*, 68(4): 376–97.

Key Note Publications (1992a) *Retailing in the United Kingdom*. 3rd edn. Hampton: Key Note Publications.

Key Note Publications (1992b) *UK Household Market: Furniture, Fittings and Decor*. 1st edn. Hampton: Key Note Publications.

Key Note Publications (1992c) *UK Household Market: Household Appliances and Housewares*. 1st edn. Hampton: Key Note Publications.

Key Note Publications (1992d) *UK Clothing and Footwear Market*. 2nd edn. Hampton: Key Note Publications.

Kowinski, W.S. (1985) *The Malling of America: An Inside Look at the Great Consumer Paradise*. New York: W. Morrow.

Laaksonen, Martti (1993) 'Retail Patronage Dynamics: Learning about Daily Shopping Behavior in Contexts of Changing Retail Structures' (Special Issue: Retail Patronage Dynamics), *Journal of Business Research*, 28(1–2): 3–174.

Laaksonen, Pirjo (1994) *Consumer Involvement: Concepts and Research*. London: Routledge.

Langrehr, Frederick (1991) 'Retail Shopping Mall Semiotics and Hedonic Consumption', *Advances in Consumer Research*, 18: 428–33.

McDonald, W.J. (1994) 'Time Use in Shopping – The Role of Personal Characteristics', *Journal of Retailing*, 70(4): 345–65.

Martineau, Pierre (1957) *Motivation in Advertising: Motives That Make People Buy*. New York: McGraw-Hill.

Mayer, Robert Nathan (1978) 'Exploring Sociological Theories by Studying Consumers', *American Behavioral Scientist*, 21(4): 600–13.

Moore-Shay, Elizabeth S. and Wilkie, William L. (1988) 'Recent Advances in Research on Family Decisions', *Advances in Consumer Research*, 15: 454–60.

Moschis, George P. (1976) 'Shopping Orientations and Consumer Uses of Information', *Journal of Retailing*, 52(2): 61–70.

Moschis, George P. (1985) 'The Role of Family Communication in Consumer Socialization of Children and Adolescents', *Journal of Consumer Research*, 11: 898–913.

Moschis, George P. and Churchill, Gilbert A. Jr (1978) 'Consumer Socialization: A Theoretical and Empirical Analysis', *Journal of Marketing Research*, 15: 599–609.

Newman, Joseph W. and Staelin, Richard (1972) 'Pre-Purchase Information Seeking for New Cars and Major Household Appliances', *Journal of Marketing Research*, 9: 249–57.

Nielson (1992) *The British Shopper 1992/93*. Oxford: NTC Publications.

Packard, Vance (1986) *The Hidden Persuaders*. Harmondsworth: Penguin.

Peters, John F. (1989) 'Youth Clothes-Shopping Behavior: An Analysis by Gender', *Adolescence*, 24: 575–80.

Rich, Stuart U. (1963) *Shopping Behavior of Department Store Customers: A Study of Store Policies and Customer Demand, with Particular Reference to Delivery Service and Telephone Ordering*. Boston: Harvard University Press.

Rook, Dennis (1985) 'The Ritual Dimension of Consumer Behavior', *Journal of Consumer Research*, 12: 251–64.

Rook, Dennis W. and Hoch, Stephen J. (1985) 'Consuming Impulses', *Advances in Consumer Research*, 12: 23–7.

Rust, Langbourne (1993) 'Parents and Children Shopping Together: A New Approach to the Qualitative Analysis of Observational Data', *Journal of Advertising Research*, 33(4): 65–70.

Schindler, Robert M. (1989) 'The Excitement of Getting A Bargain: Some Hypotheses Concerning the Origins of and Effects of Smart-Shopper Feelings', *Advances in Consumer Research*, 16: 447–53.

Schudson, Michael (1986) *Advertising: The Uneasy Persuasion*. New York: Basic Books.

Scott, Rosemary (1976) *The Female Consumer*. London: Associated Business Programmes.

Sharp, Harry and Mott, Paul (1956) 'Consumer Decisions in the Metropolitan Family', *Journal of Marketing*, 21: 149–59.

Sherry, John F. and McGrath, Mary Ann (1989) 'Unpacking the Holiday Presence: A Comparative Ethnography of Two Gift Stores', in Elizabeth Hirschmann (ed.), *Interpretive Consumer Research*. Provo, UT: Association for Consumer Research. pp. 148–67.

Soloman, Michael R. (1992) *Consumer Behavior: Buying, Having and Being*. Needham Heights, MA: Allyn and Bacon.

Somner, Robert, Wynes, Marcia and Brinkley, Garland (1992) 'Social Facilitation Effects in Shopping Behavior', *Environment and Behavior*, 24(3): 285–97.

Stephenson, Ronald P. and Willett, Ronald P. (1969) 'Analysis of Consumers' Retail Patronage Strategies', in P.R. McDonald (ed.), *Marketing Involvement in Society and the Economy*. Chicago: American Marketing Association. pp. 316–22.

Stutteville, John R. (1971) 'Sexually Polarised Products and Advertising Strategy', *Journal of Retailing*, 47(2): 3–13.

Tatzel, Miriam (1982) 'Skill and Motivation in Clothes Shopping: Fashion-Conscious, Independent, Anxious, and Apathetic Consumers', *Journal of Retailing*, 58(4): 90–7.

Tauber, Edward M. (1972) 'Why Do People Shop?', *Journal of Marketing*, 36: 46–59.

Thompson, Craig J., Locander, William B. and Pollio, Howard R. (1990) 'The Lived Meaning of Free Choice: An Existential–Phenomenological Description of Everyday Consumer Experiences of Contemporary Married Women', *Journal of Consumer Research*, 17: 346–61.

Tigert, Douglas J., Ring, Lawrence J. and King, Charles W. (1976) 'Fashion Involvement and Buying Behavior: A Methodological Study', *Advances in Consumer Research*, 3: 46–52.

Venkatesh, Alladi, Sherry, John F. Jr and Firat, A. Fuat (1993) 'Postmodernism and the Marketing Imaginary', *International Journal of Research in Marketing*, 10(3): 215–49.

Ward, Scott (1981) 'Consumer Socialization', in Harold H. Kassarjian and Thomas S. Robertson (eds), *Perspectives in Consumer Behavior*. 3rd edn. Glenview, IL: Scott Foresman. pp. 380–96.

Ward, Scott, Wackman, Daniel B. and Wartella, Ellen (1977) *How Children Learn to Buy*. Newbury Park: Sage.

Ward, Sue (1971) 'A Study of a Shopping Centre', in Max K. Adler (ed.), *Leading Cases in Market Research*. London: Business Books.

Wertz, Frederick J. and Greenhut, Joan M. (1985) 'A Psychology of Buying: Demonstration of a Phenomenological Approach in Consumer Research', *Advances in Consumer Research*, 12: 566–70.

Westbrook, Robert A. and Black, William C. (1985) 'A Motivation-Based Shopper Typology', *Journal of Retailing*, 61(1): 78–103.

Williams, Robert H., Painter, John J. and Nicholas, Herbert R. (1978) 'A Policy-Oriented Typology of Grocery Shoppers', *Journal of Retailing*, 54(1): 27–43.

Wolgast, Elizabeth (1953) 'Do Husbands or Wives Make the Purchasing Decisions?', *Journal of Marketing*, 23: 151–8.

Woodside, Arch and Motes, William (1979) 'Perceptions of Marital Roles in Consumer Decision Processes for Six Products', in Beckwith et al. (eds), *American Marketing Association Proceedings*. Chicago: American Marketing Association. pp. 214–19.

Zikmund, W.G. (1977) 'A Taxonomy of Black Shopping Behavior', *Journal of Retailing*, 53(2): 61–72.

Psychology

Coshall, John T. and Potter, Robert B. (1986) 'The Relation of Personality Factors to Urban Consumer Cognition', *Journal of Social Psychology*, 126(4): 539–44.

Csikszentmihályi, Mihály and Rochberg-Halton, Eugene (1987) *The Meaning of Things: Domestic Symbols and the Self*. Cambridge: Cambridge University Press.

Dittmar, Helga (1989) 'Gender Identity-Related Meanings of Personal Possessions', *British Journal of Social Psychology*, 28: 159–71.

Dittmar, Helga (1991) 'Meanings of Material Possessions as Reflections of Identity: Gender and Social Material Position in Society', *Journal of Social Behavior and Personality*, 6(6): 165–86. Special Issue: To Have Possessions: A Handbook on Ownership and Property.

Dittmar, Helga (1992) *The Social Psychology of Material Possessions: To Have is To Be*. Hemel Hempstead: Harvester Wheatsheaf.

Lave, Jean (1988) *Cognition in Practice: Mind, Mathematics and Culture in Everyday Life*. Cambridge: Cambridge University Press.

Lunt, Peter K. and Livingstone, Sonia M. (1992) *Mass Consumption and Personal Identity: Everyday Economic Experience*. Buckingham: Open University Press.

Potter, Robert B. (1984) 'Consumer Behavior and Spatial Cognition in Relation to the Extraversion–Introversion Dimension of Personality', *Journal of Social Psychology*, 123: 29–34.

Potter, Robert B. and Coshall, John T. (1985) 'The Influence of Personality-Related Variables on Microspatial Consumer Research', *Journal of Social Psychology*, 126(6): 695–701.

van Raaji, Fred W. (1988) 'Het Winkelgedrag van de Consument' [Consumers' Shopping Behaviour], *Psycholoog*, 23(5): 208–17.

Sociology

Appadurai, Arjun (ed.) (1986) *The Social Life of Things: Commodities in Cultural Perspective*. Cambridge: Cambridge University Press.

Baudrillard, Jean (1981) *For a Critique of the Political Economy of the Sign*. St Louis, MO: Telos Press.

Baudrillard, Jean (1988) *Selected Writings*, ed. Mark Poster. Cambridge: Polity Press.

Bauman, Zygmunt (1983) 'Industrialism, Consumerism and Power', *Theory, Culture & Society*, 1(3): 32–43.

Bauman, Zygmunt (1987) *Legislators and Interpreters: On Modernity, Post-Modernity and Intellectuals*. Cambridge: Polity Press.

Bauman, Zygmunt (1988a) *Freedom*. Milton Keynes: Open University Press.

Bauman, Zygmunt (1988b) 'Sociology and Postmodernity', *Sociological Review*, 36(4): 790–813.

Bauman, Zygmunt (1990) *Thinking Sociologically: An Introduction to Everyone*. Oxford: Basil Blackwell.

Bauman, Zygmunt (1991) 'Communism: A Post-Mortem', *Praxis International*, 10(3–4): 185–192.

Bauman, Zygmunt (1992) *Intimations of Postmodernity*. London: Routledge.

Beng, Huat Chua (1992) 'Shopping for Women's Fashion in Singapore', in Rob Shields (ed.), *Lifestyle Shopping: The Subject of Consumption*. London: Routledge. pp. 114–35.

Benjamin, Walter (1983) *Charles Baudelaire: A Lyric Poet in the Era of High Capitalism*. London: Verso.

Bocock, Robert (1992) 'Consumption and Lifestyles', in Robert Bocock and Kenneth Thompson (eds), *Social and Cultural Forms of Modernity*. Cambridge: Polity Press. pp. 119–67.

Bocock, Robert (1993) *Consumption*. London: Routledge.

Bourdieu, Pierre (1992a) *Distinction: A Social Critique of the Judgement of Taste*. London: Routledge and Kegan Paul.

Bourdieu, Pierre (1992b) *Language and Symbolic Power*. Cambridge: Polity Press.

Buck-Morss, Susan (1990) *The Dialectics of Seeing: Walter Benjamin and the Arcades Project*. Cambridge, MA: MIT Press.

Burrows, Roger and Marsh, Catherine (eds) (1992) *Consumption and Class: Divisions and Change*. London: Macmillan.

Campbell, Colin (1987) *The Romantic Ethic and the Spirit of Modern Consumerism*. Oxford: Basil Blackwell.

Campbell, Colin (1990) 'Character and Consumption: An Historical Action Theory Approach to the Understanding of Consumer Behaviour', *Culture and History*, 7: 37–48.

Campbell, Colin (1991) 'Consumption: The New Wave of Research in the Humanities and Social Sciences', *Journal of Social Behaviour and Personality*, 6: 57–74. Special Issue: To Have Possessions: A Handbook on Ownership and Property.

Campbell, Colin (1992) 'The Desire for the New', in Roger Silverstone and Eric Hirsch (eds), *Consuming Technologies: Media and Information in Domestic Spaces*. London: Routledge. pp. 48–63.

Campbell, Colin (1994) 'Consuming Goods and the Good of Consuming', *Critical Review*, 8(4): 503–20.

Campbell, Colin (1995) 'The Sociology of Consumption', in Daniel Miller (ed.), *Acknowledging Consumption*. London: Routledge. pp. 96–126.

Campbell, Colin (forthcoming) 'Shopping, Pleasure and the Context of Desire', in Gosewijn van Beek and Cora Govers (eds), *The Global and the Local: Consumption and European Identity*. Amsterdam: Spinhuis Press.

Carroll, John (1979) 'Shopping World: An Afternoon in the Palace of Modern Consumption', *Quadrant*, August: 11–15.

Carter, Erica (1984) 'Alice in the Consumer Wonderland: West German Case Studies' in Gender and Consumer Culture', in Angela McRobbie and Mica Nava (eds), *Gender and Generation*. London: Macmillan. pp .185–214.

Certeau, Michel de (1984) *The Practice of Everyday Life*. Berkeley and Los Angeles: University of California Press.

Certeau, Michel de (1985) 'Practices of Space', in Marshall Blonsky (ed.), *On Signs: A Semiotics Reader*. Oxford: Basil Blackwell. pp. 122–45.

Chaney, David (1983) 'The Department Store as a Cultural Form', *Theory, Culture & Society*, 1(3): 22–31.

Chaney, David (1990) 'Subtopia in Gateshead: The Metrocentre as a Cultural Form', *Theory, Culture & Society*, 7(4): 49–68.

Chapman, Rowena (1988) 'The Great Pretender: Variations on the New Man Theme', in Rowena Chapman and Jonathan Rutherford (eds), *Male Order: Unwrapping Masculinity*. London: Lawrence and Wishart, pp. 225–48.

Chapman, Rowena and Rutherford, Jonathan (eds) (1988) *Male Order: Unwrapping Masculinity*. London: Lawrence and Wishart.

Clammer, John (1992) 'Aesthetics of the Self: Shopping and Social Being in Contemporary Urban Japan', in Rob Shields (ed.), *Lifestyle Shopping: The Subject of Consumption*. London: Routledge. pp. 195–215.

Clarke, John and Critcher, Charles (1985) *The Devil Makes Work: Leisure in Capitalist Britain*. Basingstoke: Macmillan.

Comer, Lee (1974) *Wedlocked Women*. Leeds: Feminist Books.

Connor, Steven (1989) *Postmodernist Culture: An Introduction to Theories of the Contemporary*. Oxford: Basil Blackwell.

Corrigan, Peter (1989) 'Gender and the Gift: The Case of the Family Clothing Economy', *Sociology*, 23(4): 513–34.

Deem, Rosemary (1983) 'Women, Leisure and Inequality', *Leisure Studies*, 1: 29–46.

Deem, Rosemary (1986) *All Work and No Play*. Milton Keynes: Open University Press.

Douglas, Mary and Isherwood, Baron (1980) *The World of Goods: Towards An Anthropology of Consumption*. Harmondsworth: Penguin.

Edgell, Stephen (1980) *Middle-Class Couples: A Study of Segregation, Domination and Inequality in Marriage*. London: George Allen and Unwin.

Ehrenreich, Barbara (1983) *The Hearts of Men: American Dreams and the Flight from Commitment*. London: Pluto Press.

Ewen, Stuart (1976) *Captains of Consciousness: Advertising and the Social Roots of the Consumer Culture*. New York: McGraw-Hill.

Ewen, Stuart (1988) *All Consuming Images*. New York: Basic Books.

Falk, Pasi (1991) 'Consumption as Self-Building', in *The Growing Individualisation of Consumer Lifestyles and Demand*. Amsterdam: ESOMAR. pp. 13–25.

Falk, Pasi (1994) *The Consuming Body*. London: Sage.

Falk, Pasi (1995) 'Three Metaphors of Modern Consumption', *Arttu!*, 3: 24–6.

Featherstone, Mike (1991a) *Consumer Culture and Postmodernism*. London: Sage.

Featherstone, Mike (1991b) 'The Body in Consumer Culture', in Mike Featherstone, Mike Hepworth and Bryan S. Turner (eds), *The Body: Social Processes and Cultural Theory*. London: Sage. pp. 170–96.

Fiske, John (1989) 'Shopping For Pleasure', in his *Reading Popular Culture*. London: Unwin-Hyman. pp. 13–42.

Fiske, John (1991) *Television Culture*. London: Routledge.

Fiske, John (1992) 'Women and Quiz Shows: Consumerism, Patriarchy and Resisting Pleasures', in Mary Ellen Brown (ed.), *Television and Women's Culture: The Politics of the Popular*. London: Sage. pp. 134–43.

Fiske, John (1994) 'Radical Shopping in Los Angeles – Race, Media and the Sphere of Consumption', *Media, Culture and Society*, 16(3): 469–86.

Fiske, John, Hodge, Bob and Turner, Graeme (1987) 'Shopping', in their *Myths of Oz: Reading Australian Popular Culture*. London: Allen and Unwin. pp. 95–116.

Fraser, Nancy (1987) 'What's Critical About Critical Theory: The Case of Habermas and Gender', in Seyla Benhabib and Drucilla Cornell (eds), *Feminism as Critique: Essays on the Politics of Gender in Late-Capitalist Societies*. Cambridge: Polity Press. pp. 31–56.

George, Alison and Murcott, Anne (1992) 'Monthly Strategies for Discretion: Shopping for Sanitary Towels and Tampons', *The Sociological Review*, 40(1): 146–162.

Gershuny, Jonathan and Jones, Sally (1987) 'The Changing Work–Leisure Balance in Britain, 1961–1984', in John Horne, David Jary and Alan Tomlinson (eds), *Sport, Leisure and Social Relations*. London: Routledge and Kegan Paul. pp. 9–50.

Giddens, Anthony (1991) *Modernity and Self-Identity*. Cambridge: Polity Press.

Gottdiener, Mark (1986) 'Recapturing the Center: A Semiotic Analysis of Shopping Malls', in Mark Gottdiener and Alexandros Ph. Lagopoulos (eds), *The City and the Sign: An Introduction to Urban Semiotics*. New York: Columbia University Press. pp. 288–302.

Green, Eileen, Hebron, Sandra and Woodward, Diana (1989) *Women's Leisure, What Leisure?* London: Macmillan.

Gronmo, Sigmund (1984) *Compensatory Consumer Behavior: Theoretical Perspectives, Empirical Examples and Methodological Challenges*. Oslo: Norwegian Fund for Market and Distribution Research.

Gronmo, Sigmund and Lavik, Randi (1988) 'Shopping Behaviour and Social Interaction: An Analysis of Norwegian Time Budget Data', in Per Otnes (ed.), *The Sociology of Consumption*. Oslo: Solum Forlag. pp. 101–18.

Hafstrom, Jeanne L. and Schram, Vicki R. (1986) 'Husband–Wife Shopping Time: A Shared Activity?' Urbana, IL: University of Illinois, Department of Family and Consumer Economics, Working Paper Series No. 122.

Hall, Trish (1990) 'Shop? Many Say Only if I Must', *New York Times*, 28 November.

Harvey, David (1989) *The Condition of Postmodernity*. Oxford: Basil Blackwell.

Haywood, Les, Kew, Francis and Bramham, Peter, in collaboration with Spink, John, Capenerhurst, John and Henry, Ian (1990) *Understanding Leisure*. Cheltenham: Stanley Thornes Publishers.

Hebdige, Dick (1988) *Hiding in the Light: On Images and Things*. London: Routledge and Kegan Paul.

Henley Centre (1991) *Leisure Futures*. London: Henley Centre for Forecasting.

Henwood, Melanie, Rimmer, Lesley and Wicks, Malcolm (1987) *Inside the Family: The Changing Roles of Men and Women*. Occasional Paper No. 6. London: Family Policy Studies Centre.

Huyssen, Andreas (1986) 'Mass Culture as Woman: Modernism's Other', in his *After the Great Divide: Modernism, Mass Culture and Postmodernism*. Basingstoke: Macmillan. pp. 44–62.

Jameson, Fredric (1989) 'Postmodernism and Consumer Society', in Hal Foster (ed.), *Postmodern Culture*. London: Pluto Press.

Jameson, Fredric (1991) *Postmodernism, Or the Cultural Logic of Late Capitalism*. London: Verso.

Keat, Russell, Whiteley, Nigel and Abercrombie, Nicholas (eds) (1994) *The Authority of the Consumer*. London: Routledge.

Kellner, Douglas (1989) *Jean Baudrillard: From Marxism to Postmodernism and Beyond*. London: Polity Press.

Kellner, Douglas (1992) 'Popular Culture and the Construction of Postmodern Identities', in Scott Lash and Jonathan Friedman (eds), *Modernity and Identity*. Oxford: Basil Blackwell. pp. 141–77.

Langman, Lauren (1992) 'Neon Cages: Shopping for Subjectivity', in Rob Shields (ed.), *Lifestyle Shopping: The Subject of Consumption*. London: Routledge. pp. 4–82.

Lee, Martyn J. (1993) *Consumer Culture Reborn*. London: Routledge.

Lewis, George H. (1990) 'Community Through Exclusion and Illusion: The Creation of Social Worlds in an American Shopping Mall', *Journal of Popular Culture*, 24: 121–36.

Lynd, Robert S. and Lynd, Helen Merrell (1929) *Middletown: A Study in Contemporary American Culture*. London: Constable and Company.

McCracken, Grant (1987) 'The History of Consumption: A Literature Review and Consumer Guide', *Journal of Consumer Policy*, 10: 139–166.

McCracken, Grant (1989) '"Homeyness": A Cultural Account of One Constellation of Consumer Goods and Meanings', in Elizabeth C. Hirschman (ed.), *Interpretive Consumer Research*. Provo, UT: Association for Consumer Research. pp. 168–83.

McCracken, Grant (1991) *Culture and Consumption: New Approaches to the Symbolic Character of Consumer Goods and Activities*. Bloomington: Indiana University Press.

Marcuse, Herbert (1964) *One-Dimensional Man*. London: Routledge.

Mason, Roger (1981) *Conspicuous Consumption: A Study of Exceptional Consumer Behaviour*. Farnborough: Gower.

Miller, Daniel (1987) *Material Culture and Mass Consumption*. Oxford: Basil Blackwell.

Miller, Daniel (1993) 'Christmas against Materialism in Trinidad', in Daniel Miller (ed.), *Unwrapping Christmas*. Oxford: Oxford University Press. pp. 134–53.

Miller, Daniel (1994) *Modernity – An Ethnographic Approach*. Oxford: Berg.

Miller, Daniel (ed.) (1995) *Acknowledging Consumption: A Review of New Studies*. London: Routledge.

Miller, Daniel (1997) *Capitalism – An Ethnographic Approach*. Oxford: Berg.

Moore, Suzanne (1991) *Looking for Trouble: On Shopping, Gender and the Cinema*. London: Serpent's Tail.

Moorhouse, Herbert (1983) 'American Automobiles and Workers' Dreams', *Sociological Review*, 31(3): 403–26.

Morley, David (1986) *Family Television: Cultural Power and Domestic Leisure*. London: Comedia.

Morley, David (1992) *Television, Audiences and Cultural Studies*. London: Routledge.

Morris, Meaghan (1988) 'Things to do with Shopping Centres', in Susan Sheridan (ed.), *Grafts: Feminist Cultural Criticism*. London: Verso. pp. 193–225.

Mort, Frank (1988) 'Boy's Own? Masculinity, Style and Popular Culture', in Rowena Chapman and Jonathan Rutherford (eds), *Male Order: Unwrapping Masculinity*. London: Lawrence and Wishart. pp. 193–224.

Mort, Frank (1989) 'The Politics of Consumption', in Stuart Hall and Martin Jacques (eds), *New Times: The Changing Face of Politics in the 1990s*. London: Lawrence and Wishart. pp. 160–172.

Mort, Frank and Thompson, Peter (1994) 'Retailing, Commercial Culture and Masculinity in 1950s Britain: The Case of Montague Burton, the ''Tailor of Taste'' ', *History Workshop: A Journal of Socialist and Feminist Historians*, 38: 106–27.

Nava, Mica (1992) *Changing Cultures: Feminism, Youth and Consumerism*. London: Sage.

Nicholson-Lord, David (1993a) 'Consumers Made Wary by End of Eighties Boom', *Independent*, 23 February.

Nicholson-Lord, David (1993b) 'New Man Image Takes a Battering', *Independent*, 21 December.

Nixon, Sean (1992) 'Have You Got the Look? Masculinities and Shopping Spectacle', in Rob Shields (ed.), *Lifestyle Shopping: The Subject of Consumption*. London: Routledge. pp. 149–69.

Oakley, Ann (1974) *The Sociology of Housework*. Bath: Martin Robertson.

Oakley, Ann (1980) *Housewife*. Harmondsworth: Penguin.

Otnes, Per (ed.) (1988) *The Sociology of Consumption: An Anthology*. Oslo: Solum Forlag.

Pahl, Jan (1989) *Money and Marriage*. London: Macmillan.

Pahl, Jan (1990) 'Household Spending, Personal Spending and the Control of Money in Marriage', *Journal of the British Sociological Association*, 24(1): 119–38.

Prus, Robert C. (1993) 'Shopping with Companions: Images, Influences and Interpersonal Dilemmas', *Qualitative Sociology*, 16(2): 87–110.

Prus, Robert C. and Dawson, Lorne (1991) '''Shop 'Til You Drop'': Shopping as Recreational and Laborious Activity', *Canadian Journal of Sociology*, 16(2): 145–64.

Radley, Alan (1991) 'Boredom, Fascination and Mortality: Reflections upon the Experience of Museum Visiting', in Gaynor Kavanagh (ed.), *Museum Languages: Objects and Texts*. Leicester: Leicester University Press. pp. 65–82.

Radway, Janice A. (1987) *Reading the Romance: Women, Patriarchy and Popular Literature*. London: Verso.

Rapping, Elaine (1980) 'Tupperware and Women', *Radical America*, 14(6): 39–49.

Ravo, Nick (1992) 'The Born-Again Penny-Pincher', *International Herald Tribune*, 17 January.

Riesman, David with Glazer, Nathan and Denney, Reuel (1961) *The Lonely Crowd: A Study of the Changing American Character*. New Haven: Yale University Press.

Robins, Kevin (1994) 'Forces of Consumption: From the Symbolic to the Psychotic', *Media, Culture and Society*, 16(3): 449–68.

Rogge, Jan-Uwe (1989) 'The Media in Everyday Family Life: Some Biographical and Typological Aspects', in Ellen Seiter, Hans Borchers, Gabriele Kreutzner and Eva-Maria Warth (eds), *Remote Control: Television, Audiences, and Cultural Power*. London: Routledge. pp. 168–79.

Rutherford, Jonathan (1992) *Men's Silences: Predicaments of Masculinity*. London: Routledge.

Seiter, Ellen, Borchers, Hans, Kreutzner, Gabriele and Warth, Eva-Maria (1989) *Remote Control: Television, Audiences, and Cultural Power*. London: Routledge.

Sellerberg, Ann-Mari (1994) 'The Paradox of the Good Buy', in her *A Blend of Contradictions: Georg Simmel in Theory and Practice*. New Brunswick: Transaction Publishers.

Sennett, Richard (1976) *The Fall of Public Man*. Cambridge: Cambridge University Press.

Shields, Rob (ed.) (1992) *Lifestyle Shopping: The Subject of Consumption*. London: Routledge.

Silverman, Roger and Hirsch, Eric (eds) (1992) *Consuming Technologies: Media and Information in Domestic Spaces*. London: Routledge.

Sofer, Cyril (1965) 'Buying and Selling: A Study in the Sociology of Distribution', *Sociological Review*, 13: 183–209.

Soiffer, Stephen S. and Herrmann, Gretchen M. (1987) 'Visions of Power: Ideology and Practice in the American Garage Sale', *Sociological Review*, 35: 48–83.

Starkey, Mike (1989) *Born to Shop*. Eastbourne: Monarch Publications.

Steiner, Robert L. and Weiss, Joseph (1951) 'Veblen Revised in the Light of Counter-Snobbery', *Journal of Aesthetics and Art Criticism*, 9(3): 263–8.

Stone, Gregory P. (1954) 'City Shoppers and Urban Identification: Observations on the Social Psychology of City Life', *American Journal of Sociology*, 60: 36–45.

Szalai, Alexander (ed.) in collaboration with Converse, Philip E., Feldham, Pierre, Scheuch, Erwin K. and Stone, Philip J. (1972) *The Use of Time: Daily Activities of Urban and Suburban Populations in Twelve Countries*. The Hague: Mouton.

Taylor-Gooby, Peter (1985) 'Personal Consumption and Gender', *Sociology*, 19(2): 273–84.

Tomlinson, Alan (1989) 'Consumer Culture and the Aura of the Commodity', in Alan Tomlinson (ed.), *Consumption, Identity and Style: Marketing, Meanings and the Packaging of Pleasure*. London: Routledge. pp.1–38.

Veblen, Thorstein (1953) *The Theory of the Leisure Class: An Economic Study of Institutions*. New York: Mentor Books.

Warde, Alan (1992) 'Notes on the Relationship between Production and Consumption', in Roger Burrows and Catherine Marsh (eds), *Consumption and Class: Divisions and Change*. London: Macmillan. pp. 15–31.

Warde, Alan (1994a) 'Consumers, Identity and Belonging: Reflections on Some Theses of Zygmunt Bauman', in Russell Keat and Nigel Whiteley (eds), *The Authority of the Consumer*. London: Routledge. pp. 58–74.

Warde, Alan (1994b) 'Consumption, Identity-Formation and Uncertainty', *Sociology*, 28(4): 877–98.

Weinbaum, Batya and Bridges, Amy (1979) 'The Other Side of the Paycheck: Monopoly Capital and the Structure of Consumption', in Zillah R. Eisenstein (ed.), *Capitalist Patriarchy and the Case for Socialist Feminism*. New York: Monthly Review Press. pp. 190–205.

Wheelock, Jane (1990) 'Families, Self-Respect and the Irrelevance of "Rational Economic Man" in a Postindustrial Society', *Journal of Behavioral Economics*, 19(2): 221–36.

White, Daniel R. and Hellenick, Gert (1994) 'Nietzsche at the Mall: Deconstructing the Consumer', *Canadian Journal of Political and Social Theory*, 17(1–2): 76–99.

Whitehead, Ann (1984) ' "I'm Hungry, Mum": The Politics of Domestic Budgeting', in Kate Young, Carol Wolkowitz and Roslyn McCullagh (eds), *Of Marriage and the Market: Women's Subordination and its Lessons*. London: Routledge and Kegan Paul. pp. 93–116.

Williams, Raymond (1983) *Keywords*. London: Fontana.

Williamson, Judith (1988) *Consuming Passions: The Dynamics of Popular Culture*. London: Marion Boyars.

Willis, Susan (1989) ' "I Shop Therefore I Am": Is There a Place for Afro-American Culture in Commodity Culture?', in Cheryl A. Wall (ed.), *Changing Our Own Words: Essays on Criticism, Theory and Writing by Black Women*. New Brunswick: Rutgers University Press. pp. 173–95.

Wilson, Elizabeth (1985) *Adorned in Dreams: Fashion and Modernity*. London: Virago.

Wirth, Louis (1964) 'Urbanism as a Way of Life', in Albert J. Reiss (ed.), *Louis Wirth on Cities and Social Life*. London: University of Chicago Press. pp. 60–83.

Witherspoon, Sharon (1985) 'Sex Roles and Gender Issues', in Roger Jowell and Sharon Witherspoon (eds), *British Social Attitudes: The 1985 Report*. Aldershot: Gower. pp. 55–94.

Journals: special issues on consumption

The Canadian Geographer (1991), 35(3). Special Issue on West Edmonton Mall.
Culture and History (1990), 7. Special Issue: Consumption. Copenhagen: Akademisk Forlag.
Journal of Social Behavior and Personality (1991), 6(6). Special Issue: To Have Possessions: A Handbook on Ownership and Property.
Media, Culture and Society (1994), 16(3). Special Issue: Relations of Consumption.
Sociology (1990), 24(1): Special Issue: The Sociology of Consumption.
Theory, Culture & Society (1988), 5(2–3). Special Issue: Postmodernism.

Useful bibliographies on consumption

Auyong, Dorothy K., Porter, Dorothy and Porter, Roy (1991) *Consumption and Culture in the 17th and 18th Centuries: A Bibliography*, ed. John Brewer. Los Angeles: UCLA Centre for 17th and 18th Century Studies and the William Andrews Clark Memorial Library.
Rudmin, Floyd, Belk, Russell and Furby, Lita (1987) *Social Science Bibliography on Property, Ownership and Possessions: 1580 Citations from Psychology, Anthropology, Sociology and Related Disciplines*. Monticello, IL: Vance Bibliographies.

Index